Advance Praise for *Widgets*

Widgets is required reading for every leader and manager to shake off habits rooted in the past.

—*New York Times* Bestselling Author Curt Coffman
Coauthor of *First, Break All the Rules*

This book serves as a powerful countervailing force to the increasing momentum toward "widgetizing" everyone and everything in the supposed interest of productivity. Given the increasing proportion of leaders inclined toward robo-management, *Widgets* should be required reading for anyone even thinking about managing real people.

—Annette Templeton, former global chief of principals, Gallup, Inc.

Rodd is fascinated by people—what motivates them, how they think, how they learn, how they act. He's also a great storyteller. He combines both in this book, and his spot-on observations are applicable in the corporate world, the military, and at home. Great read. Fast read. Invaluable read.

—Rear Admiral Dennis J. Moynihan, U.S. Navy (Ret.)

I love how Rodd distilled a significant body of research into ideas that are so insightful, ideas that resonate viscerally to both the leader and the led. I think that's what's most compelling about *Widgets*. The New Rules are timely and inspiring. They replace old views on engagement with a contemporary focus on reciprocity. What struck me most is how strongly the data supports the resilience and commitment of people to customers and to doing something meaningful—despite how poorly companies and leaders are engaging them today—and how eager people are to do great things for leaders that create the right culture.

—Jeff McCaulley, chief executive officer, Smiths Medical

A highly readable, research-grounded, and relevant approach to employee engagement by one of the most respected thinkers on the subject. This is a frame-breaking book that puts people first and opens an important new chapter in management and leadership. A fascinating, thought-provoking, must-read book.

—Ken Bartlett, Ph.D., professor of human resource development,
University of Minnesota

If a highly engaged workforce serves as a moat that protects an organization from competitive threats, Rodd Wagner reminds us that a moat without water is nothing more than a ditch.

—Robb Webb, chief human resources officer, Hyatt Hotels

Rodd Wagner listened to the voice of the employee and faithfully defined what they need to give their best efforts. His focus on reciprocity as the key motivator is right on target. His challenge to leaders who have talked the talk, but not walked the walk, is passionate and insightful. *Widgets* is an important book.

—Leigh Branham, author of *The 7 Hidden Reasons Employees Leave*, coauthor of *Re-Engage*

As an executive in charge of a company's culture, I find this book a must-read. More important, it's imperative we put it into practice. *Widgets* is Rodd's best work.

—Jess Elmquist, executive vice president, Life Time

How to best motivate employees and teams is the eternal question we face as leaders, because motivated employees make the difference between companies that perform well and those that struggle. It's clear the rules for bilateral loyalty have changed, and both employees and managers need to know how to adapt to the new environment. Rodd addresses those changes head-on. *Widgets* is a crucial book for executives to determine how they will lead in the coming decade.

—Pam Stegora Axberg, senior vice president, Optum

Too many of today's well-intentioned approaches end up depersonalizing workplaces and customer service. Rodd's book is a bold step toward restoring humanity in the equation of what drives business success.

—Tom Rieger, bestselling author of *Breaking the Fear Barrier*

Widgets is a captivating book with important and actionable insights into the psychological and behavioral drivers of employee engagement. A must-read for executives and anyone else who seeks to engage, motivate, and positively affect employees and people in general.

—Dr. Ran Kivetz
The Philip H. Geier Professor
at Columbia University Business School

widgets

The 12 New Rules for Managing Your Employees
As If They're Real People

RODD WAGNER

New York   Chicago   San Francisco   Athens   London   Madrid
Mexico City   Milan   New Delhi   Singapore   Sydney   Toronto

2 3 4 5 6 7 8 9 0   DOC/DOC   1 2 0 9 8 7 6 5

ISBN   978-0-07-184778-0
MHID   0-07-184778-2

e-ISBN 978-0-07-184779-7
e-MHID   0-07-184779-0

Library of Congress Cataloging-in-Publication Data

Wagner, Rodd.
  Widgets : the 12 new rules for managing your employees as if they're real people / by Rodd Wagner.
     pages cm
  ISBN 978-0-07-184778-0 (hardback : alk. paper) — ISBN 0-07-184778-2 (hardback : alk. paper) 1. Supervision of employees. 2. Employee motivation. 3. Communication in management. I. Title.
  HF5549.12.W343 2015
  658.3—dc23

                                                                    2014044610

McGraw-Hill Education books are available at special quantity discounts to use as premiums and sales promotions or for use in corporate training programs. To contact a representative, please visit the Contact Us pages at www.mhprofessional.com.

The New Rules of Engagement[SM] and the New Rules index[SM] are registered service marks of BI WORLDWIDE. The New Rules index and its associated metrics detailed in the Appendix are copyright protected by BI WORLDWIDE, 2014, and are used here with permission of the company. They cannot be reproduced without permission.

To my daughter, Noelle

—RGW

Contents

Where Are You
on the New Rules Index?

BEFORE YOU DIVE INTO THIS BOOK, OR ANYTIME ALONG THE WAY, YOU have an opportunity to find out what's working and what's not for you as an employee. At WidgetsTheBook.com, you can take the New Rules self-assessment developed from the research behind this book. After spending about five minutes rating the same aspects explained in *Widgets*, you will receive your current New Rules index, a percentile showing how your experiences at work compare with those of others. You'll also get advice on how to take charge of your life at work, plus the latest blog posts, podcasts, and other information from the author. You can return at any time to see how your level changes with events at work.

INTRODUCTION

"Human Resources"

YOUR PEOPLE ARE NOT YOUR GREATEST ASSET.

They're not yours, and they're not assets. Assets are property. You don't own your people. Many of them don't trust you. Some don't like you. Too many won't stick it out with you. And the ones you need most have the credentials to walk out fastest if you treat them poorly.

Your employees are not "full-time equivalents." No college graduate, upon landing her first big job, calls her parents to announce, "I'm now an FTE!" No hardworking employee considers himself part of the company's "headcount." "Headcount" is for cattle. Your employees are not "talent." They are not "human capital," to be saved, spent, or loaned like money. They are not "overhead." They are not the numbers each is assigned when hired. They are not, as one staffing firm refers to them, "inventory," or as one home improvement chain called them, "aprons." They are not, as tech people sometimes call them, "meatware."

Above all, employees are not "human resources."

Money is a resource. Land is a resource. So are water, oil, trees, buildings, computers, gold, coal, cattle, and coffee beans. Resources are rarely unique. One load of two-by-fours is much like another. Resources are the raw materials from which a business creates a product.

Humans are not resources. No manager talks about having coffee with one of her "humans." No father holds his young son and hopes he will one day grow up to be a great "resource." It is difficult to have the right relationship between a company and its people when the corporate function responsible for doing so goes by a euphemism.

You might as well call them widgets, flesh-and-blood widgets. That's what the term "human resources" means. That's how they are too often treated. In trying to get a better seat at the executive table with number-crunching departments like Accounting and Operations and Marketing, the executives in charge of the hiring, culture, payroll, insurance, and training were seduced into using impersonal metrics for persons. Business lost its bearings in how to deal with people.

Once people are seen as widgets—as "human resources"—it's much easier to apply to them the kinds of Operationspeak that should be reserved for raw materials. They are "downsized," "attritted," "onboarded," "blended," "change-managed," "diversity-trained," "e-taught," "force-ranked," "matrixed," "requisitioned," or "made redundant." In the human resources machinery, people's entire working lives too often are reduced to a series of clicks on an automated "selection system" and sorted by computer into "As," "Bs," and "Cs" for the hiring manager. They are stereotyped by their generation, rated on their "competencies" and their computer-calculated "strengths," combined for a "group dynamic" designed by an "industrial psychologist," tracked by a "human resources information system," and tagged with a Myers-Briggs Type Indicator. They are analyzed for target "behaviors." They are ordered to pee in a cup and hand it over.

The temptation to treat people like widgets is not new. Charlie Chaplin made a movie about it in 1936. Henry Ford is reputed to have complained, "Why is it that I always get the whole person when what I really want is a pair of hands?" More than a century ago, Frederick Winslow Taylor, the pioneer of time-and-motion studies, tried to engineer an optimal system where the employees best served the machinery around them. "It is only through enforced standardization of methods, enforced adoption of the best implements and working conditions, and enforced cooperation that this faster work can be assured. And the duty of enforcing the adoption of standards and enforcing this cooperation rests with management alone," he wrote in his book, *The Principles of Scientific Management*.[1]

Taylor would have been ecstatic to have the kinds of HR tools available now. He would have pounced on a book like *The Brave New World of eHR: Human Resources Management in the Digital Age*. "Electronic human resources," says the book, is "a new world order for managing human resources in organizations—a world where scientists and practitioners in the industrial/organizational psychology field have much to say and much to offer in order to promote the effectiveness and optimization of eHR technologies and services." It describes a world in which people are "e-recruited," "e-selected," "e-compensated," e-trained, and e-managed, and where they don't need to—maybe could not if they wanted to—talk to a real person for support. "Welcome to the new world of eHR," says the book. "Things will look a bit different here. No longer will you deal with an HR professional to handle your HR needs. The HR portal will take care of you. Need to change your address? How about some online training? Want to check on your latest performance review? The portal is here to help."[2]

Too many corporations have become people-chewing machines, places where you are more likely to get an access code by which a computer gets to know you and spits out your top "themes" than you are to get a manager to take you to coffee every month and work with you individually, person to person. When people apply for a job now, they force-fit their unique selves into electronic boxes hoping not to run afoul of the secret algorithm that, because of the increased applications e-applying allows, must sift through hundreds or thousands of submissions.

No wonder one HR executive who had applied anonymously through his own company's e-selection system got rejected, or the e-selection system of another took in 25,000 applications for a standard engineering position and reported back that not one person was qualified.[3] "Job applicants have been changed into these bits-and-bytes kind of package for a software program that screens them as they apply for a job," reported Mitchell Hartman on the radio program *Marketplace*

Money. "These systems are persnickety. They're software; they're not human-ware."[4]

Few HR professionals meant for it to come to this. Most are highly principled people who want their companies' employees to have a great experience at work. And there is compelling statistical science behind much of the machinery. But the road to treating people like widgets is paved with good intentions and great software.

An entire industry has emerged to help companies address their employee engagement and other "human resources" issues. The consultancies made more problems than they solved. Rather than addressing the issues, they complicated them. They created models and metrics, "team feedback" processes and "action-planning" systems, cold acronyms and catchphrases. They too often attacked the widget problem with more ways to process people as widgets.

As their answers to people problems, the competitors in the employee engagement business created a lot of shapes. One company based its model on a big Maslowian pyramid. Another created a model based on an endless four-stage cycle, each stage pointing at its neighbor. It looks like four boxes blaming each other. Another model looks like the distributor cap for a six-cylinder engine, or maybe a nuclear bomb, everything coming together at once to create a critical mass of fissionable employee engagement. Not to be outdone, another consulting firm made a model that looked a lot like a board game. Employees who landed on one of the squares were called "hamsters."

Most people do not like to be compared with rodents.

There were other shapes as well. A flower. A thing that looked like an arrow shot through an orange. One that looked like a molecule, with labeled electron bubbles circling labeled proton bubbles. And many more. Each of these shapes and its associated survey and process is supposed to ensure employees are more engaged and therefore working harder for their employers.

But they don't. And they won't, until leaders and managers do better at treating each employee as an individual, stop ruling by fear, make pay a nonissue, and quit burning out their people. Performance won't get better until leaders realize why making their companies cool places to work is good business, or at least stop doing things that are so uncool. Firms won't match their potential until their leaders become far more transparent than in the past, stop snuffing out the meaning in their employees' work, and plan for the futures for their people as much as they do for their companies.

Employees will withhold much of what they could do until they are better recognized for what they already do. Organizations will underperform until leaders stop abusing tribal metaphors and unite their employees as the temporary team they are, until managers let their employees lead, until they better synchronize company breakthroughs with employee accomplishments.

Each of these aspects is a powerful driver of workers' commitment to the company, the intensity of their work, or both.

Even the organizations that advise other companies on their employee engagement become widget factories. One of them rated a meager 2.7 on a 5-point scale among its current and former employees who volunteered assessments on Glassdoor.com. Only 44 percent approved of the CEO, and only 40 percent would recommend the company to a friend.[5] "Management are pure bullies," wrote one former employee. One of his colleagues wrote that senior leaders there need to stop "believing that parts (people) are just interchangeable cogs in your big wheel."[6]

The company's website insists, "Our people are our priority."[7]

Another major engagement player squeaked out a rating of 3.0, with only 50 percent approving of the CEO and 47 percent inclined to recommend the company to a friend.[8] "Cost cutting, reduced hours with increased expectations, and management that, generally, has nothing to do with the minions," wrote one consultant. "There are serious employee engagement issues, which (the company) completely disregards. They know. They just don't care. Truly something you want to see from a human-resources-related service company."[9]

That firm's website says he's wrong. "We care about people and the role of work in their lives," it asserts.[10]

As they do at so many of those firms' clients, the initiatives often backfire and make things worse because the company's leaders can't handle the truth. Their surveys are not confidential. "If you put anything less than 4 out of 5 on your biannual employee engagement surveys, then you should have your resignation ready to go," cautioned an employee of one engagement consultancy. The supervisors who are worst at managing are the best at playing Find the Hamster.

Employee engagement is in a rut. It's become hackneyed. It's routinized. Commission a survey. Beg people to participate. Get the results back. Distribute scorecards. Train some trainers; unleash them on the company. Cajole the CEO into using the word "engagement" in his next speech. Ask managers to do some team sessions, which maybe half will do before tucking the forms in a desk drawer. Leave the way managers are selected, coached, supported, and held accountable untouched. Let the executives feel good that they checked the employee engagement box. Go quiet for 9 or 10 months until it's time to start the Sisyphean cycle all over again. Lather. Rinse. Repeat.

Seeing the failures of traditional employee engagement methods, seeing companies struggle to keep up with a changing workforce, the team behind this book went into the field. We asked more pointed and predictive questions of employees around the world. We drew from our experience and distilled what we were seeing at hundreds of international companies, many of which shared confidential data and plans with us. We questioned fundamental assumptions. What emerged from the research, from the clear patterns inside those organizations, and from what we've seen work were 12 imperatives.

Call them the New Rules of Engagement. They address issues of individualization, fearlessness, pay, well-being, and enjoyment of time on the job. They reflect what leaders and managers need to know about transparency, meaning, employees' perceptions of their future, and recognition. They distinguish real collaboration from platitudes about teamwork, and democratization from the old suggestion box. They show how crucial it is for employees to have the chance to do something incredible. They inoculate against widgetry. They are the company investments that create employee intensity.

The team behind this book asked employees around the world a hundred questions about the aspects outlined above. To statements such as, "I work because I love it, not because of the money," or "My manager understands me," we gave participants five possible responses: strongly agree, agree, neutral, disagree, or strongly disagree. The average response to the vast majority of questions falls just north of the line between neutral and agree. Ask someone about his or her job and the most common response is a statistical shrug.

Excited about your future with this organization? "Sort of."

Are the top leaders of your company honest? "I suppose."

Does your manager understand what motivates you at work? "A little."

Not exactly what the company website said, and not the kind of energy levels that are most healthy for the business.

Average responses, of course, can mask wide ranges among individual responses. They do here as well.

For simplicity of explanation, our researchers divided employees into four groups. We did so cautiously, however, because in the past categorizing people made the widget problem worse. Grouping together a wide swath of people into a single description runs along the cliff's edge of stereotyping. People have high or low engagement for various lengths of time and for many reasons. At some point in our careers, most of us will spend at least a little time in each of these categories.

With those caveats, the continuous range of New Rules levels can be logically divided into the following groups.

The demoralized group: Nineteen percent of the U.S. workforce answer neutral or lower, on average, to the key questions in the study. These are the people whose companies have most seriously failed them, those most consistently treated like widgets. "Every day at this job, a little piece of me dies," said one person in this category a few months before he resigned. Only 4 percent of this group strongly agree their managers meet with them on a regular basis. Thirty-eight percent worry about losing their jobs. Forty-six percent say the managers at their companies use fear to get people to work harder. Many report getting yelled at. Nearly two out of three say they are burned out. "You are micromanaged here and treated like machines instead of people," one demoralized person wrote in the survey. "There is no regard for your life outside of work."

The frustrated group: The responses of 23 percent of American workers fall between neutral and halfway toward "agree." Although not completely beaten down, and occasionally giving positive responses, this group regularly encounters gaps in how well the company is organized and run. "There are no thought-out ideas or plans by upper management," said one person in this range. "I'm doing double work because one manager likes something one way and another likes it differently." Asked if they love their jobs, 54 percent are neutral, and another 22 percent disagree or strongly disagree.

The encouraged group: Almost one out of three employees (29 percent) gives answers averaging from "agree" down to a point halfway between "agree" and "neutral." They like their jobs. Things are not so bad that they are eager to get out, nor are they invigorated enough to deliver their best. This group talks a lot about how their jobs are almost great. Almost. For example, asked if their job brings out their best ideas, 60 percent agree, but only 7 percent strongly agree. They are motivated but uninspired. "My boss is extremely supportive and encouraging, but the hoops the main organization puts in place are discouraging," said one. Because of these day-to-day obstacles, much of the potential of the encouraged group is untapped.

The energized group: Three out of ten employees have the kinds of jobs that the other seven envy. Their responses to the key questions average from "agree" to "strongly agree." That doesn't mean they don't sometimes give a negative appraisal of some aspect, but those problems are exceptions to their overall experience, and they are happy to cut their employer some slack. "My work gets recognized and they understand how hard I am working for the company," wrote one person in the energized category. Asked what gets in the way of their motivation, many say "nothing." Seven of ten say their managers regularly meet with them. Nine of ten say they've received incredible recognition. Only 9 percent say they're burned out. They love their jobs, and they return the favor to their employers. There are no widgets here.

For the better part of two or three decades, businesses have been enamored of Six Sigma, the improvement of processes and the fine-tuning of equipment to ensure that 99.99966 percent of whatever the company produces is free of defects. We've gotten used to the benefits. Smartphones, tablets, and computers work as well as they do because the most important components are built to microscopic specifications in conditions cleaner than a hospital operating room.

If executives obsess over product quality, shouldn't they also obsess over the experience of working at their firms? What is the corresponding failure rate in creating the kind of workplace that best supports the Six Sigma processes, the innovations, the customer experience, and the financial performance the company needs? Without question, it's at least 19 percent (the proportion of those demoralized). With little debate, it's 41 percent (those demoralized plus those frustrated). And one could make a case it's as high as 70 percent (all but those who are energized). No firm would countenance that kind of sloppiness in production, safety, technology, accounting, or brand standards.

People need better. Their companies could do so much better by them and through them if they only stepped back long enough to take stock of an incorrect view of human nature, wrong strategies, and bad habits that worked their way into "human resources" and the executive suite over the course of a century, punctuated by some serious blunders in the last few years.

The purpose of this book is not just to excoriate and warn. It's a guide to better understanding human nature on the job and to understanding each of the New Rules that emerged from the team's extensive research.

It's a guide for ferreting out and fixing all the ways your company treats its people like widgets.

The Reciprocal Employee

HUMANS ARE A SORRY SPECIES.

We can't lift more than our own weight, if that. We're lousy swimmers and can't hold our breath very long under water. We don't run very fast or for very long. Exposed to the sun, we burn. Poorly dressed in the cold, we freeze. We bruise and cut easily. We're unconscious one-third of the time. Our young take forever to mature. We can't smell predators coming. We can't fly.

We would be extinct were it not for our brains.

Our unique advantage, secured inside the closest thing we have to a shell, is a three-pound organ, wrinkled to maximize crucial surface area, sucking up a disproportionate amount of oxygen and glucose, and thinking, thinking, thinking, to keep the slow-running, poor-swimming, nonflying, easily chilled or overheated weakling to which it's attached from meeting what would otherwise be its fate.

It's worked out fairly well. Envying the other animals their fur, we made traps to capture them. Lacking teeth and claws, we made spears and bows and arrows. Wanting wings, we invented airplanes. By our wits and our tools we can get to work at 60 miles per hour in any kind of weather and work and live most of our lives indoors. We are soft, but we are smart.

We are impressed with ourselves. "What a piece of work is a man!" wrote Shakespeare in *Hamlet*. "How noble in reason, how infinite in faculty! In form and moving how express and admirable! In action how like an angel! In apprehension how like a god! The beauty of the world! The paragon of animals!"

Our genius has not included understanding the nature of our brilliance. We're not smart enough to know how we're smart. Until quite recently, we got it wrong. Somehow we got the idea that we are much further removed from primitive instincts than we really are. These off-target assumptions became the foundation of most workplace strategies.

From the beginnings of economics, the prevailing theory assumed that people were "rational agents" who "maximized" their "utility"—that they were selfish and calculating, logical and informed, constantly considering their options in pursuit of a better one, lazy if no one policed them, disloyal if it served their purposes. A human is "a being who inevitably does that by which he may obtain the greatest amount of necessaries, conveniences, and luxuries with the smallest quantity of labour and physical self-denial with which they can be obtained," wrote philosopher John Stuart Mill.[1]

Economic Man, or *Homo economicus*, he was called. He was a lousy worker if not closely monitored, wanting as he did the highest amount of pay for the least amount of work. But he was predictably rational. If you wanted him to do something, attach a dollar to it. If you wanted him not to do something, threaten to dock his pay or fire him if he did. Tell the widget what was expected of him at work; then enforce it. The philosophy was best encapsulated by comedian George Carlin: "Most people work just hard enough not to get fired, and get paid just enough money not to quit."[2]

In college management textbooks, and just enough in real life to be persuasive, it made sense. These rational beings "solve any problem as well as an economist would," said University of Chicago professor

Richard Thaler. On paper, he observed, "the agents of the economy, as assumed by economists, have been getting smarter and smarter for the last 60 years."

There was only one problem: *Economicus* doesn't exist.

Real employees—real people—routinely fail to react as the rational models predict. Given the chance to get free matching money by enrolling in a company 401(k) program, a large proportion do nothing. Aware of the serious risks of smoking, too many start, and too many pass up the company's free cessation program. They fail to take much of their paid vacation.[3] They often leave companies, not for more money, but for more meaning in their work. They eat doughnuts instead of vegetables. They fail to exercise. *Economicus* may have gotten more calculating and programmable in textbooks, but "human beings are just as dumb as we always were, just as human," said Thaler.[4]

What got lost in the models of rationality is that human nature was formed over tens of thousands of years living and dying in conditions poles apart from the modern workplace. We employees are the exponential-great-grandchildren of people who survived tens of thousands of years living in small groups, facing death by everything from the weather, accidents, and starvation to predators and enemies.

"Our modern skulls house a stone age mind," wrote two evolutionary psychologists in the late 1990s. "The key to understanding how the modern mind works is to realize that its circuits were not designed to solve the day-to-day problems of a modern American—they were designed to solve the day-to-day problems of our hunter-gatherer ancestors. . . . [O]ur minds are . . . very sophisticated computers, whose circuits are elegantly designed to solve the kinds of problems our ancestors routinely faced."[5]

In primitive conditions, the people who did best were those who worked together with people who looked out for them. Those who decided to go it alone or, worse yet, put too much effort into working with people who gave nothing back or betrayed their trust, were at greater risk of dying. That cruel fact, repeated generation after generation after generation, makes us who we are. And what we are more than anything is reciprocating. A disproportionately large part of our high-maintenance brains is dedicated to recognizing people and tracking their reputations so we know with whom to invest and from whom to withhold our hard work.

Over the last decade, as the discoveries of evolutionary psychology and behavioral economics have reached critical mass, the hyper-rational *Homo economicus* lost favor in the scientific literature. *Homo reciprocans*—the reciprocal human—gained ground because reciprocity better explains why people do what they do, both off the job and at work.

Most simply, reciprocity is the human reflex to return what one receives—good for good, bad for bad. It's a boomerang. It's the Golden Rule right side up ("Do unto others as you would have them do unto you") and upside down ("Do unto others as they have done to you").

It's the obsession from childhood on with what's fair. It's honking the horn when someone cuts you off on the highway or reflexively waving a thank you when someone lets you merge. It's not feeling right with your colleague until you buy her lunch to reciprocate for the time when she bought yours. It's the satisfaction you get watching a movie to see the good guy prevail and the bad guy die, preferably by the poetic justice of his own evil plan backfiring.[6]

It's why people voluntarily spend $40 billion a year in tips to those who serve them.[7] It's why a guy in line at Burger King in front of a foul-mouthed brat demanding pie from his spineless mother decided to buy and leave with every pie in the place.[8] It's the reason why a Starbucks barista admitted, "I give decaf to customers who are rude to me."[9]

Before there were police, courts, or written contracts, reciprocity was the way fairness was enforced. In most situations, it still is. If the other person deals well with you, you deal well with him. If he abuses your trust, you withdraw or retaliate. "A man ought to be a friend to his friend and repay gift with gift," states the *Edda*, a thirteenth-century collection of Norse epic poems. "People should meet smiles with smiles and lies with treachery." Reciprocity is, as a National Public Radio report put it, one of the "social rules that we're only vaguely aware of but which have incredible power over what we do."[10]

Being the primary social reflex of human nature, reciprocity is the most important concept for any leader seeking to motivate his or her employees. Engagement is the intensity employees deliver in their work in reciprocation for the investments their companies make in their experience at work.

A purely rational "agent"—a widget—would constantly be looking for a better, higher-paying job. In real life, people display a high degree of loyalty to their employers, sometimes even at the cost of losing opportunities elsewhere, unless they believe their bosses are taking advantage of that loyalty. A purely "utility-maximizing" creature would not care whether he makes money in retail or healthcare or investments, because money is money. Real people get deeply involved in the missions of their organizations.

Homo economicus is selfish. *Homo reciprocans* is often motivated by principle, by a sense of obligation, or for the satisfaction of doing something good for someone else. Having been betrayed, *Economicus* moves on, unwilling to waste time and effort just to get even and get nothing in return. *Reciprocans* holds a grudge. He gets a charge out of posting a scathing review of his former employer on Glassdoor.

Ironically, this exceptionally deep, exceptionally ancient quality of humans was the foundation for the rules to change so quickly. Human nature has not changed during our working lives. It can't change that fast. The rules have changed because a highly reciprocal creature was placed in a dramatically different work environment.

"Cultural evolution is now the dominant evolutionary force that's acting on our species. Think about the changes that have occurred . . . just in the last few generations as a result of industrialization and computers and the post-industrial world," said Daniel Lieberman, a professor of human evolutionary biology at Harvard University. "It's not evolutionary change of the sort Darwin described, for the most part. It's cultural change."[11]

What happened when the reciprocal employee, *Mercenarius reciprocans*, went through the Great Recession? How does she react when given social media like LinkedIn and Glassdoor to augment her tracking of reputations? What happens to her innate need for fairness when pay levels become increasingly public? How healthy can a creature evolved for burning calories in hard physical activity be if made to sit for hours at a computer, on a plane, or in a rental car on the way to the hotel? Where inside a cubicle will she get reinforcement of her successes? In a working world rife with layoffs and uncaring CEOs, which teams will she join? Whom will she follow, and why?

These questions are only beginning to be answered.

Tucked inside a U.S. government report is a chart that shows how badly scrambled the relationship between employee and employer became in the span of just a few years.[12]

The chart tracks the ratio of unemployed people per job opening from 2003 to today. From mid-2003 to early 2007, there were between 3 and 1.5 unemployed people per job opening—too few people for too many jobs. Companies were falling over themselves to attract and keep their people. They poached key employees from their competitors, who in turn stole key employees from someone else. If you had talent, you had options. Résumé not a perfect fit for the posted role? Close enough. Want to telecommute from a small town in the mountains near a trout stream? With the growth in technology and companies' desperation for people, it could be arranged. Need a signing bonus to help make the decision? Here's the check.

"I quit," said one man to his boss. "I'm out of here."

"You can't just up and quit," said the manager. "You owe the company two weeks notice."

"Well," said the now former employee, "in, like, two weeks, you're going to notice that I haven't shown up for, like, two weeks."

The supply of "talent" in developed countries was "running dry," the *Economist* magazine warned in a 2006 article headlined "The Battle for Brainpower." "Obsession with talent is no longer confined to blue-chip companies such as Goldman Sachs and General Electric," it reported. "It can be found everywhere in the corporate world, from credit-card companies to hotel chains to the retail trade."[13]

In 2006, three-quarters of senior HR managers said attracting and retaining people was their top priority. Nearly two-thirds worried about companywide personnel shortages. One in three said they had hired below-average candidates "just to fill a position quickly." One-third of employees said they had recently been approached by another firm hoping to lure them away. Companies worried about being "employer of choice" because the choice was the employee's. In some cases, they tried to control the market. "I am told that Google's new cellphone software group is relentlessly recruiting in our iPod group," Apple CEO Steve Jobs wrote to an executive at the rival company. "If this is indeed true, can you put a stop to it?"[14] The number of people who quit hovered around 3 million per month, while the number who were fired or laid off was only 1.8 million per month.

Then everything changed.

The housing bubble burst. The subprime market collapsed. The stock market lost over half its value in 17 months.

In the early months of what came to be called the Great Recession, companies stopped bringing on more people but held onto those they had. Job openings fell, eventually dropping from 4.5 million to below 2.5 million. As it became apparent the downturn would be longer and more severe than any in memory, businesses started sending people home for good. The number of involuntary terminations rose by roughly 40 percent. "This company's story with terminations is like mine with beer," said one statistician working for a name-brand firm. "I didn't have my first beer until college, but once I did, I really liked it. These guys didn't get rid of anyone for decades, but once they did, they really liked it."

The ultimate weapon employees have is to quit and go to a better job. At the back end of the Great Recession and for some time afterward, that "you'll notice I haven't shown up for two weeks" leverage was gone. From November 2008 through March 2010, more people were involuntarily terminated than quit on their own. Suddenly it was the recently humbled job candidates who were seeking to be employee of choice to an increasingly picky group of hiring managers. The number of unemployed people per job opening shot up to nearly seven.

Many people who would have quit in a better economy didn't. They stayed in place, relieved to have a job, outwardly enthusiastic and compliant to maintain that position but inwardly agonized. They confided to their close friends they were "holding their breath" or "keeping their heads down." Many companies took advantage of their newfound strength. If you don't like the long hours, doing more with less, don't forget the supply of widgets is high, they were told in so many words. The leaders of those companies forgot that the reciprocal employee has a long memory and a recession eventually ends.

And so it did.

Employees regained leverage much more slowly than they lost it, but incrementally they did regain it. The number of unemployed people per job opening dropped to six by late 2009, to five by mid-2010, to four by 2011, to three by early 2013, and to two by late 2014. Since April 2010, resignations have outnumbered terminations. However slowly, they eventually returned to prerecessionary levels.[15]

Even as job creation lagged, news about labor shortages in many categories was again common. One in five over-the-road trucks in Tennessee was sitting parked because there was no one to drive it.[16] "There is labor out there, but not for the quality of work we do," one Michigan homebuilder told the *Detroit Free Press*.[17] Reports of poaching the competition's people were increasing. "One of the ways that businesses have of addressing the shortage of skilled labor is to go after each other's employees," said the head of one building industry trade group.[18]

Now comes the day of reckoning. "There's no polite way to say it—workers have had it," wrote *Miami Herald* workplace blogger Cindy Krischer Goodman. "In 2012 we lost our happy-to-have a job mindset and now we want appreciation. For some of us it's been a few years since we've had a raise or bonus."[19]

The implicit deal between an employee and a company is not what it was. Fundamental assumptions have been disrupted. Young people who were in high school or college then are in the workforce now, bringing new expectations. Experienced employees saw their trust betrayed, and they vowed never to let it happen again. Technologies that not so long ago didn't exist now define how work is done, how life at work is discussed, how jobs are left behind or taken, and how companies are known. The way that firms look at their employees changed; the way that those reciprocal employees look at their employers changed even more.

Even a decade ago, would it have been imaginable that someone like 25-year-old animator Marina Shifrin would use a dance video posted on YouTube to quit her job? "For almost two years I've sacrificed my relationships, time, and energy for this job. . . . I quit! I'm gone," state the video captions over footage of Marina dancing at the office, turning out the lights, and leaving.[20] Would it have been seen by 18 million people and added to a growing gallery of "I quit!" viral videos?

Would the company have responded with its own video of Marina's former colleagues also dancing, touting the company's rooftop pool and the fact that "We're hiring!"? YouTube didn't exist a decade ago. Stunts like that would kill a career, not restart it. Not that employees ever accepted the widget treatment, but today's workers have no tolerance for it, and they have the social media tools to blast it when it happens.

Employers are too slow to catch on. Most weren't very good at looking out for their employees before the recession. Much of what they were doing correctly before the downturn got swept away in waves of fear, worries about self-preservation, and overestimates of their power over employees.

It's not that corporations are bad and people are good. Corporations are powerful, and people are reciprocal. How an enterprise wields its power determines how its employees will deliver. Most companies are quite unprepared for what they now have on their hands—more individualistic, mercenary, impatient, thrill-seeking, connected, and loud workers than have ever been seen before, people who trust business less than any previous workforce and who, regaining power, will require better leadership and managing than at any time before.

Things shifted. When most executives weren't watching, a new contract was executed. "The past is a foreign country," wrote novelist L. P. Hartley. "They do things differently there." And so they did. Their models of employee engagement were designed for conditions increasingly foreign to today's workplace. The rules have changed.

Once you read the New Rules in depth, they may seem to be common sense. That's a trick our human minds play on us with sociological truths. It's a phenomenon that led physicist-turned-sociologist Duncan J. Watts to write his book *Everything Is Obvious, Once You*

Know the Answer. "Coming into it as a physicist, I had a little of the arro-gance that physicists have that everything other than physics is sort of trivial, that everything to do with people is trivial. It can't be that hard. It's not rocket science. I was pretty humbled trying to learn sociology, because once you have to think through all these problems, you realize how complicated they are and how difficult they are to solve," he told an interviewer "Unlike the physical sciences, where it's relatively easy to see how difficult they are, it's actually difficult to see how difficult sociology is."[21]

Even if you diminish the insights here as common sense, applying them is no cakewalk. It's common sense not to eat doughnuts, not to stay up too late, to send regular personal notes to your customers, to spend lots of quality time with your children, to exercise every day, and to unplug during vacations. How are those no-brainers going?

The research behind this book, behind the New Rules, makes clear that they are, in fact, rules. Follow them and get the benefits—fewer sick days, lower turnover, greater customer focus, more innovation, to name a few. Each rule emerged from the in-depth analyses as some-thing important enough to employees' experience at work that they will reciprocate it with increased commitment to the organization and intensity in their work. It comes through strongly as well in their comments.

"I'm driven by doing something that's never been done before," said a 56-year-old man in the computer hardware industry.

"The camaraderie among us motivates me," said a 48-year-old banker. "We are truly a team. Being able to see the effect that my job has on customers is very rewarding. We work hard, but we play hard, too."

"I enjoy the challenge of the work. I love knowing that I'm helping others," said a 38-year-old insurance company employee.

Because of the power of positive reciprocity, leaders who invest heavily in the experience of working at their companies gain excep-tional intensity from their employees. "A lot of the current research on employee morale and managing people in general in organizations sug-gests that this may be the only remaining competitive advantage that organizations have," said Michael D. Johnson, assistant professor at the

University of Washington. "Organizations that do this well tend to do really well financially."[22]

SOME YEARS AGO, A GROUP OF EXECUTIVES MET TO DISCUSS THEIR company's employee engagement strategy. The company was under pressure. Its stock was down. Its key products were at risk of being commoditized.

To maintain margins, the business had done a wave of layoffs. Leadership told the employees no further layoffs were anticipated. However, not long thereafter, when results again were disappointing, and under pressure from the board of directors, the company ordered more people terminated.

Not surprisingly, this took a toll on the morale of the surviving workers, many of whom recently saw valued colleagues given pink slips, saw little upside at the company, or worried about the security of their own jobs. In the midst of all this, the company did an employee survey. Although some people undoubtedly inflated their survey responses out of fear, many also responded candidly. Given all that had occurred, they were worn out.

One of the executives, fresh from a massage at a senior leadership team off-site meeting, didn't appreciate the workers' candor. "Disengaged employees are like a cancer," he told the rest of the executive team between bites of his three-course meal. "They should be cut out."

His sentiment was unusual only for the fact that he admitted it so bluntly. Some executives—those with the nicest offices, making the policies others must follow, paid many multiples more than those they supervise—are bothered that their people aren't perfectly chipper regardless of the emotionally grinding circumstances. And the execs freak out just as some engagement advisors hope they will when those consultants use descriptions of the "actively disengaged" that are both hyperbolic and wrong.

In many quarters, "disengaged" has come to mean not that the employee made a wrong turn into the clutches of a cruddy manager or a widget factory, but that he has a character flaw. The symptoms are confused with the disease. "A disengaged workforce," wrote Cass Business School professor Stefan Stern, "is a silent killer as far as companies are concerned."[23]

Gallup vilifies the "actively disengaged" as "busy acting out their unhappiness." "Every day," it claims, "these workers undermine what their engaged coworkers accomplish."[24] Globoforce included among its profiles of "five famously disengaged employees" the traitors Brutus and Benedict Arnold. "In retrospect, good practices around recognition, culture management, and talent management would have made a big difference for these employees," it said.[25]

The most "disengaged" are "corporate terrorists," claims one self-described "HR pro" and blogger. These people "are the ones trying to sabotage everything you're trying to do," he asserts. "Your goal should be to remove the terrorists every time you catch them planting the cultural equivalent of an IED."[26] These insults are an amateurish smear job.

Imagine a person works for the U.S. Central Intelligence Agency, drawn to it by fictional spy movies and its very real mission to "preempt threats and further U.S. national security objectives by collecting intelligence that matters."[27] Suppose that over the course of several years, the spy finds, as one wrote on Glassdoor.com, that "the best and worst employees were treated exactly the same in many cases" and that "many levels of management are almost uniformly awful."[28] Or perhaps he just burns out on travel to hostile or dangerous countries and "having to lie to everyone about what you do for a living and how your day was at work."[29]

Is he "cancer"? Is he a cultural "terrorist," planting workplace "improvised explosive devices" among his colleagues? Is he "acting out his unhappiness"? Is he "undermining what his engaged coworkers accomplish"? Is he Benedict Arnold?

Of course not. That would be treason. He is simply reacting naturally to the conditions in which he finds himself. In workplaces where the mission is far less crucial, "undermining" and planting metaphorical

IEDs might not be criminal but would still be irresponsible at best. The vast majority of people are better than that, even when they become frustrated or demoralized. As one astute executive quipped, "It's not like they want to be disengaged."

In the New Rules studies, people on the high end of the engagement scale—people whose companies are following the rules well—score high on every indicator of commitment to and intensity for their employers. Obligation to work hard? Wanting to stay? Planning to stay? Willingness to work hard for customers? Looking for ways to improve the way they work? Delivering their best ideas? Recommending the company as a great place to work? All of them are not only high, but close to pegging the meter.

As would be expected, the more a company fails to follow the New Rules, the more each of these intentions fades. However, each does not fall off at the same rate.

Wanting to stay and recommending the company as a great place to work are the first casualties of poor leading and managing. An employee's best ideas disappear at nearly the same pace. As conditions degrade, being proud of working for the company slides and wanting to work somewhere else increasingly converts itself into real plans to leave.

Three key intentions prove the most resilient to mediocre or poor leadership and managing. The obligation to work as hard as possible fights back against frustrating conditions, as does an employee's determination to find better ways to work. And the last thing an employee surrenders to a bad employer? "I am willing to work especially hard for my organization's customers" averages well on the positive side of the scale even as the employee's rating of conditions is negative.

Frustrated or demoralized employees often say they still believe in the kind of work their organization does; they want to deliver high-quality work, even if they don't see it coming from the rest of the enterprise; and they do not believe customers or clients should suffer because of the situation in which they find themselves. But the lack of support eventually wears them down. As one person who had finally surrendered to poor conditions told the research team, "I do not feel challenged. I feel like my work is meaningless."

What these patterns indicate is a much higher degree of maturity, sense of responsibility, and professionalism in the reputedly "actively disengaged" than companies and consultancies have attributed to them. Some consultants tally the "cost of disengaged workers" when they should be calling it the "cost of disengaging your workers"—a minor edit with major implications. The blame-the-victim assumptions only make it more likely people will pretend to be engaged right up until the day they give their notice, and allow the true causes of frustration and demoralization to fester inside a firm.

The choice of what kinds of attitudes your employees bring to work is yours. Because people so strongly reciprocate what they receive, a company gets the engagement it deserves. Because engagement is so closely tied to results, a company also gets the performance it deserves.

THE FIRST RULE

Get Inside
Their Heads

DAVID MCCULLOUGH JR. IS A HIGH SCHOOL ENGLISH TEACHER.

Until 2012, few people would have known of him except for the fact that he shares his name with his famous father. The elder David McCullough wrote *Truman* and *John Adams* and *1776*. He's won two Pulitzer Prizes. You would recognize his voice on more than a dozen PBS films.

His son worked in relative obscurity at Wellesley High School outside Boston. Then he gave a graduation speech.

"Your ceremonial costume (is) shapeless, uniform, one-size-fits-all," McCullough the younger told the graduates. "Whether male or female, tall or short, scholar or slacker, spray-tanned prom queen or intergalactic X-Box assassin, each of you is dressed, you'll notice, exactly the same. And your diploma, but for your name, exactly the same."

"All of this is as it should be, because none of you is special."

"You are not special. You are not exceptional."

"Contrary to what your U9 soccer trophy suggests, your glowing seventh grade report card, despite every assurance of a certain corpulent purple dinosaur, that nice Mister Rogers, and your batty Aunt Sylvia, no matter how often your maternal caped crusader has swooped in to save you, you're nothing special."

The English teacher listed examples of all the attention lavished on each of the teenagers marching that day. "You've been nudged, cajoled, wheedled, and implored. You've been feted and fawned over and called 'Sweetie Pie,'" he said. "And certainly we've been to your games, your plays, your recitals, your science fairs. Absolutely, smiles ignite when you walk into a room and hundreds gasp with delight at your every tweet."

However, he said, "Astrophysicists assure us the universe has no center; therefore you cannot be it." The audience laughed and applauded.

It didn't take long for the speech to go viral. It hit the national network newscasts. The comments "raised numerous eyebrows last Friday," said one report.[1] It was a "bust-your-chops commencement address," said another.[2] The YouTube replay of the address got 2 million hits.[3]

McCullough was caught off guard by the amount of attention his speech attracted. E-mails filled his inbox. His phone rang constantly. He got a book deal.[4] "For a middle-aged high-school teacher and suburban dad, it has been a dizzying experience," he wrote.[5]

"With three memorable words—'you're not special'—David McCullough Jr. went from a popular English teacher at Wellesley High School to an Internet sensation and among last spring's most memorable commencement speakers," reported *The Boston Globe*.[6] He'd hit a nerve.

You may believe McCullough is right. You may have been nodding your head reading bits of his speech, thankful someone finally put a few cracks in all the mirrors surrounding people today. Think whatever you want. It's too late. Whatever the English teacher's or your own opinion of it, the newest graduates, the newest employees, are used to being treated as though they are special.

"Wait a minute!" a father exclaimed at seeing one of the hockey players in his son's video game. "That guy has your name and your number on his jersey!"

"And my same helmet, my same gloves, my same stick," his son added without moving his eyes from the screen as he continued playing.

"When will they adapt?" asked commentator Emily Matchar in the *Washington Post*. "They won't. Ever. Instead, through their sense of entitlement and inflated self-esteem, they'll make the modern workplace adapt to them. And we should thank them for it. Because the modern workplace frankly stinks, and the changes wrought by Gen Y will be good for everybody."[7]

Millennials didn't invent the importance of individualization. They were, after all, raised by the alleged hedonists of the "me generation." Generation Y is simply the most recent class graduating into a culture that has been growing increasingly individual for decades.

With post–World War II wealth, baby boomers "did something only aristocrats (and intellectuals and artists) were supposed to do— they discovered and started doting on Me!" wrote Tom Wolfe in 1976. "They've created the greatest age of individualism in American history! All rules are broken! . . . Neither arguments nor policies nor acts of the legislature have been any match for them in the past. And this one has the mightiest, holiest roll of all, the beat that goes . . . *Me . . . Me . . . Me . . . Me . . .*"[8]

The big difference today is the Internet. Professionally and personally, it put "Me" on steroids. Résumés used to be documents stuffed in a drawer somewhere, updated for a job search, and seen by only a few people. Most workers were anonymous to all but their colleagues and a small circle of outside contacts. Now everyone has a LinkedIn page dedicated to him or her, seen by hundreds of connections, available to hundreds of thousands.

A sizable chunk of employees have a Facebook page, jammed with trumpery, gibberish, unsolicited political screeds, and pictures of what they are having for breakfast. (In late November 2014, the online publication *Quartz* actually published "The complete guide to Instagramming your Thanksgiving dinner."[9] Mmmmm, Grandma, pass me a photo of those yams.) Every smartphone has two cameras— one to take pictures of what you see and another one, Narcissus, to take selfies. It used to be that mass communication of personal musings was restricted to newspaper columnists and radio talk show hosts. With Twitter, blogs, Instagram, Tumblr, Pinterest, podcasts, and YouTube, everyone is, should he so choose, editor, publisher, columnist, TV producer, and talk show host.

The employee who arrives at your office on Monday morning is fresh from a weekend of posting news about her, her, her, and getting likes and shares and comments from her wide social network. With the reinforcement of all that attention, she is the hero of her own life story. And you want her to widgetize herself for the workweek? To be one of many? To be ignored?

Good luck getting that toothpaste back in the tube. From the employee's perspective, being treated as a unique individual and showered with a lot of attention is as baked into the employment deal as is the pumpkin in that Instragrammed pie.

THE MOST FUNDAMENTAL OF THE NEW RULES OF ENGAGEMENT IS "Get Inside Their Heads."

Employee engagement is an individual phenomenon. Every person's motivations, abilities, and goals are unique. Each person's reasons for needing or wanting to work differ. Everything, including the New Rules themselves, needs to be adapted to the circumstances and personality of the individual worker. The most important imperative to prevent employees from being treated like widgets is to ensure each is led and managed in a way that fits his or her personality. That can happen only if someone takes the time to really decipher that employee, to get inside his or her head.

The larger the business, the greater the temptation to create economies of scale, to process the "human resources." Sometimes it's unavoidable. No large enterprise has the time to design orientation, training, an insurance plan, or even a job description for each employee. But as soon as there's only one cake for all the employees who had a birthday that month, the train has pulled into Widgetville. Too often, one-size-fits-all decisions get made on issues that are exceptionally one of a kind.

This is most painfully apparent when large firms pursue the admirable goal of eliminating racial and sexual discrimination. They count widgets by whether they are Latino, African American, Asian, or Native American; male or female; young or old. They become adept at categorization rather than individualization. Sometimes they issue clumsy advice like the Target Corporation memo on Hispanics that made headlines in 2013. "Not everyone wears a sombrero," it said. "Food: not everyone eats tacos and burritos. . . . Music: not everyone dances to salsa."[10]

Companies lose sight of the fact that people in any group—race, gender, or age—are more dissimilar than they are alike. They don't realize that as multiracial relationships proliferate, as more employees start to identify themselves with terms such as "Blackanese," "Filatino," "Chicanese," "Korgentinian," and "Juskimo," HR is going to run out of those obnoxious boxes for employees to check.[11] They fail to understand that the ultimate "diversity" program is working for a company that insists each person is managed, coached, given opportunities, and recognized as a category of one.

There are any number of people inside a company who could improve the experience of an employee. The people in information technology can set him up with the latest tools. The people in benefits can work through the right way to use the company's insurance to pay for his kid's braces. The leader of another department could recruit him for a new role. The CEO could give him a major opportunity to shine. But none of these people is likely to see the employee very often or to know him very well.

Each employee also has dozens of people who understand him, who know his abilities and goals, his past successes, his life outside of work, how he collaborates, and what best motivates him. His best friends (people who, despite the assumptions of an old engagement survey question, don't work at that company) know things he tells no one else. His friends in other departments and his colleagues are, to a large extent, "inside his head." But none of them has the wherewithal to make his life at work much better.

There is only one person in both groups, only one person who has the time and frequent contact to get inside an employee's head and the authority to marshal the company's resources on that employee's behalf.

For any given employee, there is only one person who can bring the First Rule to life: his or her manager. This is the reason why nearly every study of employee attitudes and motivation points to the manager—one's immediate supervisor—as a major differentiator between a great job and a poor one.

People are often promoted to management for their years of service or for their expertise in the department's work (or, unfortunately, for currying favor with the higher-ups), not their drive and aptitude with people. Companies try to save money by increasing the managers' "span of control" or their nonmanagerial workload to the point they don't have much time for their employees. Great managing is rarely well recognized. Sometimes supervisors simply become lazy. The cause doesn't matter much because the employee experiences the same thing: neglect.

Getting inside someone's head takes time—regular conversations. In the United States, 7 out of 10 employees say their managers meet with them regularly. In India, it's 8 out of 10. The remaining, neglected minority in each region of the world ranges from those whose managers occasionally make time to the person whose firm developed a bad habit of assigning supervisors two time zones removed from those they were supposed to be supporting and changing those assignments frequently. "I couldn't identify my manager in a police lineup," he said.

Twenty-one percent of American employees strongly agree that "my manager understands me." In the United Kingdom, Canada, and Brazil, the percentages are in the mid-teens. In Australia, it's just 9 percent. The vast majorities of these people whose managers are inside their heads also say, "I love my job." "My manager treats me like I am his most valued and trusted resource in this organization," one respondent wrote at the end of his New Rules of Engagement survey. At the other extreme, 5 percent in the United States strongly disagree that their managers understand them; only 19 percent of that group say they love their jobs.

When someone has a highly involved manager, reciprocity becomes personal. Performing poorly would not just be letting down the organization; it would be failing that manager, which is a tougher burden to carry. The greatest sense of obligation to work hard quadruples between the low and high ends of the manager attentiveness scale. "If you have a motivated staff who feels wanted and needed, you'll hit the bottom line every time," one employee wrote. "Neglect your staff and treat them as just a number, and you'll have low morale, and chances are you'll be struggling to hit your financial goals."

Managers can fire employees; employees can fire their managers also—by quitting. Among those Americans whose managers are most clueless, 2 out of 3 say they wish they were working somewhere else and 4 of 10 say they plan to leave their jobs in the coming year. "Our manager is not very involved most of the time," wrote one woman preparing to quit. "My manager just doesn't care," said another.

In the late 1990s, Gallup coined a saying that's become an engagement bumper sticker: "People join companies, but they leave managers." It's not that simple. People leave because of benefits over which their manager has no control. They leave straight salary for stock options. They leave leaders with no vision or conscience. They leave bad companies to go to better firms. They abandon financially sinking ships for sound ones. They leave stagnation here to find accomplishment there. But, yes, they leave managers also.

A tuned-in manager is what the statisticians call a "necessary but not sufficient" condition of a great job. The supervisor cannot create engagement alone. Companies that expect it are setting up their managers for failure. But if managers are asleep at the switch, they leave a void for employees no one else can fill, because no one is in a better position to get inside their heads.

WHEN PEOPLE CALL A TOLL-FREE LINE TO BUY AN AIRLINE TICKET OR get help configuring a printer, they are often talking to an employee of Wipro. Based in India, Wipro provides telephone and online chat support for companies around the world.

Like most call center firms, Wipro struggles to keep employees, many of whom burn out and resign shortly after completing their training. The work is stressful, and it is complicated by the fact that employees are expected be someone else, to "de-Indianize" their accent and attitude to reflect that of the customers calling in.

Not long before David McCullough gave his "You're not special" speech, three researchers got permission to try different orientation strategies with groups of new employees at the company to see if making them feel special would increase their commitment to the organization.

One group of employees was given an orientation session that focused on the firm. A Wipro senior leader talked briefly about the company's values and why it is an outstanding organization. A star performer at the company spoke about the same topic. The new recruits were asked to spend 15 minutes writing answers to the following questions:

- "What did you hear about the company that was most intriguing or appealing to you?"
- "What did you hear about Wipro today that you would be proud to tell your family about?"
- "What did you hear about Wipro that makes you proud to be part of this organization?"

The recruits in this group talked briefly about their answers. Finally, they were given a badge and two fleece sweatshirts with the Wipro name and were asked to wear them during their training.

Another group of employees received nearly identical treatment, but rather than emphasize the company, the focus was put on them as individuals. The senior leader talked about how working at Wipro would allow each person to express himself or herself. The recruits were asked to reflect on the following questions:

- "What three words best describe you as an individual?"
- "What is unique about you that leads to your happiest times and best performance at work?"
- "Reflect on a specific time—perhaps on a job, perhaps at home—when you were acting the way you were 'born to act.'"
- "How can you repeat that behavior on this job?"

Members of this group were also given fleece sweatshirts and a badge, but theirs bore the name of the employee rather than that of the company.

The experiment was conducted only during orientation. From there, the two groups began doing identical jobs, taking calls and dispensing advice. Even so, six months after their orientation, the group whose first experiences at Wipro were focused on them as individuals suffered 21 percent lower turnover than the group focused on the positive aspects of the enterprise.

Complementary discoveries emerged after employees at a chapter of the Make-a-Wish Foundation were encouraged to come up with personalized, unofficial titles such as "Minister of Dollars and Sense," "Goddess of Greetings," "Heralder of Happy News," or "Duchess of Data." Even the researchers were struck by how such a simple, individualizing thing could strengthen people dealing with the emotional burdens of arranging last wishes for terminally ill children.

"Although the psychological benefits of self-reflective job titles that employees described seemed somewhat implausible at first, our initial uncertainty waned after many hours of interviews in which employees made spontaneous comments about the value of self-reflective titles as a way to cope with stress in a heart-wrenching environment," wrote three professors from the Wharton School and London Business School.

"As organizations seek to create consistency between employees, employees are at risk of losing the 'me' within the 'we,'" wrote the researchers. During their interviews, the Make-a-Wish employees "described how creating and using a self-reflective title opens the door for colleagues to view one another as human beings, not merely role occupants," wrote the researchers. And there was no harm in it; the employees still had their official titles for purposes of HR keeping everything straight.[12]

For decades, many organizations have encouraged their employees to subordinate much of their individuality to the corporation. You can find it most commonly among the flight attendants of major airlines (Southwest being a prominent exception). It also shows up in major retailers, bank call centers, hotels, rental car companies, and fast-food outlets. The company wants a standard, brand-compliant approach. "The last thing I want is our front-line people exercising their judgment," a corporate brand manager once blurted out in an unguarded moment. The firm wants uniform widgets following a uniform script.

"The goal of many organizations' socialization practices is to help newcomers adopt a new organizational identity. In fact, many organizations require newcomers to wear standard wardrobes and follow detailed verbal scripts, forbid personal possessions, and enforce appropriate displays of emotion—all measures designed to suppress individuality," wrote the authors of the Wipro study. The approach backfires. Perhaps it would have worked better a generation or two ago, when companies and employees were more loyal to each other, but "You're not special" just doesn't fly anymore.

"Tactics emphasizing employees' personal identities ultimately may be more effective at strengthening employment relationships," wrote the researchers. "We contend that while newcomers do seek to reduce uncertainty and fit in, they also yearn for authenticity. Namely, they want to feel that they can behave authentically in the environment where they spend the majority of their waking hours—to be recognized for who they are rather than being subsumed by an organizational identity."[13]

WHILE THE DIRECT CONNECTION BETWEEN ONE PERSON AND A billion-dollar enterprise employing tens of thousands is made on the front line, the way a company treats its people is ultimately a reflection of the CEO and his or her team. They write the policies. They set the expectations of managers and other leaders. They set the tone.

Which would be fine were it not for the fact that powerful people are handicapped in understanding those who work for them.

Every person has in his brain a network of what have come to be known as "mirror neurons." This wiring allows a person to put himself in the place of someone else, not just logically but empathically. It's the system that makes hockey fans "feel" a hard check into the boards that they only see. It allows someone to "taste" in her mind the soda she sees another woman drinking across the room. It's one of the most important ways one person can intuit what another is feeling. It's how one person gets inside another's head.

In 2013, three researchers randomly assigned volunteers to think and write about being in different levels of the pecking order. "Please recall a particular incident in which you had power over another individual or individuals," the first group was told. The second group was directed to "please recall a particular incident in which someone else had power over you."

Immediately after putting themselves in one of the two mindsets, the subjects were shown a video of a hand squeezing a ball. Even something so simple activates a person's mirror neurons, sending signals to the volunteer's hands as though he or she were squeezing the ball. That's the natural human response.

But those who had just thought about being powerful didn't mirror the actions of the hand in the video as strongly as those who put themselves in a dependent mindset. "When people were feeling powerful, the signal wasn't very high at all," said Sukhvinder Obhi, one of the authors of the study.[14] "The mirror activation, if you like, seemed to be low."

"In other words," said National Public Radio reporter Chris Benderev in his story on the study, "when people felt power, they really did have more trouble getting inside another person's head."[15]

Stories of out-of-touch executives are so common they've become axiomatic. They entertain us in TV shows such as *The Office* or movies such as *The Devil Wears Prada*.

"There you are, Emily. How many times do I have to scream your name?" asks hypothermic boss Miranda Priestly in the movie.

"A-a-actually it's Andy. My name is Andy," says her new assistant. "Andrea, but everyone calls me Andy."

Her boss laughs sarcastically. "I need 10 or 15 skirts from Calvin Klein."

"Okay, what kind of skirts?"

"Please bore someone else with your questions. And make sure we have Pier 59 at 8 a.m. tomorrow. And remind Jocelyn I need to see a few of those satchels that Mark is doing in the pony. And then tell Simone I'll take Jackie if Maggie isn't available."

It's funny in the movie. It's not funny if you're the person reporting to an executive who has let the office go to his or her head.

A trainee for one industrial firm happened to be seated next to the head of her new division at a company dinner. "He bragged the entire time about his new game room, complete with a number of taxidermy heads of animals he had killed himself," she said. "He talked about how large the new addition was: 3,500 square feet. My whole house at the time was 1,800 square feet. I felt like screaming."

One CEO was traveling with an underling to a number of the company's facilities around the United States. The enterprise had recently been a takeover target. The deal had fallen through. Had the firm been purchased, the CEO and the rest of the senior team would have been rewarded handsomely. The employee would have been "made redundant" and terminated.

"It's too bad that sale didn't go through," the CEO commiserated to his employee on their road trip. "I would have been the $7 million man."

His subordinate was dumbfounded: "I couldn't believe he said that."

Perhaps his mirror neurons weren't working.

An organization's failure rate on the First Rule cannot be charged solely to managers. Leaving a trail of out-of-touch anecdotes for the business press, outright mocked on *Undercover Boss*, many executives are the ultimate causes of their firms being impersonal places to work. "The higher the management, the less involved they seem to be with the day-to-day employee issues of the company," one manager complained. "Walk the floors occasionally and meet the people who make you look good."

Some executives are prone to seeing their people as widget costs on the financial statements more than they see them in real life. They often fail in their direct supervision of the other C-level leaders to set an example of the individualization that should cascade through the whole firm.

A few million in salary and stock options ought to buy more. It ought to buy more of a leader's time with the troops. It ought to buy some strategies for looking out for each individual. It ought to buy a CEO who is not only a great leader but a great manager—and a great person. And, ironically, it ought to buy more awareness that the money, perks, and power of the office could make an executive empathetically tone deaf, with a countervailing intensity for working around the handicap to get inside his or her people's heads.

THE SECOND RULE

Make Them Fearless

BILL HEWLETT HAD A DIFFICULT DECISION TO MAKE.

It was 1970, three decades removed from the iconic garage in Palo Alto where Hewlett-Packard had been started. Hewlett's partner, David Packard, was temporarily away from the company, serving as U.S. deputy secretary of defense.

The country was in a recession. Orders to HP had slumped, coming in substantially below capacity. Revenues and profits were down. The company needed to cut 10 percent of its costs.

Some of the company's managers, used to organizations hiring and firing in concert with profits, apparently jumped the gun and began terminating people. Loyal and hardworking employees were being blindsided. Hewlett rushed out a memo to his managers.

"An increasing number of cases are coming to my attention in which employees are being terminated with little or no warning that their performance has been unsatisfactory," he wrote. "In some cases, evaluations have been glowing up to the time that an individual is released. There is no excuse for this. It is not humane. It is not HP-like. It is not justified."

Hewlett told his managers that no one should be terminated without having "advance warning through written evaluations" and without having been "advised constructively" on how to improve. Whenever possible, the company, not the employee, should try to find somewhere else in HP where he or she could succeed. The employee should not be "turned loose to find his own job somewhere in HP," he wrote. "Before any adverse action is taken, it should be well thought out," he continued. "We must recognize that each of our people represents an individual with problems, families, etc."

But there was still the issue of needing to cut costs, which could not be done without trimming the payroll. Hewlett issued another directive: Nearly everyone, himself included, would take off work every other Friday and take a corresponding 10 percent cut in pay. Production would be shut down on that day. Only salespeople, whose activity would create the orders needed to reverse the trend, were exempt. One company vice president called it "the Nine-Day Fortnight."

"Usually in business, it is the little guy on the line who takes it on the chin, while management and higher-ups stay at work," wrote Hewlett in announcing the decision. "It is only right that everyone share in the pain, up and down the line."[1]

Six months later, orders were again flowing into Hewlett-Packard at their normal rate. Production resumed on the second Fridays. "Some said they enjoyed the long weekends even though they had to tighten their belts a little," wrote Packard. "The net result of this program was that effectively all shared the burden of the recession, good people were not released into a very tough job market, and we had our highly qualified workforce in place when business improved."

With his directives that employees should not be let go without notice and that the whole company would get through the recession together, Bill Hewlett took fear out of the equation.

Two motivations come through in Hewlett's and Packard's explanations of their decisions. The first is loyalty, executives feeling a strong sense of responsibility for the people who are an integral part of the company. Why should Hewlett or Packard care about "releasing" people into a lousy job market? Because to the two executives, their employees were not widgets.

All the evidence indicates that kind of concern generates a reciprocal commitment from the employees when fear is removed. "Inside HP, where many employees had already resigned themselves to an inevitable layoff, the Nine-Day Fortnight produced an upwelling of gratitude, even love, for Hewlett-Packard—and Bill Hewlett in particular—that would carry the company for the next two decades," wrote Michael S. Malone in his book *Bill & Dave.*

The second motivation is what economists call "labor hoarding." Loyalty is the ethical reason for trying to keep people during a downturn; labor hoarding is the practical reason. A recession doesn't last forever. When it's over, the company is going to need talented people. If too many of them are lost during the slowdown, the firm will be at a disadvantage during the recovery and better years that follow. Better to keep what Packard called their "highly qualified workforce" with the company.

That's what happened in the past. Quite consistently, economic studies show that for each 1 percent decrease in output, employment would drop only half a percent. While productivity suffered in the short term, companies were ready for growth during the recovery.

But something happened over the last two decades. In the last few recessions, more companies cut loose good people. They dropped employees faster than they had in the past. "Firms proved keener to cut workers than hours," reported *The Economist* magazine. "In the 1973–75 recession, . . . employment cuts accounted for less than a third of the reduction in man-hours. The remainder was achieved by shortening the working week or year." In the Great Recession, "the split was reversed."[2]

Economists argue over the causes. Maybe today's recessions are structural, tougher to recover from. "And to the extent that firms know this, they have less reason to hoard labor," wrote economist and *New York Times* columnist Paul Krugman. "They're not going to need those laid-off workers for a long time."[3] Maybe the decline in labor unions made companies less concerned about invoking their wrath. Maybe companies are trying to keep a lid on permanent employees to reduce the cost of new healthcare insurance requirements. Maybe so much more of executive compensation coming from stock options has given those leaders a powerful incentive to "release" people in ways Hewlett and Packard would not.

Whatever the causes, the unwritten social contract between companies and workers has changed—more mercenary, more driven by a bargain cut for the needs of each here and now than a long-term working relationship. "There's been a generational shift toward a less committed relationship between the firm and the worker," said one bank economist.[4] Northwestern University professor Robert Gordon says American workers have come to be seen as "disposable."[5] They are at greater risk of being treated as widgets.

THE SECOND OF THE NEW RULES OF ENGAGEMENT IS "MAKE THEM Fearless." Once you are inside your employees' heads, it is essential you ensure they are not so distracted or paralyzed by fear that nothing else matters.

Fighting fear has always been an imperative for companies that want to perform at the highest levels. It's substantially more important in the wake of the Great Recession. Three years after the recession technically ended, three-quarters of Americans believed the economy was still in its throes.[6] In our studies, one out of four employees says, "I worry a lot about losing my job." Just over half believe they could get another job matching their current pay. The rest are not so sure. Even those who do not regularly worry about their jobs can be rattled surprisingly easily.

There is no more primal emotion than fear. It's a survival instinct. We are hardwired to experience and react to it. Because the human brain evolved a powerful fight-or-flight response against mortal dangers, people struggle to give measured responses to the nonlethal dangers of a poor performance evaluation, the potential closing of a company plant, or a boss who yells. The only time a manager is justified in yelling at an employee is to shout, "Duck!"

"You may have had this experience: You alter an employee's routine or change the way he's evaluated, and you get a reaction that's far bigger and more negative than anything you expected," wrote two professors in a *Harvard Business Review* blog.

"What did you do wrong? Probably nothing except underestimate his fear of death."[7] Yes, death.

An emerging field of research suggests that we have a need for consistency, fairness, and meaning as a way of delaying or putting out of our minds The Inevitable. Because fear is more reflex than choice, people generally have little control over it or its consequences. The fearful employee may lock up and become timid. He becomes compliant and avoids risk. He lays low. He becomes a yes man. The research shows he procrastinates.[8] His spine dissolves. He allows himself to be mistreated, deciding it's better to be an employed widget than a more dignified but jobless real person.

Or just as bad for the business and the employee, he gets angry. He rallies his fellow union members, or he switches from internally collaborative to competitive. He does his work begrudgingly. He watches the clock. He snickers to himself when the equipment breaks. He flips off the phone when his boss calls.

Regardless of whether it taps into deep worries about mortality or just makes him mad, fear is proved to be exceptionally toxic to productivity, health, energy, commitment, and collaboration. This reflex is at the heart of the failure of what's come to be known as "rank-and-yank" performance appraisal systems that threaten some percentage of the employees with loss of pay or being fired if they don't outperform their peers. The father of this fear factor, Jack Welch, prefers the more nuanced term "differentiation," as if the euphemism makes it any less Darwinian.[9]

"Labeling people with any form of numerical rating or ranking automatically generates an overwhelming 'fight or flight' response that impairs good judgment," wrote three experts specializing in neuroscience. "This neural response is the same type of 'brain hijack' that occurs when there is an imminent physical threat like a confrontation with a wild animal. It primes people for rapid reaction and aggressive movement. But it is ill-suited for the kind of thoughtful, reflective conversation that allows people to learn from a performance review."[10]

Logically, many fearful employees want to flee to a job somewhere else. Of those Americans most concerned about their jobs, 56 percent wish they were working somewhere else, compared with only 22 percent on the most secure end of the scale.

To some degree, job insecurity is just part of life. Often there's nothing a company can do to counteract the threat to a person's livelihood. Interest rates, oil prices, and the stock market don't care who gets left behind. People in an increasingly virtual world don't read as many newspapers as they used to, use as many office supplies, write as many checks, or send as many letters. They are using computers less and tablets more. Changing tastes in food, fashion, or music leave some firms devastated just as they make others appear as if out of thin air. "Creative destruction," the economist Joseph Schumpeter called it. Employees know this, and they generally don't hold it against their employers if the company handles the decline compassionately and transparently, as Bill Hewlett handled the 1970 recession.

Fear is the crudest of managerial tactics. It's an emotional baseball bat, threatening to beat the hell out of the employee's sense of security and well-being. One out of five workers in the United States and China feels its impact, agreeing with the statement "Management uses fear to motivate employees to work harder." The proportions are one out of three in the United Kingdom and India and one out of four in Canada and Latin America. This perception is roughly twice as powerful at killing commitment and intensity as just worrying about losing one's job.

So why do powerful people use fear? Because in the short term and in limited ways, it works. Of course you can scare someone into doing what you want. People work harder on both ends of the intimidation scale than they do in the middle. But there is a vast difference between working hard voluntarily and doing so because you are freaking out. It's a J-shaped pattern. Fearful employees scramble to find ways to improve the way they work, to cover their butts, but the drive is not as strong, as effective, or as honest as it is among those who are fearless. One set of experiments found that people experiencing anxiety are more likely to engage in "self-interested unethical behaviors" and to rationalize their misconduct as not as serious as similar acts by others.[11]

The drive to help customers runs high among those who are being managed by fear, but here, too, it's an unhealthy and unsustainable motivation. Sometimes employees find in the appreciation of their customers the recognition they don't get from their managers. "I love my clients," said one employee of a firm that decimated its culture in the recession. "It's my company I can't stand." In a similar vein, a Connecticut state park ranger said the best thing about his job is "meeting great people and working out in the field." Staying outside minimizes his time with "bullying, sociopathic managers," he wrote.

Because it's so powerful, fear tempts leaders and managers who lack confidence or competence in their abilities to motivate through meaning, trust, individualization, recognition, accomplishment, and positive reciprocity. When they pick up that baseball bat, they should not be surprised at how quickly people scatter or fight back.

✿

CIRCUIT CITY WAS A STAR AMONG COMPANIES.

From 1982 to 1997, its stock did 18.5 times better than the overall market, the best 15-year return of any public company. It was featured in the bestselling book *Good to Great* as one of 11 exemplary organizations that showed "why some companies make the leap and others don't."

Part of its success, according to the legend, was its way of dealing with people. When the enterprise operated as Wards Company TV stores in the 1950s, founder Samuel S. Wurtzel took a personal interest in his employees.

"He did not care how much education or what kind of manners a salesperson had, as long as he could sell," wrote his son and successor, Alan Wurtzel. "He also did not care about race. When the all-white sales force threatened to quit *en masse* because he had decided to give a smart, personable African-American service technician a chance to prove himself on the sales floor, Sam faced down the revolt." The older Wurtzel and business partner Abraham L. Hecht "built a fiercely loyal and devoted following among their employees and their families."

The younger Wurtzel, who was CEO from 1973 to 1986 and a board member until 2001, says he operated from 12 "Habits of Mind," concepts such as "Evidence Trumps Ideology" and "Encourage Debate." His eighth habit is "Mind the Culture: Create a caring and ethical culture where employees can make mistakes without fear of adverse consequences. . . . Understand, exemplify, and reinforce the company's positive history and culture."[12]

Reviewing draft chapters from *Good to Great*, Wurtzel wrote author Jim Collins a note about how to manage people. It ended up in the book. "I spent a lot of time thinking and talking about who sits where on the bus. I called it 'putting square pegs in square holes and round pegs in round holes,'" he wrote. "Instead of firing honest and able people who are not performing well, it is important to try to move them once or even two or three times to other positions where they might blossom."[13]

By 2007, Circuit City was a different company. Wurtzel was gone, as was the guy who came after him. The company was under the command of Philip Schoonover, who defected from Best Buy in 2004 and within two years was running the rival enterprise.

The company was already in trouble. It had become complacent. It built stores in poorly trafficked sites. It stopped selling appliances. It was slow to see trends in consumer electronics. Its online presence was unimpressive. Cash that could have been used to reinvigorate the brand and its stores was spent repurchasing shares, thus bolstering the stock price while the underlying business was drifting.

Worse yet, largely unknown to those outside, a culture of fear was building inside the organization. Chief Information Officer Mike Jones wanted no part of it and resigned in late 2006 "to pursue other interests," according to the company's press release. "I left," he explained years later, "because I began seeing the decline in our business, and rather than building one strong, cohesive team, founded on trust and support, we were building our team around fear and intimidation," he said. "Those elements are not aligned with my definition of success."

A few months after Jones's departure, the firm committed a staggering blunder with its employees. Circuit City announced it "made a business decision, with respect to certain positions, to separate from employment hourly associates whose pay rate is 51 cents or more above established pay range." Translation: The company would fire those who, by greater performance and experience, were paid the most.[14] "It had nothing to do with their skills or whether they were a good worker or not," said company spokesman Bill Cimino in announcing the news. "It was a function of their salary relative to the market."[15]

Wired magazine blogger David Becker snarked that with the terminations, Circuit City had solved "that nagging problem of clerks being overly helpful and knowledgeable."[16]

The irony that "Our associates are our greatest assets" was the first of Circuit City's company values posted on its website was not lost on the media. "Clearly, the company doesn't value them as 'great assets,'" said *USA Today*. "If it did, it would realize that firing employees because they've performed well enough to earn raises demoralizes everyone else. What kind of inducement is it for employees to work hard and excel if their reward might be a pink slip? And why would people want to shop at a store where the low premium on service is so loudly trumpeted?"[17]

On top of its other problems, Circuit City hardwired fear through its organization. In less than two months, analysts said negative reciprocity and the loss of talented employees were taking their toll. The cost-cutting move boomeranged back as a much bigger revenue-cutting mistake. The firm "cast off some of its most experienced and successful people and was losing business to competitors who have better-trained employees," reported *The Washington Post*.[18]

The leadership of the company was "feudal and paranoid," an employee relayed to Wurtzel. "Initially, Schoonover appeared to be a visionary leader. We all wanted him to succeed. He proved to be a ruthless, superficial, and vindictive person. He was an embarrassment to everyone. We never had a chance after he settled into power."[19] With the company in a tailspin, Schoonover resigned in September 2008. *Businessweek* crowned him one of the worst managers of the year.[20]

Five months later, Circuit City announced it was going out of business.

Alan Wurtzel wrote a book about the demise of the company his father started and he once led. He called it *Good to Great to Gone*. He dedicated it to the former employees of Circuit City. "For over sixty years these dedicated men and women gave their best to provide customers with a great shopping experience," he wrote. "This book is dedicated to those who, through no fault of their own, lost their livelihood and their dreams when the company faltered and then collapsed."

FOR AS LONG AS THERE HAVE BEEN LARGE CORPORATIONS, THE MOST common implicit contract between them and their employees has been a mutual long-term commitment. Never mind the legal notices of "at-will" status signed on the first day. Assuming the employee was a good hire, the company wanted to keep him or her indefinitely, and it expected loyalty from the worker. In return for that loyalty, the company would provide security and stability.

Work hard. Look out for the company. Wear the company golf shirt. Enjoy the company picnic. You're indispensable, one of us. Stay longer, and the company's contributions to your 401(k) will become vested. We'll give you more vacation. You'll get a better office. We'll promote you to management.

It worked. In many places, it still does. But for most firms, the decline of labor hoarding, accelerated by the Great Recession, changed the old rules. It altered the implicit contract faster than companies changed their underlying assumptions. Many enterprises still demand old-school devotion from their employees as long as they need those people at the company, but they want the option to call "game over" whenever it suits their short-term needs. Any student of game theory knows that won't play.

"Most of the companies . . . particularly the larger ones, went through about a 10-year period of worrying about attraction and retention," said Wharton management professor Peter Cappelli in a 2009 podcast.[21] "Just before this downturn, if you looked at the CEO priority lists, in the top three typically were attracting and retaining talent. And they went right from that, in sort of whiplash fashion, into laying people off. Even inside these companies, they realized this was a little bizarre to do."

When a company starts laying off people, a cascading series of unintended consequences begins. By definition, layoffs are designed to be concentrated on those the company can get by without. But they rattle everyone, causing the remaining employees to reevaluate their jobs. The proportion of people most committed to staying at the company gets cut in half, from 31 percent to 14 percent. The proportion who wish they were working somewhere else jumps 50 percent, from 21 percent to 31 percent. Who bolts fastest? The most talented, of course—the people the company can least afford losing. People in the middle—looked on neither poorly enough to be let go nor favorably enough to escape quickly—are stuck. The firm has sentenced itself to years of lackluster performance.

"I think the best people have already left," said an executive of a company that had seen several waves of layoffs before he arrived. "Let's face it: What happens when a business struggles? The best people see the signs. They go out looking for a job, and they leave. Once they leave, a wave of the next-smartest people says, 'What am I doing here?' and they leave. And the people who are left? Their mediocrity is exposed."

Or seeing their colleagues take the metaphorical bullet creates that mediocrity. The New Rules research indicates the performance of those who survive the layoffs takes a hit. Creativity, customer focus, sense of obligation to the company, pride in working for it, and inclination to recommend it as a good place to work all run lower than in companies that have not laid off people in the previous year.

In trying to justify the ejection of so many previously "greatest assets," some companies throw dirt. "It wasn't working out with him," they'll say, or "She wasn't a good fit." They might as well complete the sentence with ". . . and should you ever resign or be fired, we're going to say the same thing about you." Anything but the most dignified treatment of former employees is immature and caustic.

Employees who feel they have been burned become highly motivated and capable competitors—people who know all the weaknesses of their former employer, who meet for drinks with other expatriates, form alumni networks on LinkedIn, and write scathing reviews on Glassdoor. Taking jobs at client organizations, they bar the door to the company they once represented. Getting a call or e-mail from someone thinking about joining the old place, they'll give them an earful. Widgets sometimes have a nasty bite.

Leaders have two distinct alternatives to avoid this type of backlash.

The first is to staff lean enough, operate conservatively enough, and hoard labor to avoid the need to make people fearful. "There are a number of employees who have seen the economy go down, and stay down, for such a prolonged period of time that there has actually been a reverse boomerang to a certain degree where employees have more loyalty than perhaps they did before," employment attorney and Wharton advisor Philip Miscimarra said in the midst of the recession. If they keep their jobs "and have seen employers that have reacted in a helpful and responsible way, the people who are continuing to be with organizations trying to do more with less, in some respects have greater energy and a greater commitment to the organization than they had before."[22] In rare cases, such firms can even scoop up highly talented employees in a buyers' market.

The second option is to openly acknowledge a different arrangement in which, since the company can't give loyalty, it also does not expect to get it. Such arrangements, whose prevalence is a matter of debate,[23] require a far more deliberate strategy for managing people.

As a holdover from the old rules, too many companies and their people are playing make-believe: "We pretend we're going to employ you forever; you pretend you're going to stay forever." That fiction continues until one or the other abruptly says goodbye. Whichever one was left behind feels misled. "If I work hard, you're not supposed to toss me," or "If we gave you a good and stable job, you're not supposed to quit."

To the degree they take hold, deliberately temporary relationships with employees will change everything about the deal. If a company can't commit to keeping certain employees indefinitely, or if those employees are among the one in three who doesn't "see a way to get ahead at my current organization," it can't complain when those people are more actively and even publicly planning their next move. If a manager wants to hang onto a key employee longer, he must make that additional time more valuable than her alternatives.

With some of the best employees perpetually on the market, companies will have to spend more time recruiting and orienting them, pay more to keep them, ensure if they do leave it's on the best of terms, and be open to some of them coming back for a second or third stint. They will need to ensure that those employees can simultaneously see the end of their current jobs and yet, by virtue of their ever-strengthening credentials, not worry about job security. And someone will have to change how the 401(k) takes five years to fully vest.

"The key to the new employer-employee compact . . . is that although it's not based on loyalty, it's not purely transactional, either. It's an alliance between an organization and an individual that's aimed at helping both succeed," wrote three entrepreneurs, including LinkedIn cofounder Reid Hoffman, in the *Harvard Business Review*.[24]

Both these approaches work because they give the employee, if not traditional job security, high degrees of predictability and control, which reduce fear. That's the ultimate gauge of the Second New Rule of Engagement. How much fear is each employee experiencing? What's its source? What's its toll? And what can you legitimately do to reduce it? Only leaders who agonize over these types of questions are able to truly make their employees fearless.

THE THIRD RULE

Make Money
a Non-Issue

ABOUT A DECADE AGO, FOUR PROFESSORS FROM FRANCE AND BELGIUM put bowls of plain and crispy M&Ms in front of volunteers and asked them which tasted better. It was a trick. The researchers didn't care which kind of M&Ms were better.

The taste test was a ruse to see how much candy the volunteers would eat after the experimenters got them thinking about money. Before the subjects got the candy, half of them had been asked to fantasize about what they would buy if they won 25,000 euros in a lottery. The other half were asked to think about what they would buy if they won only 25 euros. The people who envisioned lot of money ate more M&Ms.

Money is like food, the professors concluded.[1]

Five years later, another group of researchers scanned the brains of volunteers while they were shown videos of money being torn apart. Seeing currency being destroyed agitated the parts of the subjects' brains that recognize tools.

Money is like a tool, these scientists decided.[2]

That's not the whole story, said yet another team of researchers. People are too obsessed with and addicted to money to think of it like just a tool. Money makes people do all kinds of irrational things, like keep pursuing it long after they have more than they will ever need. "In a range of situations, money is found to have a value and an emotional charge that is not predicted by its economic use," they wrote, which is kind of funny given that there's nothing more quintessentially "economic" than money. "Money derives some of its incentive power," they observed, "from providing the illusion of fulfillment of certain instincts." Something weirder is going on.

Money, they argued, is like a drug.[3]

These comparisons tie scientists in knots. Unlike food or a tool, whose usefulness is obvious, the value of money is learned. Even before they can speak, toddlers know to eat marshmallows and hit stuff with a toy hammer, not vice versa. Only later do they learn that a $5 bill from Grandpa gets ice cream or a comic book or other stuff all over town. "What makes the piece of paper in my hand count as money is the fact that we, collectively, accept and recognize that the piece of paper has the status of money," states one study.[4]

The intaglio printing, the official seals, the engraved portrait of a founding father, the security thread, the watermark, the high-quality cotton paper with tiny red and blue threads, the light-shifting ink, and a little-publicized pattern of circles that shuts down color printers[5] are not just intended to foil counterfeiters. They are designed to convince you what you are holding is more than what it really is.

A piece of paper.

"All the fonts, the busy filigree, the micro patterns. It's just dreadful," podcaster Roman Mars remarked about U.S. banknotes. If it were just about practicality, American currency should have a cleaner, more colorful, less easily counterfeited design. But there are what Mars calls "compelling and pretty understandable reasons for its particular brand of horribleness." The greenback doesn't change much. It communicates stability.[6] The U.S. Bureau of Engraving and Printing does not want the druggy "realness" of its money—the thing that makes your brain freak out seeing Ben Franklin torn apart—to become an issue.

"Money is a shared illusion," said Adam Waytz, a psychologist and assistant professor of management at Northwestern University. "We have a lot of beliefs in various systems, whether it's the universe or government or organized religion, that serve more of an existential function to give us a sense that there is some order in the world."[7]

Pay is supposed to bring order to the work world. Compensation is supposed to be the company's most powerful tool, a means of tapping need and greed to get workers to line up with the executives' and shareholders' financial goals. "Money is the crucial incentive because, as a medium of exchange, it is the most instrumental. No other incentive or motivational technique comes even close to money with respect to its incremental value," states a 1980 academic treatise on the subject.[8] In a world staffed by *Homo economicus*, that 35-year-old statement would be spot on.

But if you're doling out magic paper to *Mercenarius reciprocans*, things are going to get weird.

THE THIRD NEW RULE IS "MAKE MONEY A NON-ISSUE."

Nothing illustrates better than pay the difference between the theoretical, fictional "agents" that inhabit economics textbooks and the flesh-and-blood people that companies have on their payrolls. Money motivates, but not in the ways people typically believe it does. It's exceptionally complicated, scaring away the most timid engagement consultancies from even asking about it, and creating a minefield for leaders and comp managers.

Mess it up, let it become an issue, and it will often become *the* issue.

The most basic fact about money is that most of us want more. Duh. Nearly half of Americans say, "I believe I should be paid a lot more money," and another 3 in 10 are ambivalent on the statement. The proportions are similar in Australia, Canada, the United Kingdom, and India. Frustrations with pay are higher, closer to 6 in 10 believing they should be paid much more, in China and Latin America. You'd be hard-pressed to find anywhere in the world where more than about 1 in 5 people say they should not be getting much more in their paycheck.

The strange thing about the range of answers to straight pay questions is that rather than being "the crucial incentive," it has a surprisingly weak connection to people's drive to work hard. In the United States, responses to the question "What percentage of your full effort are you currently delivering in your work?" average nearly the same for those who feel well paid, poorly compensated, or somewhere in between. In Australia, satisfaction with pay has no statistical connection to one's sense of obligation to work hard. Pay more, get more? It's not that simple.

Maybe it's because employees don't believe that harder work will get them higher pay. One survey of decision makers at 121 companies found that a quarter admitted employees who "fail to meet performance expectations" would still be getting bonuses. One-fifth of companies confessed there would be little difference in the bonuses paid to those who performed well and those who performed poorly. A *Washington Post* column on the study was headlined "Why Slackers Still Get Bonuses."[9]

Money also fails as "the crucial incentive" because it does not buy happiness. "Despite the popular theorizing, results suggest that pay level is only marginally related to satisfaction," states one summary of compensation studies.[10] Between the extremes of incredible wealth and poverty, where the effects of money or its absence are stark, there is tremendous noise—lots of people who make modest amounts and are happy with their pay and lots of people who are well off and grumble.

But the most important reason why absolute compensation levels have so little effect on an employee's intensity is that pay is boring. Maybe it would more predictably drive hard work if our managers paid us more like when we were teenagers mowing lawns or babysitting, if our supervisors counted out and handed over a few Benjamin Franklins at the end of each day, plus a tip if we'd gone the extra mile. That would be something to talk about. In a direct-deposit world, no one rushes home to tell his or her spouse, "Hey, I got paid the same amount this Wednesday as I was paid every two weeks for the last six months."

Even a raise doesn't command our attention for long. Behavioral economists call it "hedonic adaptation." Seeing that your company sent a larger number from its bank account to yours feels great for the first few pay periods, after which it doesn't feel much different from getting paid at the old, lower level. The VP of compensation would like your pay to be a psychological "Ka-ching." More often, it's "Yawn."

This fact, this counterintuitive and confusing fact, does not mean that pay is not pivotal. Far from it. It only means that for the three-legged stool of attracting, motivating, and retaining employees, the second leg should be built of something other than the sheer amount of money paid to your people.

In 2013, three Harvard researchers decided to see how different levels of pay would affect the amount of work they got.

On the freelancer contracting site oDesk, they posted jobs typing in CAPTCHAs, those hard-to-read words or codes used to authenticate that a real human is accessing a website. "This is a four-hour job, with the goal of entering as much data as possible while minimizing the number of mistakes," stated the postings. "Specifically, we need as many correctly entered words as possible in four hours because we need the data for a future task and only correct entries can be used."

One of the postings offered $3 an hour for the job. Another offered $4. From those who responded and qualified by having done data entry in the past, the professors replied, "Great, you are hired" to 136 at the $4 rate and 404 at the $3 rate.

From the group promised $3 an hour, the researchers peeled away 135 and gave them a surprise. "As it turns out, we have a bigger budget than expected," they wrote. "Therefore, we will pay you $4 per hour instead of $3 per hour."

The group initially hired at $4 an hour worked no harder than those hired at $3. "When someone is paid $4, even though it is more than they are used to making or expecting, there may be no reason for them to interpret this as a gift or concession from the employer," said Deepak Malhotra, one of the researchers. "More likely, they just assume that their expectations were wrong, and $4 is 'the going rate' for this type of work."[11]

But the group that hired on at $3, then got $4 per hour, worked substantially harder. Among those who were most experienced and had worked most recently—those who best understood the generosity of the surprise pay increase—the raise "actually increased productivity more than it increased cost." The difference between being paid $4 as the market rate or being paid $4 as the market rate plus the employer's generosity may seem "innocuous," said the researchers, but it's not.

In the employee's mind, $3 + $1 is greater than $4. Generosity of pay leads to generosity of effort. Reciprocity affects the perception and effect of compensation as much as it affects everything else.

Chief financial officers and procurement managers are supposed to get things for the lowest price. In buying resources, that's imperative. A great deal on a piece of land. Optioning oil at a three-year low. Locking in high-quality, exotic coffee beans when supply is high and demand is low. A volume deal on laptops. It's just smart business.

The land certainly is not insulted that it was bought on the cheap. The oil does not burn cooler because it was acquired with a well-timed call option. The coffee is just as aromatic at the lower wholesale price. The laptops don't operate any differently.

But when a chief financial officer or some other leader applies the resource procurement strategy to people, it quickly disintegrates. People are not just another category of resources that happens to be human. They expect fairness. They appreciate generosity. Their value to the company varies greatly depending on how they believe they are being treated. Positively and negatively, they reciprocate the intentions of their employers.

A company that treats its people like widgets, that demands its people work as hard as they can for the lowest possible wages, gets the mirror response in return: people who want to work as little as they can for the highest wages they can get. Who can blame them? A company perceived as cheap implicitly gives permission to its employees to be miserly with their effort. Eventually, the company backs itself into the psychology of employees of Soviet state-owned enterprises in the 1980s:

"They pretend to pay us; we pretend to work." A firm can slog through under that kind of transactional, mutual selfishness, as many heavy with labor unions do, but the company will be at a structural disadvantage. Working relationships eventually fail when neither side really cares about the success of the other.

Employees are expected to look out for the long-term financial health of their organizations. Is it unreasonable to expect that the company should look out for the financial trajectory of the employee? In the studies that led to this book, 38 percent of employees say their companies understand this concept. Their firms, they say, are "actively helping me reach my long-term financial goals" and "want me to make more money as the organization becomes more profitable."

It's with favorable attitudes like this about the intentions behind the pay that compensation gains real traction. Among Americans who strongly agree that their firm is helping them reach their financial goals, less than 4 percent want to defect and an astounding 92 percent say their jobs bring out their best ideas. On the other extreme, among those who strongly disagree that their company wants to see them reach their financial goals, 7 of 10 wish they were working somewhere else and only 12 percent say their company gets their best ideas.

To *Economicus*—or "Econs," as behavioral economist Richard Thaler calls the fictional species—our survey statement "Over the long-term, I believe I can earn more here than I could somewhere else" would be more predictive than questions about the employees' perceptions of their leaders' intentions. It's the opposite. To real people, it's the thought that counts as much as the cash.

BECAUSE IT IS NORMALLY SO BORING, MONEY USUALLY STAYS QUIETLY in the mental background. Starting a new project, meeting a new client, getting meaningful recognition, catching up with a caring boss, and a few hundred other events are more likely to make an impression on any given day. Assuming the pay is "competitive"—whatever that means—at a level the employee found workable when she signed on, it will be on most days a non-issue. If she believes her company is looking out for her financial future, it will even be a motivator.

One aspect of pay more than any other, however, will turn money into a monster: unfairness.

Humans are competitive creatures, always comparing themselves against others. More than in absolute terms ("Will it pay the mortgage?"), they measure their pay relative to what their colleagues are making ("Am I making more than the screwup three desks over?"). What appears to make people happiest is making more money than the other guy, or at least not making less.

Given the choice between making $50,000 in a world where everyone else makes $25,000 or making $100,000 in a world where everyone else makes $200,000, half of people will choose to make less in absolute terms in order to be ahead in relative terms. From their comments after making a choice among these alternatives, those who participated in the study "seemed to see life as an ongoing competition, in which not being ahead means falling behind."[12]

"Research has shown that happiness is not related to one's absolute level of wealth," Wally tells the Pointy-Haired Boss in a classic *Dilbert* comic strip. "What matters is one's relative wealth compared to other people. So," he says, pointing to Dilbert, "if I do a good job, could you cut this guy's pay?"[13]

To have the right effect, pay and other rewards must "be perceived as fair, and procedurally justified, as well as anchored in well defined, logical, and ultimately reasonable outcomes," wrote two experts from the University of Louisville. "When context is missing, information is surprising or not transparent, or rewards are perceived as inauthentic and unfair, employees find it challenging to see the meaning in what they are doing no matter the currency, whether external or internal."[14]

Like bad seasonal allergies normally ignored but vicious when pollen is in the air, money will become a potential deal-breaker when fairness is called into question. When a candidate interviews for the job, money is an issue. If an employee reads online that both profits and her CEO's multimillion-dollar pay rose by double-digit percentages while frontline comp is capped in the low single digits, money is now an issue. If she's told by a veteran colleague that the compensation strategy is designed to always raise the bar enough to keep substantial pay increases out of reach, money is now the issue.

If a headhunter calls and offers a much bigger paycheck, money is now the issue. If she reads the 2014 *Forbes* article that states, "Staying employed at the same company for over two years on average is going to make you earn less over your lifetime by about 50 percent or more," money is now an issue.[15] If she thinks that the company's focus on improving employee engagement is really meant to placate people without paying them more, money is now the issue. Nothing short of a true interest in paying employees generously takes the heat off this flammable aspect of the relationship between the individual and the organization. Even then, convincing people that's the intent of the company is going to be a tough sell, because these days it so rarely is a firm's strategy.

"It's not really about asking for the raise but knowing and having faith that the system will actually give you the right raises as you go along," Microsoft CEO Satya Nadella told a women's technology conference in October 2014. "And that, I think, might be one of the additional superpowers that quite frankly women who don't ask for raises have."

"Because that's good karma," Nadella continued. "It'll come back because somebody's going to know that's the kind of person that I want to trust. That's the kind of person that I want to really give more responsibility to."[16] (The executive quickly retracted his remarks.)

"You never trust the system," Marla Malcolm Beck, CEO of retailer Bluemercury, told *The Wall Street Journal* after Nadella's comments. "You always take matters into your own hands."[17] Her perspective is more reflective than Nadella's of how the average employee now views her (or his) company.

Issues of fairness in compensation are only going to get worse in the coming decade. The Great Recession left in its wake what the *National Post* of Canada called a "no-raises recovery" in which "U.S. workers' wages stagnate, but (the) rich get richer." "We're sort of in uncharted territory," one economist told the newspaper. "This isn't fully behaving like prior cycles."[18]

What often kept money from being an issue in the past was that people didn't know what their executives and counterparts were earning. Not any more. Microsoft awarded Nadella a compensation package in fiscal 2014 worth an estimated $84 million.[19] He and Karma have coffee regularly across the street from the bank. The evidence indicates that as more information gets out, it's going to stir the money pot.

In 2004, journalists from the *Contra Costa Times* asked officials of Oakland, California, for the names and pay of all city employees making more than $100,000. The city said no.

The newspaper sued. It's taxpayer money, argued the publication. The pubic has a right to know how its money is being spent. "People making six-figure salaries in government service have to expect public scrutiny," said an attorney for the newspapers.

We can't tell you what each individual makes, argued the city and its labor unions. Making a person's compensation public could expose him or her to unwarranted risks from marketers, identity thieves, or abusive former spouses. Never mind that if you compared a city employee's pay one year with her pay the next, you have a pretty good idea what kind of performance evaluation she received. It's just too intrusive, they said. "It's not the city being injured. It's the employees," said an attorney representing the unions.[20]

The employees lost. The journalists made a compelling case that knowing what each public employee makes is "in many cases necessary to disclose inefficiency, favoritism, nepotism, and fraud with respect to the government's use of public funds for employee salaries," ruled the Superior Court of Alameda County.

The employees appealed to the California Supreme Court. Tough luck, said the justices. California's laws require transparency, and that transparency is crucial "to expose corruption, incompetence, inefficiency, and favoritism."[21]

With such a sweeping ruling from California's highest court, *The Sacramento Bee* in March 2008 started a website where anyone could look up the pay of any state employee. The pay books were not only open but now just a few clicks away. If you were a professor at UCLA, for example, and wanted to know what the professor down the hall pulled in, all you needed to know was the web address.

Three economics professors from Berkeley and a fourth from Princeton spotted an opportunity. The three in the University of California system got out their directories and randomly selected e-mail addresses from the Santa Cruz, San Diego, and Los Angeles campuses.

"We are . . . conducting a research project on pay inequality at the University of California," the four men wrote in the e-mail. "*The Sacramento Bee* newspaper has launched a web site listing the salaries for all State of California employees, including UC employees." The professors told them where to find it.

Like a lot of studies, this one was sneaky. The researchers wanted to see what would happen when they blabbed the news that the universities' pay records were open for inspection. "As part of our research project, we wanted to ask you: Did you know about the *Sacramento Bee* salary database website?" Many people who got the e-mail thought, "No, I did not know. But now I do!"

Twenty percent of those who were e-mailed had already checked out the website. The e-mail shot that proportion up to half. Four out of five of the people who went to the site because of the e-mail looked up the pay of the people in their own department. It appears, said the researchers, "that workers are interested in coworkers' pay—particularly the pay of peers in the same department." Of course they were.

The researchers next sent an e-mail to every employee at the three universities, asking them about how fair they felt their pay was, whether they expected a generous pay raise in the next three years, what their knowledge was of the newspaper website, and whether they were planning to quit their jobs in the next year. Thanks to the court ruling and website, the economists already knew the salaries of everyone to whom they sent the messages.

So what happens when people learn what everyone else makes? It depends. Those who are making more than the median for their department tend to shrug it off. Knowing they are making more—perhaps confirming what they already suspected—does nothing to increase their satisfaction with their pay.

But those who get the shock of learning they are making less than the majority in their departments report lower satisfaction with their pay and with the job itself. "That might be one of the reasons why employers insist on pay secrecy as part of the deal on working there. It's really going to make the lower-wage people much less happy," David Card, one of the authors of the study, told the radio broadcast *Marketplace*. (He, by the way, makes $300,000 a year as a Berkeley professor.)[22]

Those who are paid less become substantially more likely to consider looking for a new job and more likely to bolt. Two to three years after the experiment, the researchers checked to see who was still in the directory. Those who said they were going to quit—often because there were irked by lower pay—did, in fact, quit at substantially higher rates.[23]

Outside of government, the top ranks of publicly traded firms, and the occasional outlier firm, the old rule was that you could not reveal your pay. Companies would add a paragraph to their employment agreement that said something like, "For purposes of this Agreement, 'Confidential Information' means any information regarding my compensation or the details of my benefits package with the Company." These clauses are illegal under U.S. law and an increasing number of state laws, but the legacy of past practices remains.[24] Combined with people's natural sensitivity to revealing their pay, those policies generally kept a lid on the information.

Not anymore. Among the details on the increasingly influential website Glassdoor are salaries reported by current and former workers. Look up just about any large company, and you can get a fairly good idea of how they pay. "See how your salary stacks up! Compare anonymous employee salary and bonus info for any job or company," boasts the site. The *Sacramento Bee*'s list of specific names and pay to the penny, it's not. But few people need to fly blind anymore.

At the same time, what numerous commentators have called the "last taboo" is fading. "Comparing salaries among colleagues has long been a taboo of workplace chatter, but that is changing as millennials . . . join the labor force," reported *The Wall Street Journal* in 2013.

"Accustomed to documenting their lives in real time on social media forums like Facebook and Twitter, they are bringing their embrace of self-disclosure into the office with them. And they're using this information to negotiate raises at their current employer or higher salaries when moving to a new job."[25]

One 25-year-old former employee of Apple told the *Journal* he blew off the company's rule not to disclose his pay. "It just made me more curious," he told the newspaper. He quit after discovering he was twice as productive as the lowest performer on the team but being paid only 20 percent more. Pay secrecy "has become an old-fashioned, obsolete management practice that has a much larger downside than upside. It is time for organizations to enter the world of pay transparency," wrote University of Southern California business professor Edward E. Lawler III in *Forbes* magazine.[26]

As information increasingly leaks out, companies will need to be able to defend how they decide who's paid what. Overpaying for mediocrity will no longer be a secret but will instead become a bad benchmark. Those whose value to the company is not reflected in their salaries will be more likely to discover the unfairness through internal or external comparisons. They'll quit. There may be no court decision looming over most leaders that will publish what they pay, but the best of them will clean up their compensation systems as though it were.

In the past, one of the ways companies kept pay from becoming an issue was by keeping it secret. In the future, companies will have to keep pay from being an issue by making it fair.

THE FOURTH RULE

Help Them Thrive

NICHOLAS FELTON SAVES THE DETAILS OF HIS LIFE.

He records when he sleeps, where he does his work, which songs he listens to, which rooms in his house he spends the most time in, with whom he spends his time, where and when he takes photos, where and how he travels, which books he has read, and dozens of other trivia.

Since 2005, he has compiled those data, analyzed them, and summarized and graphed them into the "Feltron Annual Report."[1] The personal yearbook is a demonstration of his design abilities (he was instrumental in a redesign of Facebook) and his obsession with making sense of minutiae.

His 2012 report shows that he spent time with 488 people that year, 226 of them only once. During his waking hours, he was alone 48 percent of the time. He took 2,801 photos with his iPhone, within which were 18 different species of animals. He was seven times as likely to be found reading Facebook, Twitter, some other website, or e-mail rather than a book. Over the course of the year, he used his laptop less and his iPhone more.

He averaged 7.7 hours of sleep but hit a maximum of 11.9 hours after returning from a trip to Japan. He ate tomatoes more than broccoli, pork more than chicken, and mangoes more than blueberries.[2]

"I wanted to understand the bleeding edge of reporting and quantifying myself," Felton told *The New York Times*.[3]

Felton is just one participant in an increasing "quantified-self" trend fed by the introduction of devices and apps that measure heart rate, steps, running speed, calories, sleep quality, blood sugar, and even mood. One-third of mobile device owners in 2013 used diet and fitness apps to track their health, a proportion that was only likely to rise with the pre-installed health app Apple introduced the following year with its iOS8.[4]

"I got up this morning at 6:10 a.m. after going to sleep at 12:45 a.m. I was awakened once during the night. My heart rate was 61 beats per minute, my blood pressure, 127 over 74," said *Wired* magazine contributing editor Gary Wolf as he opened his TED Talk about the quantified-self trend. "I had zero minutes of exercise yesterday, so my maximum heart rate during exercise wasn't calculated. I had about 600 milligrams of caffeine, zero of alcohol. And my score on the Narcissism Personality Index, or the NPI-16, is a reassuring 0.31."[5]

Felton and Wolf are outliers. Most people have little interest in tracking themselves so closely. But the two men are not as unusual today as they were even just a few years ago. More and more, companies are pushing their employees to quantify themselves, to be a little like Felton, a little like Wolf, in the hope that they will make healthier choices in their lives.

The companies offer free tracking devices and discounts on insurance premiums for getting poked and prodded regularly. They subsidize gym memberships. They sponsor contests among workers to get them to walk and run more. Some outright ban cookies and doughnuts. Some started allowing only diet soda for internal meetings, which was dumb, because diet soda messes with the body as much as the sugary stuff.[6]

It used to be that employees' health was their business. As long as they showed up on time and did their work well, companies didn't care whether they jogged or smoked, ate fish or bacon, curled iron or hoisted beer. Not anymore. Now many organizations assume that if you work for them, your "well-being" is company property.

It's making for one of the most fascinating experiments in the relationship between employee and employer. In many quarters, where

people feel like their organizations are making impositions or intrusions in one of the most sensitive areas of their lives, these initiatives are
backfiring.

It didn't have to happen that way. The problems surfacing now
occurred because decision makers failed to recognize the basic differences between man or woman and machine, between economic and
reciprocal decision, between employee and widget. At least in seeking to
have it all quantified, they got the crash on tape.

THE FOURTH NEW RULE IS "HELP THEM THRIVE."

There is no escaping the fact that a person's job influences his health,
one way or the other. Policies, workloads, vacation time, boredom, manager quality, and other aspects of working at a place either can help
those employees thrive or can degrade their health, their psychological
well-being, and the performance of the enterprise. It's always been that
way, but it's gotten more serious with our new electronic leashes.

"If you're old enough," reported NBC's Brian Williams, "you remember a day when after work, you'd go home from work and maybe once
every six months you'd get an after-hours call from work, but for the
most part you didn't think about work until it was time to go back to
work the next day. Well, not anymore. Now work is in your hand, it's on
your screen, it's staring you in the face. Work expects an answer at 11 at
night when, of course, you're expected to be plugged in and available. If
you think this kind of thing can't be good for our health, you'd be right."[7]

One out of five workers in the United States agrees with the statement "I have too much work at my job to maintain a healthy lifestyle,"
according to the New Rules studies. The proportion ranges from about
a fifth to a third around much of the globe. One out of four Americans
says he or she is "burned out from my job," and another one in five is
neutral—not burned out but not too far away from it either. Although a
certain amount of stress goes with working, the evidence indicates that
it often reaches unhealthy levels.

"Burnout is an issue that business prefers not to talk about, despite the toll it can take in the workplace," observed a columnist for *The Globe and Mail* in Toronto. "Executives are eager to discuss employee engagement: Getting employees more excited about their work. But burnout, caused when employees are exhausted, overwhelmed, and ticked off with their work, isn't a topic for conversation."[8] Sixteen percent of Canadians feel their jobs make it hard for them to balance priorities at work and in their personal lives.

The grand irony of employers' efforts to get their workers to wear pedometers and use calorie counters is that those same devices inevitably show what health researchers have long known—that exceptional pressure from the job is frequently one of the greatest hazards to an employee's well-being.

We already knew job stress messes up a person's sleep—and that poor sleep is linked to increased accidents at work or when driving for the company, lower job performance, greater absenteeism, and more doctor visits, to the tune of $100 billion.[9] We recently discovered that working in a windowless office cuts three-quarters of an hour off an employee's night of sleep.[10] The evidence is accumulating that, as *The Washington Post* reported, "having a bad boss can make your work life a misery, but it can also make you sick, both physically and mentally."[11] Now the same iPhone that ensures someone's work e-mail follows her to bed can also be used to graph the restless night she had thinking about those e-mails or falling ill from a case of bad manager.

We already knew the stress hormone cortisol shoots up more on a workday than on a day off.[12] We knew that daily overdoses of the stuff could contribute to "metabolic syndrome, atherosclerosis, osteoporosis, immunosuppression, and an increased risk of coronary heart disease"[13] or even make cuts heals slower.[14] Now there are mood-tracking apps that let an employee document the accumulating daily freak-outs.

We are learning that sitting for long periods is detrimental for a species that walked through tens of thousands of years and across a few continents to get to today's cubicles.[15] Now the company-issued pedometer makes a detailed graph showing 90 minutes flat-lined for the strategy meeting, another 60 almost motionless on a conference call, 2 or 3 or 4 hours sitting on a plane, and another 45 minutes sitting in the rental car to arrive at the hotel too late to go for a run.

"It's no one's fault," said one executive who cares deeply about his people but feels powerless to avoid the conflicting messages. "The expectations for the business have become unreasonable. I can't change that. We're stuck with that. I have to make unreasonable demands of my people because my customers make unreasonable demands of them because their customers make unreasonable demands of them. You can argue its wrong and bad and stupid, and it is, but I can't help that."

Administrators of healthcare organizations have approached the leaders of some major companies asking them why so many of their female employees are having induced labor or cesarean births. The answer: The company's culture drives people so hard and has them so tightly scheduled that childbirth at the baby's own time becomes a casualty. "I was working 80-hour weeks," one working mother recalled. "I realized I had outsourced everything in my life, including my daughter." She quit to take a job that let her live outside of work.

One father knew he was in trouble when his young daughter, asked at school to draw a picture of her family, made a crayon rendering of her father separate from the rest of the group, with a suitcase in his hand. "If your own dog bites you when you come home because he doesn't recognize you," said another businessman, "you're traveling too much."

Employers can't have it both ways. They can't insist employees work around the clock and also take good care of themselves. They can't expect employees to be on call 24/7 and still make the kinds of breakthroughs that the evidence shows come most predictably with sufficient downtime. The proportion of those who say their jobs bring out their best ideas drops from 82 percent among those furthest from burnout to only 26 percent among those already in its clutches.

In a business that strikes the right balance, modest psychological sweeteners and health-tracking tools are appreciated and can help feed people's natural interest in staying fit. In a firm that continues to demand excessive hours, pedometers, healthy lunches in the cafeteria, and subsidized gym memberships won't do a thing. They risk creating cynicism and increasing turnover. The most severely burned out are

10 times as likely to be planning an exit as those on the other end of the scale.

An effective well-being strategy begins with the acknowledgment of one central fact: people have limits. Within those limits, they can be fast-thinking, accurate, alert to mistakes and hazards, positive, productive, creative, and healthy. And they'll stay. Beyond those limits, they become slower, error-prone, grumpy, ineffective, dull, and at much greater risk for disease.

Americans in particular seem to believe working more than 40 hours per week is a badge of honor (although the British and Canadians are more likely to complain about job stress). While workers in the European Union are guaranteed 20 days of paid vacation, the United States leaves the decision to the free market, the sole developed economy that does not require paid vacation or holidays. As a consequence, a quarter of American workers receive none. Among those who have paid vacation, 41 percent leave at least some of their vacation days unused.[16] The average American employee is now working the equivalent of one more month per year in longer days and more days on the job than in 1976.[17]

The research says working that many hours is foolish, as is expecting employees to work that long. "This is what work looks like now," states one summary of the evidence. "It's been this way for so long that most American workers don't realize that for most of the 20th century, the broad consensus among American business leaders was that working people more than 40 hours a week was stupid, wasteful, dangerous, and expensive—and the most telling sign of dangerously incompetent management to boot."[18]

MOST COMPANIES PAY LIP SERVICE TO "WORK-LIFE BALANCE" OR well-being. They say they offer something like "unmatched autonomy and freedom on a day-to-day basis," but in practice it means, as was once the joke at Microsoft, "You can work any 18 hours you want."

Or they offer free food and incredible on-site amenities because, with the amount of work you'll have, you won't have time to go anywhere. Or they argue that if you've got a job that really matches your strengths, working night and day is a joy.

Yet a fantastic minority of organizations get it. They understand that people rarely know their own limits and that the most dedicated employees are, by definition, at the greatest risk of pushing themselves too hard. Those hardest-working people will keep plugging along until, with little warning, they can't. To get ahead of the flat tire, sick child, emotional meltdown, or heart attack that makes it apparent the employee was overstretched, an enlightened fraction of leaders and managers are more vigilant of burnout than the workers themselves.

Slalom Consulting tries to match its people with clients in their own cities, so they can avoid airports, hotels, and time lost to the road. Every three years, an employee can take a month off at 75 percent of pay. The firm does quite well in newspaper, magazine, and Glassdoor.com survey rankings.[19]

Employees at Patagonia's Ventura, California, headquarters set their own hours, so they can time an hour or so away from business to surf in the best waves of the day or take a 30-mile bike ride over lunch inland to Ojai. "Far from slacking off, the family-owned company has doubled in size and tripled in profits since 2008, earning $600 million in 2013," reported *The Washington Post*. "Its 2,000 employees around the globe are fiercely loyal. Turnover is minimal. The company is expanding into new global markets."[20]

Bandwidth cofounder and CEO David Morken enforces policies that require employees to take all their vacation days in the year they are awarded and, while taking them, cease communication with the mother ship. "To make sure the policy is followed to the T," reported *Forbes* magazine, "when someone goes on vacation, all the folks he or she would ordinarily communicate with (employees, partners, boss, etc.) get an email, saying 'So-and-so is on vacation. If he or she contacts you for any reason, please let us know.'"[21]

CEO Bart Lorang of FullContact decided in 2012 to give his people what he calls a "paid, paid vacation." Not only do employees get their regular pay while gone, the organization will pay an additional $7,500 if the worker follows three rules: "1. You have to go on vacation, or you don't get the money. 2. You must disconnect. 3. You can't work while on vacation."[22]

It would be difficult to find an enterprise that better understands how to get the best from mortals than statistical software maker SAS Institute. Unimpressed by seeing people in the Apollo space program "treated like workers on an assembly line" during a year there in the 1960s, Jim Goodnight determined to lead a different kind of company when he cofounded and became CEO of SAS.[23]

That venture, sprung from research projects at North Carolina State University, is now the largest privately held software firm in the world. It is also, by the reckoning of *Fortune*'s annual rankings, one of the "100 Best Companies to Work For."[24] Year after year, the company reliably appears at or near the top of the list.

SAS is routinely profiled by major media, the journalists typically coming away sounding more like marketers. More than a decade ago, CBS *60 Minutes* correspondent Morley Safer gushed that working at SAS was "the good life." "A tour of its carefully tended, 300-acre corporate campus," reported *The New York Times* in 2009, "leaves little doubt why surveys, year after year, rate the SAS Institute . . . among the best places to work."[25] In 2013, *Forbes* made a big deal of SAS topping Glassdoor .com's list for work-life balance.[26] The same year, *Fast Company* called it "The World's Best Place to Work."[27] The magazine had previously labeled SAS "Sanity, Inc."[28]

"What if you worked where you were entertained with live music as you ate at one of four company cafes, your salad so fresh they're grown right on the property, and the boss encouraged you to eat lunch with your kids?" asked NBC's Kerry Sanders in an early 2014 *Today Show* broadcast. "This may not sound like any company you've heard of, where there are gyms and pools and a solar farm where sheep cut the grass, and where not one employee is crammed into a cubicle. Everyone gets an office."[29]

As part of a tradition dating back to the company's founding in 1976, there are free M&Ms every Wednesday. The company orders them by the ton.[30]

SAS employees and their families have free access to a team of nurse practitioners, family-practice physicians, registered dietitians, nurses, lab techs, physical therapists, and a psychologist.[31] Sick leave is unlimited. The company subsidizes the on-site day care and preschool. Workers can take a break to use the firm's basketball and racquetball courts, exercise rooms, swimming pool, 40 miles of trails, or the meditation garden.[32]

"People who are preoccupied wondering 'When can I fit in time at the gym?' or 'Is that meeting going to waste my whole afternoon?' can't be entirely focused on the job at hand," Goodnight wrote with creativity expert Richard Florida in a *Harvard Business Review* article. "The more distractions a company can remove, the more its employees can maximize their creative potential and, in turn, produce great work."[33]

The centerpiece of the SAS well-being philosophy, the practice that most flies in the face of a widget worldview, is the company's 35-hour workweek. Five weekdays. Seven hours per day. It seems exceptional, and it may be, even at SAS.

"While we say we have a 35-hour workweek," Chief Marketing Officer Jim Davis said in 2013, "I don't know anybody who really works 35 hours. The reality is if you trust people, and you ask them to do something—and you treat them like a human being as opposed to a commodity where you try to squeeze something out—they're going to work all sorts of hours. But they're going to enjoy those hours as opposed to 'slaving in the office.'"[34]

Yet 35 hours is still the policy. It's what behavioral economists would call an "anchor." It sets the tone for work-life balance in the company, just as a business that legislates a minimum of 2,300 hours per year sends the opposite signal. The bedrock strategy of SAS is that people who are worn out don't do anyone any good.

"After eight hours," Goodnight says, in what's become an SAS proverb, "you're probably just adding bugs."[35]

Hearing about Goodnight's approach without knowing his background, one could be forgiven for wondering if he's a sandal-wearing Marxist growing more than lettuce on the property. Far from it. He's a capitalist who in 2013 was ranked number 58 among the world's richest people. *Forbes* estimates the work of the people he's so carefully looked after have made him worth $7.2 billion.[36]

Goodnight is also a Ph.D. statistician running a statistical company. He and his leadership team make a calculated determination of which benefits give a good return on investment. "The company isn't just doling out treats willy-nilly," he and Florida wrote. "There's a deliberate process for choosing which benefits to offer (or, put another way, which distractions to eliminate)."

SAS surveys its people to learn what improvements they would like to see. If the answer is no, the company explains why not. "If the answer is yes, SAS provides the benefit," wrote the CEO. "SAS has said yes quite a lot."[37]

Early on, Stanford professor Jeffrey Pfeffer identified Goodnight's practices as a powerful example of how people with enlightened leadership reciprocate in profitable ways. The low single-digit turnover alone at SAS saves the company about $100 million a year in recruiting and training costs.[38]

But looking at the world outside SAS, Pfeffer is not impressed. "When and how did human well-being, and indeed human life, come to play such small roles in judgments about how to organize work arrangements and social policies?" he wrote in *Bloomberg Businessweek*. "If human life is indeed sacred, if we care about people and not just polar bears and endangered species, then we need to 'score' governmental and company decisions not just by their monetary effects, but also on their implications for people."[39]

It's one thing for an employee to quantify himself. It's quite another when his employer starts tracking people's bio habits. Things can get creepy.

Encouraged by his employer to download an app to track his calories and exercise as part of the new "wellness" program, one executive of a health insurance company dutifully complied. He began recording what he ate and when and how he exercised. Encouraged to build a network of friends and colleagues for social support, he went along.

"I start getting notifications anytime one of my 'friends' does something. 'Sarah just ate a salad.' 'Bill went running,'" he said. "It was annoying."

"Then, I notice that in the app under the exercises you can log is 'Sexual Activity.' Not only that, but there are three levels of 'intensity' to choose from, 'light,' 'moderate,' and 'vigorous,'" said the man. "I start to wonder, if I choose those in the app, is it going to broadcast it to my network?"

"So I decided to do a little experiment," he said. "One Tuesday I went into the app and logged vigorous sexual activity four times during the course of the morning. Sure enough, about noon, my friend John calls me and says, 'What the hell is going on over there?!'"

"I deleted the app."

(A woman to whom this story was told quipped, "Well, that app saves having to ask, 'How was your weekend?'")

Employees are grown-ups. They are supervised by people who are their managers, not their mothers. The responsibility for a worker's health rests with the employee. It's his business. Outside of the military and a few other professions where physical fitness is a job qualification, it's not the organization's place to tell him to eat his veggies, how or whether to exercise, how often to consult a doctor, or when to go to bed.

Some companies are learning the hard way that well-being initiatives can violate the privacy and dignity of employees. Few intrusions make a person feel more like a widget. Three in ten U.S. workers say "My health is none of my organization's business," and an equal proportion straddle the fence on that statement. Only half are open to taking advice about their health from their company.

"The minute someone makes me pee in a cup, I quit," said one executive who does not allow such intrusions of his people. When the story was relayed to an HR leader of one Fortune 100 firm as a reasonable reaction, she replied without blinking, "Well, we already make everyone pee in a cup."

The sales director of one "wellness" company emphasized how a call center, because it "wants workers at their desks as much as possible," could have a nurse come to the employee's desk to poke and prod between calls.[40] A national retailer urged its people to fill their prescriptions at the same store where they work.

Trek Bicycle president John Burke told an audience in Chicago in 2014 that obese employees are a liability and that he forces his into an eight-step program—a convenient public stance to take for a guy who wants to sell more bikes. He also bragged about how he told two of his employees they were too fat and needed to lose weight.[41] Taken aback, a columnist for *Workforce* magazine countered, "If obese and unhealthy employees are bad for business, then I think it's fair to argue an executive who plays 'body police' and essentially bullies employees into participating in a health and wellness program is bad for business, too."[42]

In the summer of 2013, Penn State University imposed a "Take Care of Your Health" program requiring employees to disclose problems with a supervisor, their marital status, their money worries, and fear of job loss. Women are asked whether they intend to become pregnant over the next year. Failing to cough up those intimate details would result in a $1,200 "noncompliance fee."

The program caused an uproar that made national news. The firm that administers the plan reassured the teachers that all their information was private and the company had never suffered a leak. "As an English professor, I think I am having difficulty with your definition of 'private,'" faculty member Kimberly Blockett replied. "For me, discussing my reproductive plans with an unknown entity at an insurance company does not constitute 'private.'" The school dropped the financial penalty.[43]

The people who hatched Penn State's and so many other plans aren't thinking it through. Whether such programs save any money is a matter of debate. "More than four years into the [Affordable Care Act], we conclude that these programs increase, rather than decrease employer spending on health care with no net health benefit," wrote three prominent well-being program critics in late 2014. "The programs also cause overutilization of screening and checkups in generally healthy working age adult populations, put undue stress on employees, and incentivize unhealthy forms of weight-loss."[44]

The companies selling and administering them have every incentive to inflate the numbers. They are clumsy force-feedings of online forms backed by formulas loaded with untested or faulty assumptions. "Employers' increasing efforts to cut their health care costs are on a collision course with employees' boundaries about medical privacy," observed *The New York Times*.[45]

The most crucial question behind these initiatives is whether the executives who fund them actually care about their employees' health. The thought does count. As two experts writing in a *Harvard Business Review* blog put it, "Should wellness be something you do *to* your employees or *for* your employees?"[46]

If a well-being initiative is voluntary, fun, and respectful of people's dignity; if it is grounded in a much broader strategy to give people an incredible experience on the job, with plenty of time off; if it accounts for the huge range of individual conditions; and if it is motivated by wanting to see those employees live long, healthy lives well after the time they are off the company insurance, it will succeed. Those in our studies whose companies are most genuinely looking out for them, including having a good work-life balance, are far more receptive to the firm's well-being offerings. They trust their leaders.

But if the program is coercive and snoopy; if it is a one-off program in a demoralizing and overly demanding environment; if it insists everyone fit himself or herself into the administrator's biometric parameters; and most important, if it is focused less on the employees' health than the cost of their healthcare, the so-called wellness program will fail. That kind of program is not sincerely aimed at helping them thrive.

THE FIFTH RULE

Be Cool

A FEW YEARS BACK, A RESEARCHER WITH THE COOL NAME OF ILAN
Dar-Nimrod and his friend Ian Hansen could not decide whether actor
Steve Buscemi was cool. Dar-Nimrod "could not stomach the idea that
such a geeky, sleazy-looking dude can be considered cool."

After a "heated discussion" about the actor and, more important,
the criteria, the scholars decided they should look for a scientific test
that would settle the question. "To our shock and dismay," Dar-Nimrod
wrote, "we found that despite the omnipresence of the term 'cool,' there
is no quantitative research that actually indicates what it means."[1]

Dar-Nimrod, Hansen, and four other scholars decided to do some
experiments. They published a paper about it. They titled it "Coolness:
An Empirical Investigation."

"The present studies (offer) the first systematic, quantitative exam-
ination of what characteristics recur in popular understandings of the
cool personality," they wrote. "In order to study the construct of coolness, we use a nomological net approach, examining convergent and
discriminant validity with respect to other constructs. We base our rea-
soning partly on a lexical hypothesis that the construct of coolness has

become embedded in language because it reflects a meaningful dimension of variation conveying information about persons."

Blah, blah, blah. It was, they conceded, a "decidedly uncool method."

Dar-Nimrod, Hansen, and the others asked people to describe coolness. After grouping and analyzing the responses, the researchers determined the concept overlaps heavily with qualities such as friendliness, competence, attractiveness, caring, and confidence. It casts a wide net. Cool does not "adhere to a specific, highly constrained set of characteristics," they wrote.

But when the researchers analyzed responses to separate what was merely desirable from what is distinctly cool, they got an edgier list of adjectives. Cool means being unconventional, having emotional control, thrill seeking, rebelliousness, irony, roughness, and a bit of hedonism. At the center of it all is a core of authenticity independent of what others are doing.

Still, all their research failed to settle the question that started it all. "The most frustrating thing about this research is that nine years later," said Dar-Nimrod, "we still can't agree on whether Steve Buscemi is cool or not."[2]

The Fifth New Rule is "Be Cool."

In business today, coolness is crucial. People who work for what they consider cool companies and cool leaders and cool managers and with whom they consider cool coworkers are substantially more motivated to stay and to work harder for the company. It's highly profitable to be cool.

Employees around the world are relatively liberal in their assessments of their employers' coolness. Out of 10 people in each region we studied, an average of 6 in the United States agree, "My organization is a cool place to work." It's 5 out of 10 in Canada and China, 7 in Latin America, but only 4 of 10 in Australia and the United Kingdom.

But industry matters more than country. While British workers in healthcare, government, and banking give lower marks, a healthy 58 percent of British tech employees think their organizations are cool.

Coolness is hugely connected to an employee being proud of her job, wanting and planning to stay, and recommending the company to others. Of those Americans who work in the least cool companies, 84 percent wish they were working somewhere else; only 10 percent of those who work for the coolest firms do. Coolness fuels innovation; those who strongly agree they work at a cool place are 13 times as imaginative as those on the other end of the scale.

It is almost statistically impossible today for an employee to be energized by everything else about the job and not find the company a cool place to work. This is not true of fearlessness, of pay, or of balance. People can and do say, "It's a great job, but I'm worried the company will be acquired." They sometimes say, "I love my job, but the pay is not great." Or they might say, "I love it there, but the hours are a bear." But almost no one on one hand scores their overall job high and the coolness of their company low. Coolness is not the frosting *on* the cake. It's the sugar *in* the cake.

Those statistics don't help a company if its leaders struggle to be cool.

"Am I cool, kids?" Marge asks in one episode of *The Simpsons*.

"No," her kids Bart and Lisa respond in unison.

"Good. I'm glad," she replies. "And that's what makes me cool: not caring, right?"

"No," her kids tell her.

"Well, how the hell do you be cool? I feel like we've tried everything here."

"Wait, Marge," says Homer. "Maybe if you're truly cool, you don't need to be told you're cool."

"Well, sure you do," says Bart.

Lisa adds, "How else would you know?"[3]

Therein lies the puzzle.

The most basic part of this rule is easy. Being cool starts with not being uncool. That's more than a tautology. The same aspects that, when done well, can have people amped up can also, with a few epic fails, make the place seem backward, inept, uncool. Before a business leader can work much on the upside of this element, he or she must address the fundamentals.

Take inclusion, for example. Two of the most powerful indicators of a cool place to work are whether the employees agree with the statements "My organization is open to different points of view" and "Being different is welcomed where I work." At ground level, it means the company is free of discrimination.

Big deal. No firm is going to get points for obeying the law. Maybe it meant something in the late 1960s for a company to post the mandated "We are an equal opportunity employer" in its job ads, back when the movie *Guess Who's Coming to Dinner* was groundbreaking because it told the story of interracial marriage, back when companies whose fairness was questioned would point out they did, after all, have a black employee.

More than a half century after passage of the U.S. Civil Rights Act of 1964, it's just "EOE," and those letters don't mean anything. But in the rare cases where a company either is or is perceived to be bigoted (5 percent strongly disagree being different is welcomed at their firms), the cool factor is about one-sixth what it is among those who are neutral on whether being different is encouraged.

The same is true of materials and equipment. Supplying people with what they need to do their jobs is basic. Asking whether they have what they need only reveals where the company has committed a blunder so serious that the leadership looks silly needing a survey to point it out. It's what's sometimes called a "hygiene factor," like mowing the lawn, brushing your teeth, or taking out the trash. Forgive your people if they don't fall over themselves thanking you for a bug-free computer or a copier that actually makes copies. Neglect it, however, and you should duck. It's really uncool to be outfitting people poorly.

It turns out that having dishonest leaders is also uncool. Who would have guessed? Only 4 percent of U.S. workers are exceptionally skeptical of their top leaders' integrity, but it's hard to find many in that small group who say they work at a cool place.

"We don't discriminate. We'll give you what you need to do your job. And our executives aren't crooks!" Not much of a sales pitch. Not the definition of cool. But better than failing at the basics, any of which will pop the cool balloon.

For the same reason, abject failure on any of the other New Rules will also knock the sunglasses off the company's image. Neglectful managers. Leaders who use fear. Stingy with pay. An unrelenting schedule. Hiding the truth. Letting people get stuck in one spot. Never saying thank you. Every man for himself. Keeping them in their place. Keeping them from their potential.

All so uncool.

"Cool" is believed to have its roots in Africa. It was popularized in the 1930s by saxophonist Lester Young and carried along in jazz culture until it became part of mainstream vocabulary in the United States after World War II.[4] It proved as sticky and resilient as it is difficult to tack down. Other 1960s words like "dig" and "groovy" fell by the wayside. But "cool" has always been cool.

In a large number of languages, the translation for "cool" is "cool." It is now, as *Slate* magazine observed, "our elastic container for anyone and anything with relevance and spark,"[5] a definition so broad that it would leave most executives as frustrated as Marge Simpson, asking, "Am I cool, kids?" and "How the hell do you be cool?"

Being cool—for a person or a company—means being who you are so intensely and unyieldingly that you don't care you are not someone else. It's not trying to be Google or Facebook or L.L. Bean or Apple or Starbucks or any other enterprise, even if what they are doing at their companies sparks some ideas about what you could do at yours. Any idea from the outside needs to be adapted to the personality of the organization, or it will seem a clumsy imitation, just as obvious and ineffective in the corporate world as it was in high school.

What made Steve Jobs cool—despite his very uncool way of working with others—was his vision for the design of Apple products independent of what the rest of the technology industry was creating. He hated buttons on tech devices. He was obsessed with design. He preferred turtlenecks over ties. He didn't ask others if any of this was okay. He wasn't trying to be Bill Gates.

Cool people don't care if others think they are cool. Being themselves makes them not care; not caring makes them that much cooler. It's harder for companies to pull this off, because they have marketing departments desperate to "make" them cool. There is a world of difference between organizations led by executives who have an authentic, independent vision of what they want to be and those who want to know what everyone else will be wearing when they come back to school, that are always asking "What are the best practices at other companies?" Being authentic as a company or as an executive means you are communicating "This is who I am. I am not pretending to be someone else."

There is, however, one group's opinion that a cool leader worries about: his or her employees. A cool place to work tickles the brain. Time spent there is enjoyable, rarely boring, at least occasionally fun, often different or unexpected, unique, authentic, quirky, and intense. Coolness, the researchers found, is a lot of things people want in the plain version, plus an edge.[6]

As much as people's jobs are intertwined with their lives outside of work, as much as the world outside the office has a good soundtrack and graphics, an effective leader today has to ensure that he or she has created a cool place to work. It's worth measuring, worth analyzing, worth experimenting to find the kind of experience that a firm's employees will look forward to each morning during their commute.

By the traditional line of thinking, applying this science to the workplace is nonsense. It gets in the way of getting the job done. It's frivolous. "Work is work!" Red Forman says to his son, Eric, in an episode of *That 70s Show*. "If it wasn't work, they wouldn't call it work. They'd call it 'Super wonderful crazy fun time,' or 'Skippity doo!'"[7]

Businessweek columnist Liz Ryan hears that sentiment from retired CEOs whenever she writes about leadership: "It's not supposed to be fun; that's why they call it work." they tell her. "But," she counters, "a lot has changed since those guys ran the place, like the fact that more and more of the people running companies aren't guys anymore.

"What kind of effort, creativity, or productivity are you going to get out of someone performing a job against his will?" Ryan wrote. "Are you going to tell your shareholders and customers, 'Here at Acme Explosives, our motto is, "Work's not supposed to be fun." Our employees are highly qualified individuals who don't choose to be here, but come for the money. That level of commitment helps us ensure a moderate level of customer service at all times.'"[8]

A certain amount of "skippity doo" is baked into the new engagement recipe. "Despite the sobering economic shocks of recent years, the Fun at Work movement seems irrepressible," a guest columnist observed in *The New York Times*. "Major companies boast of employing Chief Fun Officers or Happiness Engineers; corporations call upon a burgeoning industry of happiness consultants, who'll construct a Gross Happiness Index for your workplace, then advise you on ways to boost it."[9]

A few years ago, *The Wall Street Journal* reported huge increases in the number of jobs with titles such as "Ninja," Jedi," "Guru," "Rock Star," and "Evangelist."[10] Why? Why not? Ask the people who sell neckwear if they've noticed a decline in their business. Almost everyone is loosening their ties.

SOUTHWEST AIRLINES BOUGHT COMPETITOR AIRTRAN IN 2011. THE deal had many benefits. It also had created some problems.

Buying AirTran got Southwest a new or bigger presence in 63 markets such as Orlando, Milwaukee, and, most important, Atlanta's hyperbusy Hartsfield-Jackson International Airport. It put the combined airline in a better position to compete in an industry of fewer and larger competitors. It accelerated Southwest's progression from a regional airline to a truly national one.

But they were two very different airlines. Southwest had never had an accident. AirTran, back when it was known as ValuJet, suffered a 1996 crash into the Florida Everglades that killed all 100 aboard.

Southwest kept costs down by flying and having to maintain only Boeing 737s. AirTran had 52 of the 737s, but it also had 87 Boeing 717s. Southwest had one class of first-come, first-served seating. AirTran had first class. In its advertising before the merger, it portrayed Southwest passengers as cattle.

Pilot seniority lists had to be merged. Pay—Southwest paid more— had to be reconciled. Southwest did not charge reservation fees, nor did it charge for checked bags. AirTran did, something Southwest used to mock in its premerger ads.

Many of these issues were not all that different from those faced in other airline mergers or acquisitions. What made the Southwest-AirTran combination compelling was that in merging routes and landing rights and pay scales and pilot seniority, the two companies would also be squishing together two contrasting cultures.

Southwest Airlines was cool. AirTran was AirTran.

"The big task remains: Making these two very different airlines into one," reported Jeremy Hobson, host of the radio program *Marketplace*. "Think of Southwest as the Hawaiian shirt of the airline industry— comfortable and familiar. And AirTran as the Sears suit—businesslike, affordable, no frills."[11]

Adjusting to Southwest's culture could be a strange experience even for those who worked there before the acquisition. When he joined the company in 1986 as controller, future Southwest CEO Gary Kelly was skeptical of his instructions to show up for work in a polo short and Hawaiian shorts. "I thought everybody was playing a joke on me," he said. "I had my normal suit in the car—just in case." His willingness 22 years later as the top boss to don a dress, wig, and size 14 high heels for a Halloween costume as Edna Turnblad from the musical *Hairspray* was proof he had "transformed himself from a buttoned-down C.P.A. to one of Corporate America's most colorful bosses," reported *The New York Times*. The culture was full of "oddball ways," said the paper.[12]

At Southwest, at least on paper, customers come second. Employees come first. It's part of what makes the airline cool. "We know if we're doing the right thing for our employees, that ultimately it'll be the right thing for our business, which is ultimately the right thing for our customers," Southwest director of Culture Services Cheryl Hughey said in 2011.[13]

Through the years, the employees-come-first mindset meant that while Southwest's employee costs per mile flown were high, its costs per customer mile were low. Employees were paid more than the rest of the industry. The cost of a ticket was generally lower for customers. Its employees repaid the fun with productivity. Anyone who regularly flies Southwest has a story or two. While Delta or United or American flight attendants drone widget-style through the script of the preflight announcements, a Southwest employee might make it into a small comedy routine or sing it or do a rap. Or smile.

At ground level, the philosophy means Southwest is comfortable with the fact that Halloween got so out of hand that the whole day is probably a money loser. Does any work get done that day? "No. None," the chief financial officer was once quoted as saying.[14]

Because of higher productivity—a combination of higher morale and a crisp operations strategy—the company is perennially profitable in one of the toughest industries. In early 2014, Southwest announced its forty-first consecutive year of profitability.[15]

The AirTran acquisition put Southwest's reciprocal strategy at risk.

Sometimes what makes a company cool evaporates when it becomes too big, when control passes to leaders who don't share the core values, when the firm is acquired by a humorless conglomerate, or when it tries to swallow a company that is too stuffy. One highly passionate, privately held pet supply firm had, among other cool things, a "company dog" stationed at the front door to greet visitors. Then the company made the big time and was sold at a high price to a publicly held multinational. Lots of money was made, but the dog at the front door violated policy. He had to go. Best Buy hoped to get an infusion of mojo from its purchase and in-store integration of Geek Squad in 2002, but the much hipper brand and its attitude was largely subsumed in a sea of blue and yellow.

"Southwest's whole business model is built on a particular approach to managing employees. It's a big bet they are making that they can swallow AirTran," Wharton management professor Peter Cappelli observed when the merger was announced.[16]

In normal business operations, Southwest hired people one-by-one, assessing their fit with Southwest's "oddball ways." With the acquisition of AirTran, 8,000 people who were adapted to AirTran's rules were essentially hired *en masse* to join 35,000 instant colleagues at the acquiring firm. "Now this is a very different approach, taking thousands of [AirTran] employees, dumping them into the system and hoping it works," said Cappelli. "It's a pretty risky move."

AirTran has "draconian management that lets us know every day that we contribute no more to the success of this airline than any one else, that we are replaceable and there are thousands of others that would take your job given the chance," wrote one pilot. "Southwest is going to get a lot of good, friendly, talented and hard working people from this deal who are ready to take them to the next level."[17]

Some changes were easy. The AirTran dress code was relaxed. Flight attendants could wear their hair down, and neck scarves or ties became optional. Corporate office employees could wear jeans.[18] Others took time. "We got a hugging culture at Southwest Airlines," Bob Jordan, a Southwest executive who became AirTran president in 2011, told *The Wall Street Journal* that year. "I've stunned a few people, I think. Since then, I've learned to be a little more careful."[19]

As the merger progressed, some Southwest employees saw the acquiring airline losing what made it great. "The luv is gone," wrote one in March 2013, invoking the spelling of the company's stock symbol. "With the AirTran merger, Southwest employees are being forced to follow AirTran's culture, which is based on manipulation, intimidation, and fear."[20]

"Since the acquisition of AirTran, we seem to be taking on their policies and dismal way AirTran treated their employees," wrote one eight-year-veteran flight attendant a few months later. "We are Southwest, not AirTran. Management needs to focus on integrating AirTran into the Southwest philosophy and way of doing things right, rather than the other way around. We are the most successful airline in the world at Southwest. Let's do things the Southwest Way and treat your employees like assets once again."[21]

Some passengers are starting to accumulate stories more typical of the other airlines, like the passengers who missed their connection in AirTran's Atlanta by three minutes when they closed the door early and were summarily issued boarding passes for a flight three hours later by a gate agent who made no apologies. Or eye contact.[22]

While Southwest sells and repaints former AirTran aircraft, merges routes, and adds destinations on pace with plans, it will take years to know how quickly or whether the acquiring firm instills its culture in the acquired. What is clear from the combination is how protective a company needs to be of its mojo. "I guess you're always at risk of losing your coolness if you lose sight of what your core values are," said Hughey in 2014. "We've not seen anything we've had to sacrifice. If anything, our family just expanded."[23]

Coolness outperforms seriousness, but seriousness is a stronger force of nature in corporations. It's so much easier to take away the beer and to tell people hugs are forbidden, that office hours will be strictly enforced, that working remotely is prohibited, that we're not going to blow a day with a party or a retreat, and—don't be absurd— that the CEO will not be wearing a costume on Halloween. Coolness has to be given air cover from the highest levels of the organization, or it will be snuffed out with the intensity of a 1950s librarian's "schoosh!"

THE WINTER OF 2010–2011 WAS A TOUGH ONE IN MINNESOTA, EVEN BY Minnesota standards. It was cold, of course. It always is. Minneapolis was pummeled by 86.6 inches of snow, the most in 27 years.[24]

Like everyone else, BI Worldwide's people were working through the aftermath of the Great Recession. "We were all walking around here like zombies," said company president Larry Schoenecker.

As the snow finally receded and summer approached, Schoenecker decided his people needed a shot in the arm. So he sent out a company-wide memo announcing what he called "the Summer of Love."

It went like this: There would be more parties that summer on the lawn of the company's campus. The firm would hire some good bands. There would be beer. The company would organize a volleyball tournament; free team T-shirts to whoever joined a team, and redeemable recognition points for the team that won.

The dress code, which allowed jeans year-round anyway, was tossed out from Memorial Day to Labor Day, replaced by one line: "Don't wear anything that will get you arrested." Flip-flops. Cargo shorts. Tie-dyed T-shirts. Not only allowed, but encouraged.

And to put some teeth into the new nonpolicy policies, every other Friday afternoon would be additional paid time off. "If you work it right, you can get an additional three-and-a-half days of time off over the summer," Schoenecker wrote to the troops. The Summer of Love has been repeated every summer since and has become a defining characteristic of what it means to work at BIW. It makes the place cooler.

What makes a company cool is different at every firm. It depends on what uniquely resonates at each. AppNexus in New York has surprise ice cream deliveries, happy hours, scavenger hunts, birthday cupcakes, and occasional appearances from a remote-controlled flying shark. Some of their conference rooms are named after comic book heroes. There's a big, modern kitchen stocked with lots of food.[25]

Website Etsy gives every employee a $100 credit to buy stuff to decorate his or her worksite. Every Wednesday, a chef prepares lunch for the employees using mostly local ingredients. Headquarters has two office dogs.[26] Digital ad agency Space150 rebrands and remodels itself every 150 days in what its founder called "an idea so stupid it just might work."[27] Seeley Lake Elementary in Montana has bikes and cross-country skis that employees can borrow to get outside.[28]

There's a danger with this kind of "skippity doo." Overengineered, lacking genuineness, or just plain goofy, such initiatives can be counterproductive, like the awkward kid in high school trying so hard to be someone he's not that he becomes a total dweeb in the process. Force-fed fun, employees and managers can feel that in addition to their regular responsibilities they need to pretend to the Chief Happiness Officer that they are having the time of their lives.

"'Voluntary' outings . . . are really mandatory," wrote one employee of Zappos. "You are viewed as an outsider if you do not act like you're part of the Zappos college-fraternity-like lifestyle. It is very much like high school or college all over again."[29] In the research literature, faking it like this is called "emotional labor." "The most unpleasant thing about the fashion for fun is that it is mixed with a large dose of coercion," warned the *Economist* columnist. "Compulsory fun is nearly always cringe-making."[30]

The companies that really get it do their own thing in their own way, and they let their employees follow along at their own pace. The best are wrapped up in some combination of passion for the work they do and the genuine imprint of their leader's personality. The morning before the Edgar Winter Band played for the 2013 Summer of Love, Schoenecker had to explain to some of his younger employees exactly how much of a rock legend was going to be performing that afternoon on the company lawn. "I think you'll like it," he said. "Anyway, that's what you get when you let an old hippie run a company."

What makes the Summer of Love work uniquely at BI Worldwide is that it fits Minnesota, where summers are short and people are religious about them, it fits the character of the company, and the company president wasn't being anyone but himself in deciding to do it. Done genuinely and done right, these perks send an exceptionally strong signal to the reciprocating employee that his company, which controls the bulk of his waking hours, wants him to have a great time while he's at work. How could it not motivate employees?

After *The New York Times* published its story on the "Fun at Work movement," one reader pushed back hard against its insinuation that having a good time at work was a suspect idea. "I did an internship in Silicon Valley that had to be the best place *ever* to work," he wrote. "I was paid as an intern, not a huge amount, but enough to live on. No one cared what you wore to work. The facility was beautiful and the Aero chairs at every desk were wonderful."

Throughout the company's headquarters were espresso machines and popcorn machines and freezers with Ben & Jerry's Peace Pops. Catered food, beer, and wine were served on Friday afternoons. The company had games, and places to nap or take a shower.

"And, you know what? We worked our butts off for them because we felt appreciated," he wrote. "When you are writing code, it is a creative process that sometimes requires breaks to work out a problem. Whether that's a video game or a beer or throwing around a ball, it does something to your brain that allows the problem to simmer on the back burner and then the right answer just pops.

"I wasn't a kid. I was in my 40s, with 25 years of work history behind me. I had gone back to school to update my skills and it was a bit unnerving at first. But it works. And I suddenly realized what had been wrong with all those other jobs of back-biting and office politics and being scared to death of your boss. It doesn't have to be like that to work well."

Very cool.

THE SIXTH RULE

Be Boldly Transparent

Diana Mekota was looking for a job in Cleveland.

She graduated in 2009 from John Carroll University, just east of the city. Her neuropsychologist husband, having completed his internship in Rochester, New York, accepted a residency in Cleveland. "We are both thrilled to return home and be close to family," she told her alma mater in an update it posted online.[1]

Mekota reached out on LinkedIn to Cleveland's self-proclaimed "Job Bank Mother," a woman who on the side kept a list of communications and marketing jobs in northeast Ohio. "I want my subscribers to feel like everyone is my little sister or brother, and I'm looking out for them," the networker once told a conference.[2] Mekota sent a short message describing her credentials and asking to join the job bank subscriber list. The younger woman requested to be "connected" to the more established professional on LinkedIn.

She got the following reply:

Poor Judgment on Your Jobseeking Strategy
Diana: We have never met. We have never worked together. You
are quite young and green on how business connections work
with senior professionals. Apparently you have heard that I pro-
duce a Job Bank, and decided it would be stunningly helpful for
your career prospects if I shared my 960+ LinkedIn connections
with you—a total stranger who has nothing to offer me.

    Your invite to connect is inappropriate, beneficial only to you,
and tacky. Wow, I cannot wait to let every 26 year old jobseeker
mine my top-tier marketing connections to help them land a job.

    I love the sense of entitlement in your generation. And there-
fore I enjoy Denying your invite, and giving you the dreaded "I
Don't Know Diana" because it's the truth.

    Oh, and about your request to actually receive my Job Bank
along with the 7,300 other subscribers to my service? That's
denied, too.

    I suggest you join the other Job Bank in town.
    Oh wait—there isn't one.

    You're welcome for your humility lesson for the year. Don't
ever reach out to senior practitioners again and assume their
carefully crafted list of connections is available to you, just
because you want to build your network.

    Don't ever write me again.[3]

"At first, I was shocked," Mekota told the *Cleveland Plain Dealer*. She reread the response several times, thinking it must be a mistake. Disregarding the older woman's instructions, she e-mailed her back.

"I realize you told me to never write you again, but wanted to reach out as there has been a large miscommunication and I merely wanted to explain myself," she wrote. One of her friends told her not to send a résumé, Mekota said, so she sent the LinkedIn request to share her background. "I apologize if this came off as arrogant or invasive, as that was never my intention," she wrote. "I was, again, hoping to join your very impressive job board, but I understand your reservations."[4]

No reply.

So Mekota did what many millennials do when they have something to share. She shared it. She took a screenshot of the scathing reply, blocked out the names, and posted it to her friends on Facebook. And then posted it on more public sites. "I decided, with the attention and anger it was fueling, it would be best to share with sites like Imgur and Reddit."[5]

"Guess us twenty somethings should bow down to senior professionals because clearly we have nothing to offer," Mekota editorialized on Imgur under the screenshot of the scolding she received. "Just like to point out that her LinkedIn page reads: 'Frequent speaker on creating a gamechanger resume, professional presence, and how LinkedIn is a critical element of any job search.'

"So the job search continues..."

A generation ago, young people who were told to get lost by a powerful jerk suffered largely in silence. They had to. There was no Internet, Twitter, Facebook, Imgur, YouTube, or Reddit. There were no cell phones. What were they going to do? Call the local newspaper and whine to some reporter who himself had been put in his place a few times by curmudgeonly editors? Maybe they would have told friends. But the social media of that day—talking—moved a lot slower. And by the time they told their stories, they would have calmed down. It was a time when important people could show one face to those they needed and another to those they did not.

Not anymore.

"Looks like someone forgot where she came from," one person commented to Mekota's Imgur post. "She's about to learn a whole lot of stuff about the Internet she never knew before," another presciently added.[6]

It didn't take long for the woman who slammed Mekota to be identified as Kelly Blazek, recipient of the 2013 Communicator of the Year award from the Cleveland Chapter of the International Association of Business Communicators. CNN picked up the story, calling Blazek's missive "the Devil-Wears-Prada of all responses to a LinkedIn request."[7] Once the news went viral on social media and worked its way onto the mainstream wires, newspapers, and cable channels, other people came forward with their own evidence of widget treatment from Blazek.[8]

In short order, the blowback from Blazek's private correspondence with supplicants took her down. She issued an apology. "I am very sorry to the people I have hurt," she wrote. "My Job Bank listings were supposed to be about hope, and I failed that. In my harsh reply notes, I lost my perspective about how to help, and I also lost sight of kindness, which is why I started the Job Bank listings in the first place. The note I sent to Diana was rude, unwelcoming, unprofessional and wrong. I am reaching out to her to apologize. Diana and her generation are the future of this city. I wish her all the best in landing a job in this great town."

Blazek deleted her LinkedIn account; her Twitter account, @NEOHCommJobs; and all the content on her blog.[9] The Cleveland IABC chapter replaced the online story of her recognition with a statement that she and they "mutually agreed that she will return the chapter's 2013 Communicator of the Year award."

"Anti-Mentor Roasts Millennial Who Contacted Her on LinkedIn," *Time* magazine reported. "Then karma roasts her online."[10]

THE SIXTH NEW RULE IS "BE BOLDLY TRANSPARENT."

People have always communicated with others about their jobs, but never at the speed they do now nor, in many cases, with as great an audience. Leaking a document can be done in a keystroke. One thumb drive can contain file cabinets' worth of information. Everyone has a still and video camera as close as his or her smartphone. Almost nothing is secret anymore. It's never been more important to run a company so that there's nothing to hide.

The last decade was marked by a democratization of the means of publishing and broadcasting unimaginable a generation ago. Hundreds of websites trade in "user-generated content," making anyone who wants to be reporter, editor, news photographer, columnist, or talk show host, not that any of us would go by those titles. It's casual. We just post, upload, tweet, or share. No matter. The information is out there.

Kelly Blazek's comeuppance "serves as another reminder that we are held accountable for our actions, even more so in our online-driven world," said Stefanie Moore, an assistant professor specializing in public relations and social media at Kent State University. "If we're inconsistent in our interactions with our audiences online and offline, we'll be called out."[11]

Even in high-security workplaces such as U.S. Navy ships and submarines, evidence of poor leadership, where it exists, is more likely to leak out. "In years past, allegations of wrongdoing often remained mere allegations, because words alone are generally not sufficient to indict anyone, let alone a commanding officer. However, e-mails, security cameras, cellphone cameras, electronic records of calls and texts, and 'smart phones' with web access have changed the landscape dramatically," wrote a Navy captain and faculty member at the U.S. Army War College. "Subordinates have a plethora of means to document and report perceived offenses of their skippers. Furthermore, that same technology has made it increasingly difficult to deal with such transgressions quietly and privately; it is just as easy to post incriminating evidence on YouTube as to send it to the officer's superior."[12]

The need for consistency and transparency kicks in from the beginning of the employee-employer relationship. Back when a company would advertise a job in the local newspaper, *The Wall Street Journal*, or a trade publication, a prospect's first contact with the organization would often be with wherever the ad said applicants should apply. No one then could "Google" a potential employer or boss. Today, an increasing number of "Best Places to Work" surveys detail what's good and bad about a company. Tipped off by social media or with digital evidence, traditional media are discovering new ways to uncover stories about companies that in the past would have remained hidden.

When a job gets posted on LinkedIn, prospects can easily build a list of first- and second-level connections who either work there or once did. Within a few texts or e-mails, and perhaps a cup of coffee with a key informant, the job seeker can be well briefed on the organization's culture. A generation ago, a prospective employee likely would not have known that much unless and until she took the job. By then, it would be too late. Now, if a company does not have a solid digital reputation—a reputation increasingly outside its control—the best hiring prospects evaporate long before they ever make contact with HR.

Once on the job, employees are less likely than those a generation ago to trust other people, including their leaders. The trend of all generations toward greater skepticism is accelerated by the fact that millennials, as a group, are substantially less trusting than the boomers they are replacing.

"Millennials have emerged into adulthood with low levels of social trust," reported the Pew Research Center in 2014. "In response to a long-standing social science survey question, 'Generally speaking, would you say that most people can be trusted or that you can't be too careful in dealing with people,' just 19 percent of millennials say most people can be trusted, compared with 31 percent of Gen Xers . . . and 40 percent of Boomers."[13] The patterns appear stable, meaning that millennials' trust is unlikely to increase, and as they become a larger proportion of the workforce, overall trust levels are almost certainly going to keep declining.

This lack of trust upends communication strategies. If someone trusts his leaders, as employees a generation or two ago were much more likely to do, silence means things are fine. When trust levels are low, silence creates rumors that something is wrong. Employees' decision rules on whether to believe their leaders have evolved from "Trust" to "Trust, but verify," to "Verify, then trust."

In primitive times, uncertainty—not knowing where you were, who was friend or foe, what would happen next—could be life-threatening. Still an important part of our mindset, those instincts make people hate not knowing what's going on at the companies where they work. Not knowing makes them nervous enough that they simply want to leave in much the same way that their ancestors would avoid strange areas or people in favor of familiar and more predictable circumstances.

In business, the lurking danger is not a grizzly bear or another tribe making a night attack. No one is going to die. But the human mind is built for watching for those kinds of threats. Isn't it ironic that so many senior executives, when planning a major move, incorporate into their strategy the element of surprise precisely so employees do not do what they would do if they saw the change coming?

In the United States, one in four workers agrees with the statement "I'm kept in the dark on important issues at my job." Understandably, the employees who compose that one-quarter are far less likely to trust the leadership of their companies or to believe everything the firm does is honest and ethical. Fifty-three percent of this hypervigilant group also agree with the statement "I wish I were working somewhere else," a proportion nearly 3½ times greater than in the rest of the working population. The United States is typical of much of the rest of the world on corporate transparency. In most regions, including the United States, roughly 3 in 10 agree, "This organization keeps too much information from its employees." In the United Kingdom, however, it's nearly half, and among that group, only 28 percent agree, "I love my job." Among the 5 percent of the British who feel their companies are most transparent, 82 percent love their jobs.

Similar roots in transparency appear through all of an employee's intentions. Those who see greater transparency in their companies are far better able to focus on customer needs, feel a greater sense of obligation to work hard, would recommend their company as a great place to work, have a greater sense of pride in their jobs, and see those jobs as bringing out their best ideas. The converse, of course, is also true; the more companies clam up, the more they lose their employees' best efforts.

"The worst thing about this job? Not being told what's going on," a 51-year-old employee of a container manufacturer told our research team. "The most frustrating part of this job is the unknown—finding out what to do as we go along," said a 38-year-old employee of a medical center.

Where transparency is low, the relationship between employer and employee is becoming a fascinating game of Spy vs. Spy. The mindblowingly stupid idea of asking job applicants for their Facebook passwords flared up and was properly hosed down in 2012. Since then, some companies have simply refined their "tradecraft."

"LinkedIn recommendations . . . can provide valuable intelligence to companies about their employees," reported one human resources magazine. "A flurry of new LinkedIn recommendations can signal that the worker is looking for a new job," the leader of a firm that does that kind of snooping told the publication. "When you see someone accumulating many recommendations quickly, it is often a sign or an indicator they are trying to increase their relevance and persona," he said.[14]

Sometimes transparency itself is perverted into an Orwellian level of employee tracking. In the name of transparency, investment management company Bridgewater Associates records every meeting, a practice strangely lauded in the *Harvard Business Review*.[15] To many of the employees, it's creepy. Bridgewater "is completely paranoid and functions more like a prison than anything else. Prepare to have every aspect of your life probed and recorded," wrote one former employee.[16] "Cameras follow you everywhere, meetings and conversations are recorded," wrote another refugee. "Might as well live in Soviet Russia. Very, very weird place. I'd say close to a cult."[17]

Knowing they are sometimes the target of corporate surveillance; knowing that some companies are tempted to drop nasty layoff, closure, merger, or reorganization surprises on their workforce; people are increasingly gathering their own "intelligence" on current and future employers. The sources and methods of workers are starting to yield fascinating results.

ROBERT HOHMAN AND RICH BARTON HAD AN IDEA FOR A NEW BUSINESS.
Barton had already spun Expedia out of Microsoft and cofounded Zillow, spreading previously locked travel and real estate information into the market. Hohman was the president of Hotwire. An engineer by training, he led the team that built Expedia's cruise, hotel, and package booking systems. The two men had worked together at Microsoft.

"At its core, [Expedia] was a transparency play," said Hohman. "It was magical to see what happens when you take all this information that is bottled up, either in people's heads or proprietary systems, and you set it free to the masses."

The two men wondered what would happen if they did to jobs and companies what Expedia had done to flights, airlines, and other travel information. Hohman recalls the conversation going along these lines: "The one area of our lives that really needs this is work, because it's so critically important to our happiness in terms of making sure we're at the right place, making sure we're compensated fairly for what we're doing. And yet there's woefully poor information on the Internet about companies, what it's like to work there. And how do I find the right one for me?"

"You can find a million articles on which model iPhone you should buy," he said, "but there's incredibly poor information around employers. So we started talking about that and said, 'What if suddenly you could see inside employers and see their strengths and their weaknesses? That annual survey that we all take . . . what if that were completely made public—a copy was given to every employee. Most companies have a spreadsheet of salaries, too. What if that spreadsheet of salaries got mailed out to everybody in the company, and in fact somebody forwarded it outside the company and it was available to the world?"[18]

"It's about empowering the regular guy with information, data, analysis, and tools," Barton said years later.[19]

But what would happen if the files were opened? Would it all be good, or would it become a Pandora's box of unintended consequences? "We scratched our heads over that for a bit," said Hohman. "Is this a good thing, ultimately? Is it a bad thing? It was certainly an uncomfortable thing. He and I had both been CEOs of companies for many years. We ultimately decided that beyond the discomfort, it was ultimately a good thing for both employees and employers. And that is how Glassdoor was born."[20]

An employee who goes to Glassdoor is asked to anonymously rate his current or former employer's culture and values, work-life balance, senior management, compensation and benefits, and career opportunities. He's asked whether he would recommend the company to a friend and whether he approves of the CEO. What are the pros of working there? What are the cons? What advice would he give to the senior management? Each review appears individually on the site.

Any one stranger's opinion might not matter much. But when dozens or hundreds of employees weigh in, it becomes a useful and tempting read for prospective, current, and past workers. By 2014, the site had 6.5 million reviews on 325,000 companies.[21]

What is it like to work at Bain & Company, one of the top-rated firms on the site? It's staffed by "great people who really care about both their colleagues and solving client problems" but "work/life balance could be tough if traveling," say the people who work there. There are 612 Bain reviews that go into further detail. What is it like to work at Sears, one of the lowest-rated companies on the site? "Employees can't do anything to please upper management. It's never good enough," said one complaint similar to many others. "Run away as fast as you can," wrote another.[22]

Glassdoor has several weaknesses. The site suffers from what statisticians call self-selection bias; its data come only from people who decide they want to share something about where they work. And in seeking recruitment dollars from the same companies whose workers are anonymously rubbishing their bosses, Glassdoor has the same conflicts of interest traditionally faced by newspapers and magazines that covered businesses and sold help-wanted ads to those same companies. "Now that it's taking in advertising dollars from employers, Glassdoor's challenge will be to make sure that decisions to filter certain reviews don't seem to outsiders like they were motivated by relationships with sponsors," noted *The Wall Street Journal*.[23] If the company chooses to respond to a negative review, HR gets the last word.

Yet some tables are being turned. Searching "Glassdoor" and "Wall Street Journal" not only leads to articles from the highly regarded newspaper about the job website but also links to the site chirping about what it's like to work at the newspaper. (It's worse than working at Bain but better than working at Sears.) Glassdoor's CEO got a little blowback from pushing transparency when *The New York Times* asked him to reveal his salary. It was $200,000, he stammered, sending an e-mail later to the reporter saying he had been meaning to go public with his pay anyway.[24]

"Glassdoor didn't take long to get to 14 million unique visitors because people want to see what people at different companies make. They also want to see where their friends work, which is key to networking," said Barton. "It's a way to bring light to the job-hunting process."[25]

Ultimately, the information is just too juicy. The reviews may not be representative, like a well-designed and well-fielded employee survey, but they have a different kind of validity by coming in largely unfiltered, outside of the corporate-sponsored opinion gathering, from people who have been there. And the writing is sometimes quite entertaining.

"Think of Disneyland, the happiest place on Earth. Now think of the opposite of Disneyland, the unhappiest place on Earth." That's his former employer, wrote one person on Glassdoor. "Employees, embittered by bad pay, a poisonous and unsupportive work environment, managers who are waiting for them to fail, an absence of any communication, and no yearly bonus at all, want out. Search elsewhere. You don't want to work here."[26]

Reading the reviews on a company is like having coffee in a half hour with 50 former employees. Their comments have to be taken with a grain of salt, but people do that all the time. They know, for example, that what a believer in the company acknowledges as a "con" of working there is likely true, particularly if several people say it. They know that what the company's most severe critics concede as a "pro" of working there is also likely true. If nothing else, Glassdoor gives potential employees essential questions to ask before getting too serious about joining a firm.

"Before it existed," said Sonoma State University economics professor Robert Eyler, "what you saw a lot of was individualized websites and individual people doing the blogging and social media aspects of discussing their companies in an anonymous manner. What Glassdoor does is provide that way of discussing companies that a lot of people were historically reticent to engage in."[27]

"I think another thing this website shows us is that nothing is a secret," said McGill University associate professor Lisa Cohen.[28]

A few people are even starting to explore whether the caliber of employee tattling is predictive of how the firm's stock does against the market. The early results are only tantalizing, not much proof of anything.[29] But as more information leaks out from every company, publicly available "intelligence" may become as useful to investors as assessing the leadership abilities of the CEO, guessing about future interest rates, scrutinizing the newest product, sizing up debt, or any of the other more established ways of handicapping a stock. The little secrets once known almost exclusively to those who work at a company are increasingly on display.[30]

Regardless, the trend toward transparency driven in part by Glassdoor can't be stopped. Early on, some companies tried to tell their widgets not to access the website, or the companies "suggested" they—hint, hint, remember we pay you—write a glowing review. "I'd recommend reading all of the posts on this site with the understanding that . . . the entire company received a note from the chief marketing officer 'asking' that each person write an honest review of the company," one person tattled. "This is my honest review three months after severing ties with the organization."[31]

There is a fun game developing for readers of Glassdoor to spot the reviews planted by organizations to artificially boost their rankings. In the early going, it wasn't too hard. "Keep doing what you are doing," one review glows. "The Management and Exec teams have consistently worked to improve the company and its employees. There are always challenges that arise when a business is growing this quickly, what matters is how the leadership chooses to handle those challenges, and so far they have done an exceptional job."[32] Said no real employee ever.

When one company got high ratings on Glassdoor for having tough interviews, its leadership sent a link to the rankings list as a way to brag that it hired only the best. Employees who didn't know about the site now did. Once there, they not only read the page to which their employer linked; they also started reading the reviews posted by their colleagues. As the firm's culture deteriorated over the next few years and the company started firing many of those select few, those reviews got worse. The company told people not to read or post on the site. Too late.

The company "has again instructed employees not to read, talk about, or post things on Glassdoor," reported one employee.

He wrote it in a Glassdoor review.

LEADING AND MANAGING OPENLY HAS ALWAYS BEEN A WISE STRATEGY— to be motivated by the best intentions, to have the highest ethical standards, and to share information liberally throughout the company. In the past, doing so was more of a choice. Those who did so got credit for their openness. Now it's table stakes.

"Parents of millennials talked about everything in front of their children, from finances to sex," wrote a columnist for *Time* magazine, "so millennials are comfortable with the same approach from businesses and managers."[33] After spending their adolescence posting and tweeting where they are, whom they are with, what they are thinking, how they are feeling, and what they will do next, millennials don't do well with leaders who hide in the C-suite. At this point, neither does anyone else.

Transparent firms perform better. One firm specializing in corporate ethics maintains there is a connection between the transparency of a company and its immunity to scandal, litigation, and poor stock performance. "It's a fact of life that fraud, malfeasance, class-action suits, bankruptcies, and other negative events make the headlines; not companies that are fair and open in their dealings with shareholders over the long term," the company's chief executive told *Forbes*.[34]

To be boldly transparent, a company must communicate with its employees candidly and frequently. Rumors—and now online reviews— fill any vacuum. Silence is now assumed to mean either the news isn't good or the employees aren't trusted. And ulterior motives can be spotted a mile away. Most CEOs, being used to the old rules, are not prepared for the level of transparency their employees now expect.

"Trust in the person leading the company is inextricably linked with trust in the company itself," a research report by public relations firm Edelman concluded. "Actions (by the CEO) that ranked highest included communicating clearly and transparently, telling the truth regardless of how complex or unpopular it is, and engaging with employees regularly."[35]

Maybe cutbacks will be needed; waiting to tell people only makes things worse. So the strategic plan isn't finished yet; sharing what you have and asking for input might get it done faster and with greater buy-in. Perhaps you don't know what the future will hold, but that doesn't mean you can't tell employees how you will make the decisions. There are very few situations today where the best option is not the most transparent one.

The signals are clear: it's now time to share.

THE SEVENTH RULE

Don't Kill
the Meaning

ONE OF THE BEST DEMONSTRATIONS OF THE POWER OF MEANINGFUL
work revolves around the question of how long you can get a Harvard
man to play with Legos.

Beginning around 2001, the company that makes Legos began selling a line it called Bionicle. Bionicles were otherworldly action figures
with names like Tahu, Kopaka, Pohatu, and Onua. They came unassem-
bled in colorful cylinders so the child who got one could not only play
with the figure when it was done but get the satisfaction of building it.

A few years after Bionicle came onto the market, three researchers
decided to recruit male undergraduates at Harvard University to assemble the 40-odd pieces into the finished figure. (Harvard men can do this
without difficulty, the social scientists reported.)

The students were paid $3 to assemble one figure, then asked if they
would be willing to build a second for $2.70. All of them agreed. After
they built a second Bionicle, the subjects were offered the chance to build
a third for $2.40, a fourth for $2.10, and so on. The researchers wanted to
know at what point and at what wage the "employees" would quit.

For half the men, the completed Bionicles were simply placed below the work table and replaced by a new kit. But for the other half of the subjects, as each man worked on assembling a new figure, the researcher in the room would take apart the Bionicle he just finished. This second group was labeled the "Sisyphus" condition after the king in Greek mythology condemned to push a giant boulder up a hill only to have it roll down each time, forcing Sisyphus to start over. For this half of the Harvard men, the experiment consisted of "an endless cycle of them building and we destroying in front of their eyes," said behavioral economist Daniel Ariely, who included the study in his bestselling book *The Upside of Irrationality*.

The subjects in the first group also knew the Bionicles they were assembling would eventually be taken apart to be reused in the research, but they didn't have their work undone immediately and right in front of them. With what the three researchers called in their published paper "a thin veil over the futility of the task," the first group built nearly 50 percent more Bionicles. The pay rate at which their counterparts in the Sisyphus group resigned was 40 percent higher than that at which the second group said stop.[1]

Of course, some people like playing with Legos more than others, so the scientists analyzed whether that factor affected how long an undergrad kept building Bionicles. It did for the first group, for whom the work was more meaningful, but not for the Sisypheans. The difference, said Ariely, "suggests to me that with this manipulation of breaking things in front of people's eyes, we basically crushed any joy that they could get out of this activity."

One of the drawbacks of the experiment with the Harvard men is that it was not real work. It was a simple illustration based on college students assembling toys. "People were not curing cancer or building bridges. People were building Bionicles for a few cents," said Ariely in a 2012 TED Talk.[2] "So there was not a big opportunity for meaning."

That same year, two Ph.D. candidates decided to take the Bionicle experiment into a real labor market and make it more meaningful. They couldn't give anyone a chance to cure cancer, but they could give them a chance to spot it. They recruited people on Amazon's piecework contracting website, Mechanical Turk. The website trades in "human intelligence tasks," or HITs—small, repetitive operations that computers can't do. It's widget work, to be sure, but as the doctoral students discovered, that depends on how it's framed.

The researchers offered small payments for reviewing digital images of magnified tissue scans. The project hired 2,471 people in the United States and India. Some of the workers were told "your job will be to help identify tumor cells in images" to help overburdened medical researchers. "Thank you for your time and effort," the first group was told in their training video. "Advances in the field of cancer and treatment prevention rely on the selfless contributions of countless individuals such as yourself."

A second group of piece-rate workers was told only that they should look for "areas of interest." The words "cancer" and "medical" were never mentioned to them.

A third group was also told to look for areas of interest, but they were warned that, like the Sisypheans in the Lego experiment, their work would be used to test the system, but then discarded.

Everyone got the same training on what to tag and was paid the same amount. The doctoral students labeled the three groups "Meaningful," "Zero-context," and "Shredded" to reflect the way the work had been framed.

Those who believed they were helping spot cancer for medical reasons were more likely to take on the work, labeled more images, and tagged the center of the cells more accurately. "It's always nice to have [HITs] that take some thought and mean something to complete. Thank you for bringing them to MTurk," wrote one of the workers tagging what he believed were cancer cells. "I felt it was a privilege to work on something so important," wrote another, "and I would like to thank you for the opportunity."

Those in the "zero-context" condition completed fewer images, although at a similar level of quality. The drop-off might have been more serious if some of them didn't look for meaning even where it was not given. "I assumed the 'objects' were cells, so I guess that was kind of interesting," wrote one worker.

Those whose work was "shredded" did as much work, and therefore got paid as much, as the "zero-context" group, but the quality of their tags was lower. "This makes sense; if the workers knew their labelings weren't going to be checked, there is no incentive to mark points carefully," wrote the researchers. While some of those who believed they were marking cancer cells wrote notes explaining they had trouble zooming in close enough and clicking on just the right spot, "we found no such apologies or comments from people in the 'shredded' group."[3]

As for Bionicles, Lego doesn't make them anymore. After a decade on the market, they were discontinued in 2010. If the two studies of meaning at work are any clue, some of the Lego employees who developed them were deflated to see that work end, but happy to know there were plenty of Bionicles assembled and ready for action in kids' toy bins around the world.

Meaning is a funny thing that way.

The Seventh New Rule is "Don't Kill the Meaning."

If you ask someone "Why do you work?" her response will often be, "Because I need the money." If you ask her "But why do you work in your current occupation?" there's a strong chance her answer will include something about meaning.

"The thing that motivates me most is my kids," said a 28-year-old teacher who earns $37,000 a year. "I do something very few are able to do and provide something useful to everyone," said a 32-year-old, $90,000-a-year utility employee. "I like troubleshooting issues and making a repair that gets the aircraft back to making money," said a 47-year-old, $100,000-a-year mechanic.

To the Alaskan native who helps manage her tribe's financial endowment from oil-rich lands, it's "seeing people succeed because of my efforts." "I help make their lives improve," she said. "I give them hope." Could she be lured to another job for more pay? Yes. "But it would have to be for a job that is as rewarding."

Purpose-driven motivations charge through in the comments of those who participated in the research for this book. "Helping others." "Working with graduate students." "The mission." "Knowing that my decisions directly benefit people financially." "Keeping the public safe." "Doing work that matters." And from a young woman working for a bio-tech company: "Curing cancer."

Most people need meaning in their work. They need it so badly that they'll take something that others might find trivial and elevate it to integral. Their identity is intertwined with their career and often with their current job.

At various points in history, the prevailing view of work was that it was both unavoidable and distasteful. "To the ancient Greeks, work was a curse that prevented humankind from engaging in the more sublime and worthwhile pursuits of the mind and spirit," wrote one pair of academics studying the issue.[4] Pay is called compensation because it compensates the worker for being somewhere she would rather not be, doing something she would rather not do.

"If you don't want to work, you have to work to earn enough money so that you don't have to work," said Ogden Nash. "The brain is a wonderful organ; it starts working the moment you get up in the morning and does not stop until you get into the office," quipped Robert Frost. When people are treated like widgets, Nash's and Frost's view holds true.

More than any other, the Seventh Rule is where John Stuart Mill's cynical view of humans as greedy and lazy runs headlong into the reality of so many people whose psychological rewards don't start with dollar signs. This is where a company posts a job with "competitive pay and benefits" to attract *Economicus* and a sentimental *Reciprocans* shows up on a mission to do something to make a difference.

Three-quarters of Americans value the missions of their organizations. That's an exceptionally high proportion, inflated by people gravitating toward enterprises that spark their interest, but also juiced by their innate need to be part of something bigger than themselves. It's an astounding 87 percent in India. Large majorities in every region believe their jobs are important and see how their work connects to larger company goals. The proportion who disagree with these statements around the globe runs in the single digits. To no other rule are people so likely to answer positively.

A person may have a neglectful manager. The pay might be marginal. The hours might be rough. The place may be at risk of closing or being sold. Through all of it, most employees will still find meaning in their work. That says something profound about the reasons why people work.

The statement "I value my company's mission" is twice as powerful as the statement "I am paid fairly" in predicting the average employee's sense of obligation to work hard for the company, her willingness to work hard for customers, and her pursuit of better ways of getting the job done. It is a substantially stronger predictor of her being innovative in the role and being proud of working at her company. Money is important, particularly for signing on and staying. But for daily drive, meaning trumps money.

Some of the people who understand this best are those who have been "terminated." It's not just the loss of income and security that gave them a gut punch, they'll tell you. It's waking up the next morning to the realization, as one suddenly unemployed man did, that "I didn't just lose my job; I lost my purpose."

The double-edged sword of meaning is that as much as companies love their employees to wrap themselves in the corporate mission, those connections—what four researchers called "work-role centrality"—make the ever-more-common layoffs all the more painful. "Because individuals with high work-role centrality find the work role as providing meaning and fulfillment, the absence of work for these individuals . . . lead[s] to lower psychological and physical well-being," they concluded.[5]

"My calling is gone," wrote a veteran newspaper reporter knocked out by the collapse of that industry. "I used to be a top reporter in this town, and I felt an ownership of it. I am about as useful to the world as dryer lint."[6]

The patterns in the survey responses show that company leaders don't need to do much for people to have a sense of meaning in their work. People who work at an ice cream maker usually come to the company already with a love of ice cream. People who join a tech firm already think technology is cool. You don't have to sell them on the product.

Showing them how what they do leads to larger enterprise successes, connections of which they may not be aware, proves to be highly reinforcing. Recognizing not just those who score the goal, but everyone who helped get it to that end of the field, always plays well. But because meaning is an intense and individual phenomenon, attempts to amplify it by presuming to tell employees why they should value the mission run a high risk of coming across as mere sloganeering. Making meaning gimmicky, like the department store chain that created a set of company value rubber bracelets, can make an employee feel foolish for his earlier belief.[7]

"Most organizations draw together a committee of people, maybe the leadership of the company and the board, and write out the purpose statement and pick the values for that organization," said Tom Gardner, CEO of the investment site The Motley Fool. "And then they hand that down like a tablet from the mountaintop. Every new employee gets a document that they're supposed to look at, memorize, and deploy that thinking in their work from one day to the next. The problem is that you can't really own that as an individual, can you? You've been handed that purpose statement and those values."

The Motley Fool has six core values. The sixth is left blank for the employee to fill in. Gardner came across one employee who wrote in that space, "I like to have a beer at 4 o'clock on Friday."

"Why? How could that be your core value?" he asked the worker. "What does that mean? I'm not upset by it. I'm just curious."

"I like to make a transition from work to home," he replied. "I like to have a little fun in the workplace that gets me ready for the weekend. I don't want to just break at the end of Friday and then have my fun. I want to enjoy myself with people that I work with. That's why I have a beer every Friday at 4."

"I thought," said Gardner, "that's a wonderful way to express something that matters to this person at our workplace."[8]

In lifesaving or life-changing professions such as medicine, law enforcement, national intelligence, or teaching, the purpose is compelling and easy to latch onto. In the less serious occupations, people look for reasons to believe nonetheless, to either enlarge the meaning or have a high level of dedication to the work regardless of what others may think.

Sometimes an employee is pursuing a lifelong interest. She's been good at math since the first grade, and accounting seemed almost her destiny. Sometimes he takes a job because he needs the money and, along the way, finds himself drawn into the purpose of the company. In either case, the strength of a person's connection to the mission depends heavily on whether he's building Bionicles in a "meaningful," "zero-context," or "shredded" environment.

Whether someone finds purpose in his or her work is largely a consequence of how that employee is treated, how he or she is made to feel important, how genuinely the enterprise's leadership talks about the mission of the company, and whether leaders do anything to cheapen that meaning. Working at the Department of Motor Vehicles can be either full of meaning, taking license photos of 16-year-olds on one of the biggest days of their lives, or an endless slog of forms and angry people and a slow computer system. Meaning grows or gets stomped on depending on the quality of the leadership and managing.

Those who work for exemplary leaders and dedicated managers adopt the mission of the organization. They make it their own. They become personally invested in a goal they may not have anticipated when they were hired. The evidence is equally clear, however, that employees who are neglected either become cynics or, believing in the goal but unable to take the working conditions, go elsewhere to fulfill a similar mission. People naturally gravitate toward meaning at work, but that meaning can be diluted or entirely washed away.

Asked why she was quitting her call center job, one banker said, "I've always wanted to go to nursing school." But would she have stayed at the bank if her manager were better? "Yes, I would have," she said. Is it possible she would have done her entire career in banking and never gone to nursing school if the bank had been a better place to work? "There's a very good chance I would have," she said.

"In our view, meaning, at least in part, derives from the connection between work and some purpose, however insignificant or irrelevant that purpose may be to the worker's personal goals," wrote the Bionicle researchers.[9] "When that connection is severed, when there is no purpose, work becomes absurd, alienating, or even demeaning."

A FEW YEARS AGO, TWO PROFESSORS WERE IN SEARCH OF THE MEANING of work.

"Where could we find," said J. Stuart Bunderson, one of the researchers, "a group of employees who clearly don't work for financial reasons and clearly don't work for socio-emotional reasons but who probably work for a cause, for an ideology?"[10]

Friends from graduate school, Bunderson and Jeffrey A. Thompson had gotten their families together. "We were trying to decide what to do with the kids, and we thought, 'Well, the zoo's fun. Maybe we should go to the zoo,'" said Thompson.[11]

The kids went to see the animals. The professors went to see the employees.

At first blush, it's a mystery why anyone would want to work as a zookeeper. Most employees volunteer for months or years to land a position that pays $25,000 or less. Many depend on second jobs or spouses' pay to make ends meet. There is little room for advancement. It's not a high-status profession. Instead, because of all the muck and manure, it falls within the category of what sociologists call "dirty work," distasteful but necessary jobs many people prefer to avoid.

"When you're the first one to walk into the gorilla building in the morning and it hasn't been cleaned since overnight, you don't need coffee to wake you up in the morning, believe me!" one employee told the men. "Not everybody can handle it."

One zookeeper told the story of a nun who warned the class she brought to the zoo, within earshot of a worker cleaning an animal enclosure, "See the kind of job that you get when you don't finish your education!" Like most zookeepers, the one being used as a cautionary tale had a college degree.

The work is hard, a mix of manual labor, sloppy weather in the outdoor enclosures, and calls in the middle of the night if something is wrong with an animal. "You go home and you're absolutely exhausted and you don't feel like doing anything," said one employee. "It's a back-breaker."

"As we began interviewing zookeepers, we asked, 'What would be grounds for divorce? What would cause you to walk away from the zoo and from your job?'" said Thompson.

"There's not much they could do to get me to quit," one said. "I can't think what would cause me to leave," said another.

"This question didn't register for them," said the professor. "We thought, 'Bonanza! We found it. This is where we can study people who are working for a cause.'"

The secret is in the meaning zookeepers find in their work. The professors found the passion animal caretakers have for their work even reaches the level of being a "calling." The employees comments "reflected a belief that zookeeping was one's calling, one's niche, what one was meant to do, or part of who one has always been."

"It's part of who I am and I don't know if I can explain that," one person told the men. "When you use that expression 'It's in your blood, like football players and coaches who can never retire because it's in their blood, whatever my genetic makeup is, I'm geared toward animals." Being a zookeeper is much like being a craftsman, doctor, scientist, or artist, the two men concluded. In many respects, the person is his occupation and is part of a group of similarly dedicated individuals.

All this is powerful motivation for the employee to work hard regardless of the pay and the hardships. In some ways, at the highest levels of meaning, those hardships only reinforce that the employee is in a select group. Caretakers at a modern zoo often see themselves as part of much larger movements for conservation, biodiversity, and education. "Most people think, 'Oh, you should just turn these animals loose in the wild,'" said one of the people who volunteered to be interviewed. "Well, hey, there is no wild for a lot of these animals, none whatsoever. The habitat is gone. Sure, you can go turn them loose, but they're not going to find their niche because it's been removed. We've got to do something, and if captive breeding is the one thing I can do to stop extinction, then I'm fine with that."

Such a strong sense of overarching purpose can make even trivial or cumbersome tasks more significant. "The thing about this job is anything I do is ultimately for the animals, even if it's scrubbing down the back hallways," said another employee.

But this level of commitment is not free. It imposes much greater expectations on the organization. People who sacrifice for the purpose of their enterprise expect their leaders to do the same. They have little tolerance when others are not held accountable for high levels of quality. They are more likely to respect leaders who have been in the trenches. They are hesitant to let those who run their organizations know how much the work means to them, for fear their own motivations could cost them in pay and support.

"Because they believe their zoo has a moral duty related to animal care and preservation, zookeepers with a sense of calling judge management's actions and decisions against a very high standard," wrote Thompson and Bunderson.

"When I hear that $15,000 went to things that were supposed to go to animals and it didn't, that's what really makes me mad," one caretaker told them. "I think that they should be more focused. They should care as much about these animals as I do, and maybe they don't."[12]

THERE ARE THREE APPROACHES LEADERS TAKE TO THE SEVENTH RULE. Only one of them works.

Some leaders fail to understand the power of meaning. This happens most often when a corporate officer is recruited from outside the industry because of his or her financial or operational acumen. The board brings in this kind of executive to protect and grow the shareholders' money, sometimes to prepare the company for acquisition or sale, without much concern for the soul of the machine.

One of the surest ways to violate the Seventh Rule is when employees who naturally seek meaning in their work learn their leaders are mostly seeking money. If the CEO was recruited to the job by the pay package, as many are, no one should be surprised that his or her decisions are guided by the strike price of the stock options, not the mission. Seeing him or her play for cash makes the meaning-motivated workers feel like fools.

McKinsey & Company inadvertently acknowledged this common problem in May 2013 when it sent out a marketing e-mail with links to two articles. The first, "Motivating People: Getting Beyond Money," advised how to give employees the right nonfinancial incentives when money is tight. The second article, "Does your CEO Compensation Plan Provide the Right Incentives?" explained how to ensure the top exec gets the right "payoff structure," but not so much that the board has to figure out "what to say to activist shareholders and media when the CEO receives very large payouts."

At one firm, the employees noticed the head of a division stopped talking about the cool things the company would do and was spending an inordinate number of days in Florida as pivotal decisions were being made about future plans. Only when it was announced the firm was for sale did the frontline employees understand he was assiduously accumulating enough days of residency in his winter home to file his taxes there and shelter more of the large bonus he knew he'd get when the transaction was complete.

Other companies suffer another type of meaning-killing leadership. They are led by executives who understand the power of meaning—and abuse it. These folks are walking spokespeople, slick ad men and ad women, politicians. They give a great speech. They hit all the right phrases. They're faking it.

In some companies' headquarters, you can see the difference as you walk from the front door to the executive suites. The lobby features huge banners of the enterprise's biggest products or latest innovations, or the mission statement displayed across a large wall. The various departments lining the hallways—the labs and test kitchens, the operations hub, the marketing teams—display evidence of how they contribute to the mission that's displayed in the lobby. Get to the top floor or the corner offices, however, and what a visitor notices first is the high-definition TV in the waiting area tuned to CNBC, the endless stock ticker crawling across the bottom of the screen.

Eventually doubts start to form about these overly polished leaders. The telltale aloofness, the overpromising, the throw-away lines, and the "me wall" of photos of the executive shaking hands with the rich and powerful accumulate to form a more accurate portrait of his or her true motivations. You can make a fairly educated guess about the commitment of a CEO to the purpose of the firm and to his employees by calculating the ratio of times he's in front of a camera compared with how often he gets his hands dirty, obsesses over something he's doing to thank employees, or gets on a plane and goes to the company's outlying facilities.

A select few companies are fortunate to be led by executives who are just as invested in the meaning of the company's work as they hope their employees are. Sometimes the CEO succession team screens candidates for their alignment with the firm's purpose as much as their ability to manage the purse strings, and that executive is adopted into the fold. More often, the mission-driven leader comes from within. Few people doubt the commitment of a military leader who has been in the service for decades and who was once in the shoes of those he or she commands. Few people doubt the commitment of a senior executive who worked her way up in the same company over 20 years and could have made more money somewhere else.

Frequently these leaders and managers don't give as strong a speech as those who are trying to manipulate the Seventh Rule. Grandstanding turns them off. But when they do talk, the employees listen and remember. "If this ever gets to be about just the money, we should quit," one employee proudly quoted his firm's president saying.

Subtle clues come through that this person likes the job itself, not for the trappings, but for the opportunity to play a central part of what the company does. He stays when he could cash out. He seems comfortable out of the spotlight. All the gossip—every company has it—about what he's like outside the office confirms he's the same person in any setting.

Confident that the purpose of the organization is compelling by itself, he doesn't cheerlead or twist anyone's arm to go along; those who appreciate the purpose will get it.

Ultimately, only the leaders and managers for whom the organization's purpose has great personal significance are in a position to do anything to build onto the meaning their employees take from their work. When they treat the Seventh Rule with the respect it's due, their people will build the Bionicles, spot the cancer cells, clean the gorilla enclosure, or do whatever is necessary to advance the cause.

They are respectful of the deep and different reasons people find purpose in their work. They are highly protective of those sentiments and vigilant against anything that would kill the meaning.

THE EIGHTH RULE

See Their Future

FEW PSYCHOLOGICAL STUDIES ARE AS FAMOUS AS THE STANFORD marshmallow experiment.

In a series of observations begun in the late 1960s and early 1970s, psychologist and Stanford professor Walter Mischel offered children a single marshmallow on the spot or two marshmallows if they waited 15 minutes without eating the one in front of them. The study has been replicated many times. Funny videos of preschoolers being tortured by the presence of a marshmallow are all over the Internet.

Some kids eat the treat before the researcher has even finished explaining the rules. Some wait patiently for the time to pass. Many who don't eat it immediately stare at the marshmallow or consciously try to avoid looking at it. They handle it. They poke at it. They roll it around. They sniff it. They open their mouths and almost put it in before putting it down.

"If we wait, you'll give us two?" one boy, paired with a younger girl, asks at the beginning of the test.

"Yep. If you wait, you get two. Or you can eat it now—whichever you want," says the researcher as she backs out of the room.

"We're going to wait, right?" says the little girl to the boy. "We're going to wait," she confidently tells the researcher.

As soon as the door closes, the little girl sticks her tongue on her marshmallow.

"I wonder what we're going to do?" says the boy a little later. The girl takes a bite before he finishes the question.

"Are you going to eat it?" he asks.

"I just want to take one bite."

"But if you wait until she gets back, she'll give you two," the boy reminds her as she continues to eat.

"I'm waiting," says the boy several minutes later.

"I'm waiting, too," says the girl.

"No, you're eating, not waiting," says the boy.

"I can't wait," she admits.[1]

The experiment is cute by itself. It got serious after follow-up studies found that the kids who were able to sacrifice the present for the future had higher SAT scores, greater educational accomplishments, and healthier body mass ratios as high school students.

Given its alleged predictive value, the fluffy temptation has taken on exceptionally weighty implications. "I think we have found the most important factor for success," said motivational speaker Joachim de Posada in a 2009 TED Talk. "One hundred percent of the children who had not eaten the marshmallow were successful. . . . A great percentage of the kids who ate the marshmallow were in trouble."[2]

If you were the kind of four-year-old who could wait 15 minutes, so the logic goes, your odds of success were good. If you were the kind of kid who would have popped it right in your mouth, you were doomed even before entering kindergarten.

"I think I speak for thousands of my fellow Americans when I say that the first time I read about Mischel's marshmallow study—in Daniel Goleman's bestseller, *Emotional Intelligence*—I imagined myself at age 4, staring at that fateful marshmallow," wrote commentator Michael Bourne in *The New York Times*. "The tale of the marshmallows, as presented in Goleman's book, read like some science-age Calvinist parable. Was I one of the elect, I wondered, a child blessed with the moral fortitude to resist temptation? Or was I doomed from age 4 to a life of impulse-driven gluttony?"[3]

But it turns out the marshmallow test is not that simple.

More than 40 years after the original Stanford marshmallow experiment, three researchers at the University of Rochester decided to test whether decisions in the now-versus-future dilemma say as much about the environment in which the kids are placed as it does about those children's personalities.

Lead researcher Celeste Kidd, who had worked at shelters for homeless families, reasoned that eating the marshmallow would be the optimal choice for a child who was skeptical of promises about the future. "Working there gave me some strong intuitions about what kids who were in that situation would do, given the marshmallow task," she told *Businessweek*. "I'm fairly sure those kids would eat the marshmallow right away."[4] To a kid used to having promises about the future broken, "the only guaranteed treats are the ones you have already swallowed," she wrote in the paper describing their research.

To test this hypothesis, the researchers presented the kids in their study with a jar of heavily used crayons with which to color a picture, but promised if they waited—which they all did—they could use a large set of newer supplies. Half the children were brought this larger set. The promise of a brighter future was broken to the other half. "I'm so sorry. I actually don't have that big set of art supplies I told you about," the researcher said to one boy, his head hanging down at the news. "Sorry about that. But you can still use these ones to do your project."

Having been taught through the crayon experience that they were in either a "reliable" or "unreliable" environment, the researchers then conducted the classic marshmallow test.

The results were startling. Of 14 children to whom the researcher had kept her promise of the larger art set, 9 waited the full 15 minutes and got the second marshmallow. Of the 14 children burned in the first stage, stuck with the jar of used crayons when they'd been promised something better, only 1 waited long enough in the second stage to get another marshmallow. The average wait time among those in the "reliable" environment was four times what it was for those in the "unreliable" condition. "Children who were in the unreliable group were more likely to fairly quickly pick up the marshmallow and eat it," said University of Rochester professor Richard Aslin.[5]

"The difference is maybe due to a difference in expectations as to what is going to happen in the world," said Kidd. "In the marshmallow task, what you want to do is get the most amount of marshmallow possible, but there may be other considerations. Given that I have this one marshmallow now that's guaranteed, what are the chances that if I wait, there is going to be a second marshmallow later?"[6]

The Rochester marshmallow experiment does not negate the Stanford version. Self-control and delayed gratification are important qualities to anyone hoping to achieve his or her future. But the latter study qualifies the results of the former one, strongly suggesting that in addition to personal grit, getting people to bank on the future in a given place depends heavily on their confidence that there is, indeed, something worth waiting for.

Perhaps life is really just one big marshmallow experiment. If so, one of its most important questions is whether there is a second marshmallow at all.

THE EIGHTH NEW RULE IS "SEE THEIR FUTURE."

One of the coolest things about the human brain is its ability to travel through time, to go to the past and reminisce, to go to the future and envision. An optimistic view of the future is a large part of motivating hard work in the present, whether that work constitutes restraining oneself from eating a marshmallow or grinding out week after week on a project that will not see daylight for a year.

"Episodic future thought" it's called in the research literature. Sometimes it's called "preexperiencing." People do it all the time. One study found that the average person thinks about the future 59 times, or about once every 16 minutes, during the course of a day.[7] It's much of why we get out of bed in the morning, and therefore a crucial aspect of the workplace.

One of the most powerful ways to give someone a bright future is to give her a great past and present. Neuroimaging studies show that thinking about the future and remembering the past use many of the same parts of the brain. By one theory, one of the main reasons we have memories is to use them in building our futures. "We find it helpful to think of the brain as a fundamentally prospective organ that is designed to use information from the past and the present to generate predictions about the future," wrote three Harvard researchers in the prestigious journal *Nature*. "Memory can be thought of as a tool used by the prospective brain to generate simulations of possible future events."[8] Those who saw the promise of the big coloring set fulfilled are more likely to see the second marshmallow. Those who are more energized by their past at a company are more optimistic about their futures there.

We live for the future because we make it into an incredible place. Even when remembering the past, which of course cannot be changed, people are biased toward recalling the high points. "Most people perceive their lives to more often be positive than negative and the negative emotions that are associated with bad events tend to fade over time, whereas the positive emotions associated with good events tend to persist," concluded one review of the research.[9]

Time travel to the future is harder, but it's worth it. It requires more brain and more effort because it's being created from pieces of the past. Consequently, our vision of the future is hazier than that of the past. But as long as we have the mental paintbrush and fewer of the restrictions imposed by the reality of the past, we work many more "uncorrected positive illusions" into our picture of what's ahead. The future "is more emotionally positive and idyllic" than the past, wrote two Danish scientists in a 2010 paper.

Our egos are more tied up in our futures than in our pasts. When the Danish researchers asked people to evaluate past and future events on the degree to which they were or will be "important to my life," "part of my identity," and "a central part of my life story," possible future events trumped actual past events. There were more details in the past, "whereas self-narrative was higher for the future," they discovered.[10]

Children start seeing their futures—being capable, for example, of understanding the statement "We're going to the zoo tomorrow"—well before they enter school. No one needs to teach them this ability; it's built in. The only reason the marshmallow experiment works at all is that even little kids are able to mentally travel to the future, seeing themselves having two marshmallows after the 15 minutes is past even as the reality of one delicious treat sits right before them.

Not long after they gain the ability to think about being at the zoo tomorrow or at Grandma's house next week, children start thinking about what job they will hold as adults. From the psychological Lego pile of seeing their parents work, watching TV, reading books and comics, and seeing employees in different jobs around town, kids pull out pieces to construct their future selves.

The aspirations are often unrealistic, sometimes fed by their parents wanting them to shoot high. "Anyone can grow up to be president," we say, and 27 percent of kids 10 to 16 are thinking about it.[11] Yet even with fantasies about becoming an astronaut, rock star, billionaire, professional sports player, or superhero in the mix of imagined futures, "stable career preferences may emerge as early as kindergarten," one study found.[12]

By the age of 16, a young man or woman seeing his or her occupational future becomes an important predictor of whether he or she will have trouble in the job market a decade later. "Youth with undecided career ambitions earn significantly lower hourly wages in young adulthood than youth with more certain aspirations," one study concluded.[13]

But when they reach the workforce, the truth of Monster.com's famous 1999 Super Bowl commercial sets in for many employees: there is no second marshmallow.

"When I grow up," says one boy in the black-and-white ad, "I want to file all day."

"I want to claw my way up to middle management," says another.

"Be replaced on a whim," says one girl.

"I want to have a brown nose," says another.

"Be a yes man."

"Yes woman."

"Yes, Sir. Coming, Sir."

"Anything for a raise, Sir."

"When I grow up, I want to be underappreciated."

"Paid less for doing the same job."

"I want to be forced into early retirement."[14]

Among workers in the United States, a bare majority agree, "I am excited about my future with this organization." The rest are split between the 28 percent who are neutral on the statement and the 21 percent who disagree or strongly disagree. Only half know what their next career step will be at their current employer. Levels of excitement for and clarity of the future run much higher in China and India.

"Management is unclear on whether they will outsource my job in the future," a 29-year-old hospital worker in New York wrote at the end of his New Rules survey. "This company doesn't think ahead for an employee's future and growth," wrote a 33-year-old employee of an operations firm in India.

"There is no real prospect of a future with the organization. There's continual change which benefits neither the staff nor the customers, but only the shareholders," wrote a 38-year-old employee of a chemicals company in the United Kingdom. Frustrations with the future are common in Britain; more than one-third say they don't know what their next career step will be. The same proportion say their managers are little help in envisioning the next step either. One of humans' most important methods of coping with difficulties is the hope that things will improve in the future. You may not be perfectly happy with your pay now, but you probably have mentally cashed a much larger paycheck you see coming in your future, the one that will help pay for the future boat, the future cabin, or the future trip to New Zealand. You may be working 60-hour weeks, but you undoubtedly fantasize about the time a few fiscal quarters ahead when balance will return. Hope for the future, even if it's unrealistic, is a major reason why people keep pushing forward against what might otherwise be too great a burden.

Few events are more motivating than a leader, manager, or mentor seeing and believing in someone's future. "My problem looking back was that I had absolutely no role model or mentor in my small town to ask about how to go about achieving the success I wanted," said Dilbert creator Scott Adams in 2014. The inspiration for *Dilbert* came in part from doodles Adams drew when stuck in boring meetings as a middle manager at Pacific Bell.[15] But he didn't really see his future as a cartoonist until he got a call from his future editor.

"When I was trying to become a syndicated cartoonist, I sent my portfolio to one cartoon editor after another—and received one rejection after another," he once told *Fast Company*. "One editor even called to suggest that I take art classes. Then Sarah Gillespie, an editor at United Media and one of the real experts in the field, called to offer me a contract. At first, I didn't believe her. I asked if I'd have to change my style, get a partner—or learn how to draw. But she believed that I was already good enough to be a nationally syndicated cartoonist."

"Her confidence in me completely changed my frame of reference: It altered how I thought about my own abilities," said the cartoonist now syndicated in more than 2,000 newspapers, 70 countries, and 25 languages. "This may sound bizarre, but from the minute I got off the phone with her, I could draw better. You can see a marked improvement in the quality of the cartoons I drew after that conversation."[16]

If that essential optimism can't be found or is extinguished at a person's current employer, he needs to escape to rekindle it somewhere else. The reaction is part logical: Why shouldn't someone look for the best path forward? And it's part emotional: Seeing little future is too depressing to bear for long. Taking away someone's future also takes away his or her present.

Sixty percent of the time, people's reactions to the statement "This organization will do exciting things in the future" are identical to their response to the statement "I am optimistic about my future at this company." Of course, many employees can succeed personally even when the company itself struggles. Conversely, many companies prosper while leaving some employees behind. But that's not how the workers themselves see it. It is almost statistically impossible, and therefore psychologically impossible, for an employee to feel she has a bright future with the company if the company itself is not going anywhere. More to the point, it is equally unlikely that someone sees the company going places unless it is taking him along for the ride.

Among those in the United States least optimistic about their futures at their current employers, 62 percent are planning to bolt in the next 12 months. Among those most optimistic, it's less than 3 percent. Although the percentages change slightly from country to country, the connections between the brightness of a person's future and her intentions are the same. "What motivates me most are the things I will get out of this job for my future," wrote one 18-year-old British woman not planning on leaving anytime soon. As huge as the difference is, it would be larger were it not for many of the more pessimistic people being unsure they could land a job with equal pay.

"Things have changed. We can't guarantee people's futures," many company leaders will tell you. "They're on their own."

"In essence, the responsibility for career management had transitioned from the employer to the employee," concluded one summary of the trends.[17] That may be the business reality. The psychological reality is that people will continue to invest themselves most heavily in organizations where there is a future return—where there is a second marshmallow.

A HALF CENTURY AGO, WHEN A MAN JOINED IBM, HE BECAME AN "IBMer."

He would wear the IBM uniform of a dark suit and a "sincere tie." He would read IBM's company-motto-inspired *Think* magazine.

If he and his wife had a baby, they would get a letter from IBM president Thomas J. Watson Jr., son of the firm's founder. "I was so pleased to hear of the new addition to your family and realize your great happiness at this time," it would say.[18]

That kid would later play Little League baseball on an IBM team on an IBM field to earn a Watson trophy. The man and his wife were automatically members of the IBM Country Club.

Paid holidays. Life insurance. Survivor benefits. A directive 11 years before the U.S. Civil Rights Act to "hire people who have the personality, talent and background necessary to fill a given job, regardless of race, color or creed." IBM was ahead of the curve. IBM looked out for IBMers. "For much of the 20th century, IBM was the model of a dominant, paternalistic corporation," *NBC News* once noted.[19]

The IBMer would likely be promoted and relocated, at company expense, from one job and city to another, so much so that those inside the business joked that the acronym stood for "I've Been Moved." But move they did, even if it meant neighbors, friends, and kids' schools and classmates were left behind, because as the future of IBM improved, so improved the future of the IBMer. He might never need a résumé, might never need to put on one of his dark suits and sincere ties for a job interview.

"With rare exceptions we promoted from within," Watson wrote in 1987. "Virtually every IBM executive started as a salesman. Because we were growing so fast, promotions came quickly. All of our senior executives, including me, knew what it felt like to be thrown into deep water not knowing if you could swim. . . . This method worked in the main because, as young and inexperienced as these executives might be, they had come up from the bottom. They knew what IBM stood for as well as they knew their own names."[20]

Once having been made an IBMer, a hardworking person could count on the company to advance him—and later, her—to bring new opportunities as reliably as the moving van would pull in front of the house. "The model really was you joined IBM and you built your career for life there," Rutgers University Management School dean David Finegold told NBC when IBM turned 100 in 2011.[21]

IBM epitomized the hire-to-retire ethic of the time. It was not alone. You could get a job at Hewlett-Packard, General Electric, Ford, Procter & Gamble, International Paper, Sears Roebuck & Company, Goodyear, Westinghouse Electric, U.S. Steel, or any of dozens of other large corporations and work your entire career for that one company. You could see your future in the company's future. As it advanced, so would you. The question people asked each other at parties was less "What do you do?" than "Where do you work?"

There were back then, of course, people who switched employers, by choice or by force. There are now, of course, companies where people can maintain that kind of longevity. There are still today a modest percentage of "lifers" who joined the enterprise out of college and who will likely stay for the duration. But those companies and those employees are increasingly rare. In 1980, 51 percent of men aged 35 to 64 were in a job they had held for 10 years or more. Even before the Great Recession, in 2005, it was 39 percent.

The IBM of the 1950s, 1960s, and 1970s is gone. The country clubs were sold.[22] Where IBM once offered a company pension built during an IBM career, it now provides an end-of-year contribution to a 401(k) that can follow the employee to his or her next company.[23] Its employees still call themselves IBMers, but now it often has the same provisional quality as "grad student" or "renter."

IBM is not unique in having given up all but guaranteeing the future of its employees. It's just the way things are done today. It's a different world, one where employees have their own "brand" separate from that of their employers, are responsible for their own retirement savings, and must seek out their own promotions or new opportunities inside or outside the company. People are more mercenary; they have no choice. Companies increasingly recruit and cut loose people, or contract with freelancers, as the demands of the day require. And people assemble a career from jobs across a variety of employers.

"Tacking swiftly from job to job and field to field, learning new skills all the while [is] the pattern that increasingly defines our careers," observed *Fast Company*. "According to recent statistics, the median number of years a U.S. worker has been in his or her current job is just 4.4, down sharply since the 1970s. This decline in average job tenure is bigger than any economic cycle, bigger than any particular industry, bigger than differences in education levels, and bigger than differences in gender."

"For some reason I don't understand, employers seem to value having long-term employees less than they used to," Princeton economist

Henry Farber told the magazine.[24] The "company man," he concluded in a 2007 analysis of the trends, is "an anachronism." He noted, "What is clear is that young workers today should not look forward to the same type of career with one firm experienced by their parents."[25]

So what should they look forward to?

Most businesses don't have an answer to that question.

Because companies' management strategies have not kept pace with the change in their business and staffing strategies, a massive contradiction was created. Executives expect their employees to help the company build its future. Most firms have new product introduction, revenue, market share, earnings per share, and efficiency goals that stretch up to a decade into the future. You aren't a good employee if you are not committed to helping the firm achieve those goals, they either imply or say outright. And in the old days, that was true, because the implicit deal was that the company was in it for the long haul and it was bringing along its employees. That's rare anymore.

We are stuck in "a self-reinforcing cycle in which corporate time horizons have become shorter and shorter," wrote *The Washington Post*'s Steven Pearlstein. "The average holding periods for corporate stocks, which for decades was six years, is now down to less than six months. The average tenure of a public company chief executive is down to less than four years. And the willingness of executives to sacrifice short-term profits to make long-term investments is rapidly disappearing."[26]

Employees are increasingly getting the message "Help us build the future of the company, but as for your future, you're on your own. And don't forget you're an at-will employee. Our future may not include you." So many people have been burned over the past decade that we've created huge percentages of skittish employees, expected to be loyal to increasingly disloyal employers. That dog does not hunt. Only 47 percent of employees believe their careers will advance as the organization grows. For that minority, seeing a second marshmallow, they have little intention of leaving. The rest are up for grabs.

"How can we get our people to take a higher degree of ownership for the business?" asked one HR leader at a company that not that long before had laid off many of the colleagues of those employees. The simple answer: You can't. "Ownership" comes from owners, which at a minimum means an employee who gets a stake in the future of the business. The employees of that company and many others are temps—widgets—and they know it.

Another HR leader was surprised that when his company moved one of its key operations centers and all its jobs from the American Midwest to the Southeast, almost everyone chose to resign rather than, like a loyal IBMer, make the move. The employees' decisions make perfect sense in today's "unreliable" environment.

It may be impossible for most companies today to promise a bright future at those organizations. But if nothing else, an organization needs to see the potential in its people as much as it sees the potential in the firm itself. Its leaders and managers need to be deliberate in developing their employees and giving them the kinds of credentials that will allow them to build their futures somewhere, even if it's somewhere else. If they don't—if to the employee the future looks like nothing but a jar of used crayons and questions about the second marshmallow—no one can blame a worker who pops the first marshmallow in her mouth and moves on to the next experiment.

THE NINTH RULE

Magnify
Their Success

I<small>T TAKES JUST ONE CLASS PERIOD TO PASTE THE AVERAGE COLLEGE</small> professor to a wall.

College lectures are performances. Most professors want not just to educate but to entertain. They work stories and jokes into their explanations. They organize their lessons in crescendos that lead to dramatic conclusions. They want to be seen as interesting, funny, and cool.

It's always been this way. It's more intense now with social media sites like Rate My Professors, where it's open season on instructors' teaching style. More than most of them would admit, professors crave reinforcement. They want class participation. They want to pull their students' attention away from their smartphones. They want head nods and reactions and hands raised and laughter.

Combine this desire with the pacing that most teachers do, a day when the teacher arrives late, and a student instigator, and you have the ingredients for gluing the professor to the wall.

"Hey, everybody, let's do a little experiment," says the troublemaker before the teacher arrives. "The more Dr. Porter moves to the left, the more we'll pay attention to him. If he's over there, make sure you're looking at him. Laugh at his jokes. Write down what he says. The more he moves to the right, the less we'll pay attention to him. Look down. Act like you're bored. Don't make it obvious, but make it different between the right and left sides."

Those who've done this say it works every time. Over the course of the class period, without being conscious of why, the professor will start to migrate. "I noticed I was favoring the left side of the room," said one presenter on whom the trick was pulled. "I was conscious that I was doing that and made an effort to address both sides of the room equally, but somehow I always wound up playing to the left side." Something about teaching from that area seemed more comfortable, more rewarding. Something about the right side was unfulfilling, even though it was all part of the same lecture.

Executed with enough consistency and subtlety, so as not to expose the plot, it's possible for a class to stick their professor to the left wall of the room, held there by a powerful, unseen force.

That force is recognition.

"We all got a good laugh out of this exercise in behavior change," said one of its victims, "but the power of its results was clear. My behavior was definitely changed by the behavior of the group, and I didn't even know it."[1]

THE NINTH NEW RULE IS "MAGNIFY THEIR SUCCESS." THE RULE STEMS directly from the neurobiology of recognition.

If the professor's brain were being scanned as he moved from one side of the room to the other, it would show variations in the level of a crucial chemical. That chemical, a "neurotransmitter," is called dopamine. Whenever someone succeeds at just about anything, a shot of the stuff hits structures deep inside the brain on what in layperson's terms is called the "reward center." We are wired to get that primal surge for successes, particularly successes similar to those that helped our ancestors and their families survive.

Hook a trout while fly-fishing? Dopamine rush. You will not starve today.

Eat a doughnut? Dopamine is released. You now have the sugar and fat that fended off starvation for your deep ancestors who often experienced famine. Finding your next meal is now less urgent.

Drive the ball off the first tee right down the fairway? More dopamine. You are a great hunter with precise aim who will certainly bring home a deer for your family.

Kiss your date on the front porch? Dopamine surges at the prospect of progeny.

Chant with the rest of the home crowd at a hockey game? Dopamine again. You are part of a huge tribe prepared to defend itself against the other tribe.

"At a purely chemical level," *Time* magazine explained, "every experience humans find enjoyable—whether listening to music, embracing a lover or savoring chocolate—amounts to little more than an explosion of dopamine in the [psychological reward center], as exhilarating and ephemeral as a firecracker."[2]

In experimental settings, dopamine increases when someone listens to music,[3] scores in a video game, or gambles and wins. Recent research shows that go-getters release it differently into their brains than do slackers.[4] People whose dopamine response is impaired don't learn as well, because they are deprived of the emotional charge of getting the right answer. In a neurobiological sense, dopamine is the fuel of motivation and learning.[5]

Dopamine surges not only when someone succeeds but also when his leaders and colleagues acknowledge his success. Because our ancestors survived better working together than fending for themselves, we are social creatures eager to be applauded for our work, whether by chants at the campfire or likes on Facebook. Recognition can release as much dopamine as the act that earned it—or more.

When the instructor moved to the left of the room, the attention he got released more dopamine. When he moved to the right, the students' neglect took it away. And so he kept moving to the left, toward the recognition, toward the dopamine. It was a good lecture when he delivered it on the left side. It was a good lecture when he delivered it on the right. But the psychological rewards of giving the lecture were amplified only on the left.

"Dopamine [is] a kind of pleasure accountant," wrote Steven Johnson in his book *Mind Wide Open: Your Brain and the Neuroscience of Everyday Life*. "It anticipates rewards that it expects the brain to receive, and sends off an alarm if the reward exceeds or falls below the anticipated level. It's not unlike what a stock analyst does in watching quarterly earnings reports: if the company meets expectations, there's no news. But if the company shows an unexpected loss or a surprise profit, then there's something to talk about. If you're expecting a certain reward . . . and the reward comes through as promised, the dopamine in your system remains level. If you're denied the reward, dopamine production drops accordingly. And if the reward turns out to be better than expected . . . then your brain releases extra dopamine to signal the good news."[6]

Shortsighted leaders around the world make excuses for their failure to make a big deal of their employees' accomplishments. Professionals should be sufficiently motivated by the intrinsic rewards of the work itself, they claim. "No news is good news," they say in the United States. "Nicht gescholten ist lob genug" (Not scolding is praise enough), they say in Germany. "L'absence de reproches est un compliment silencieux" (Absence of criticism is a silent compliment), say the French. "A menos que te digam o contrário, você está indo bem!" (If you are not told otherwise, you're doing fine), say the Brazilians. "Por algo se te paga" (You are being paid for a reason), they say in Spanish-speaking Latin America. In Russian, it's "К сожалению, в связи с экономическим кризисом и недостатком средств, мы не сможем в этот раз вознаградить вас" (Unfortunately, due to economic crisis and lack of funds we cannot recognize you).

The problem with all these statements is not that they are illogical; programming a machine to continue until halted is a no-brainer. It's that they don't take into account the unyielding facts of evolutionary psychology. The core of behavioral economics is understanding the difference between what works in computer code and what works inside the human skull. Executives and managers who subscribe to any of the statements above are battling against a flat-out law of neurobiology. No one ever won that tug-of-war. People crave dopamine. In a contest between human nature and logic, human nature always wins.

Only one in four Americans is confident without reservation that if he or she does good work, it will be recognized. Another 4 in 10 are confident, but with some hesitation. How could an employee predict if she will be recognized? She can't know for certain, so she makes an educated guess based on whether her manager and her colleagues have recognized her hard work in the past. The two variables—past recognition and anticipation of future recognition—are almost perfectly correlated.

For the same reason that a fly fisherman will stay in an area of the river where he's catching trout, employees keep "casting" where they get recognition. Those who anticipate recognition for their future successes feel a greater obligation to work hard, give a higher proportion of their full effort, look for ways to improve the way they do their work, and deliver more of their best ideas to the company.

On the other hand, if accomplishments are met with nothing more than a "silent compliment," the brain unavoidably sees little appreciation coming and starts searching for alternatives. Eighteen percent of U.S. employees are neutral on whether their good work will be recognized, and 17 percent outright doubt it will. Canadians come in at similar levels. The proportions skeptical of future praise increase to 20 percent in Australia and 24 percent in Great Britain. Maybe reinforcement can be had working on another project, for another manager, or at another company. In the research literature, this phenomenon is sometimes called behavioral "extinction."[7] The employee may have been doing great things for the firm, but those actions were snuffed out by the lack of reinforcement. What a company does not recognize, it should not expect to see repeated.

Much like a fly fisherman who's getting no strikes, the employee leaves that spot on the river. Those who are least confident in future recognition are 17 times as likely to be thinking of leaving as those most confident that hard work will be matched with strong praise. The proportions actively planning to leave multiply 14 times between the high and low ends of the recognition spectrum.

In nearly every country, lack of recognition gets excused by confusing it with compensation. The Portuguese sometimes say, "És bem pago pelo que fazes" (You are already well paid for what you do). The Australians sometimes say, "Getting paid is the same as being recognized." But it's not. The brain processes transactional and social exchanges differently. There is no better illustration of the contrast than the classic episode of the TV show *Seinfeld* in which Jerry gives Elaine a birthday present, which, when unwrapped, turns out to be a stack of currency.

"Cash?" says Elaine as she pulls the money from the box.

"What do you think?" asks Jerry.

"You got me cash?"

"Well this way I figure you can go out and get yourself whatever you want," Jerry explains, logically. "No good?"

"What are you, my uncle?"

"Hey, c'mon! That's $182 there," he says. "I don't think that's anything to sneeze at."

Meanwhile, Kramer enters with his present.

"Oh, what is this?" exclaims Elaine. "You got me something?"

"Ya, open it," says Kramer.

Inside the wrapping paper she finds a bench she had told both men she wanted.

"The bench! You got me the bench! I love it!" she squeals, hugging her friend.

"It's pretty good, huh?" Kramer says to Jerry. "You remember when we were standing there and she mentioned it? I made a mental note of it."

"Well, goody for you," says Jerry.

"Ya, well I'm very sensitive about that. Someone's birthday comes up, I keep my ears open," says Kramer. "So what'd you get her?"

"A hundred eighty-two bucks," Jerry says, sheepishly.

"Cash?! You've gotta be kidding, what kind of gift is that? That's like something her uncle would give her."[8]

Recognition is not pay. Pay is not recognition. The two should not be confused. What a person is due in base and bonus is a calculated financial transaction, x dollars per hour, y percent commission on the total sale. Recognition is a social exchange at least an arm's length from a dollar amount.

In our research, questions about pay and about recognition reflect quite distinct elements of a person's work experience. Answers to the statements "I am paid fairly" and "I am confident that if I do good work, it will be recognized" are correlated because the firms and managers who look after one are more likely to look after the other. Yet the answer to one question does not predict the answer to the other; one in five workers, for example, disagrees or is neutral on being paid fairly, yet is confident of future recognition.

Several of the New Rules of Engagement operate somewhat independently from the others. Pay is one of them. Recognition is not. So it's possible for someone to say he or she has a great job, but it doesn't pay very well. But because dopamine is such a fundamental psychological need, it's exceptionally rare for someone to rate her recognition low and her job high. It just doesn't happen. It's the reason a bad job is often called a thankless one. A low-recognition company is a lousy place to work. A high-recognition culture leaves a unique mental impression on its people.[9]

Assume an employee, a fly fisherman on the weekends, works late for the better part of a month and through a couple of weekends on a crucial company project and brings it in on deadline. The client is delighted. Let's say his manager has $400 in his budget to recognize this type of above-and-beyond effort. If he gives the employee the money, the worker might splurge and buy himself the new fly rod he's been wanting. But he's more likely to commingle the money with what's in his regular bank account, where it will be spent on routine expenses like the mortgage or his kid's hockey fees. "Research has shown that people are more likely to spend windfall money on utilitarian rather than hedonic items," states one summary of the evidence. "This implies that an employee would not purchase the award that they most want, lowering the value of the cash incentive provided by the firm." If he did the math, the employee might realize the extra money worked out to about $7 per extra hour. He could have made more mowing the neighbors' yards. Even if he buys the fly rod, "it will be the 'employee's money,' and the link to the firm will be broken," states the research paper.[10]

But if the man's manager either knew which fly rod he wanted and got it for him or gave him the ability to choose it from a range of options, the hard worker would have something that would make a repeated mental impression. Every time he used the fly rod, he would remember it came to him as thanks—not payment—for a job well done.

Numerous studies done on "noncash" recognition indicate that it gives more bang for the buck because, as Kramer understood, it's not about the bucks. It's about giving a dopamine surge through something personally meaningful—whether a fly rod, a bench, the spotlight at an all-manager's meeting, a letter from the CEO, or the chance to work on a prized account—to the employees who you want to repeat those successes.

SOMETHING ABOUT US LOVES APPLYING A RATIO TO HUMAN NATURE.

For centuries, artists, biologists, architects, astronomers, and philosophers have obsessed over the Golden Ratio of 1.61803 and what it might say about how we see the world or fit into it.[11] We like intelligence quotients, grade point averages, body mass indexes, personal bests, batting averages, and golf handicaps. How incredibly convenient when a person can be reduced to a number.

We are intrigued by Leonardo da Vinci's famous *Vitruvian Man*, the drawing of a man inscribed by a circle and a square. "The measurements of man are in nature distributed in this manner, that is: a palm is four fingers, a foot is four palms, a cubit is six palms, four cubits make a man, a pace is four cubits, a man is 24 palms, and these measurements are in his buildings," da Vinci wrote above the human figure.

Given our enthrallment with ideal proportions, it was only a matter of time before someone came up with a mathematical ratio for the amount of reinforcement a person should receive.

The numbers came from Barbara L. Fredrickson of the University of Michigan and Marcial F. Losada of the Universidade Católica de

Brasília. A research team under Losada's direction observed 60 management teams as they made their strategic plans, coding their comments as positive or negative. They found that those who performed best in "profitability, customer satisfaction, and evaluations by superiors, peers, and subordinates" had higher ratios of positive to negative comments. Intriguing stuff. It made sense. So far, so good.

Fredrickson and Losada compared the positivity ratios in the business teams with those in marriages that endured and those that eventually ended. "Within married couples," they wrote, "greater marital happiness is associated with less predictability from moment to moment as spouses interact, and yet, over time, these marriages are the ones most likely to last." This was stretching it. Running a business and two people taking long walks on the beach are very different endeavors.

Then Fredrickson and Losada got whackadoodle. They took the observational research on business teams and marriages and tried to apply to them the highly involved formulas used to calculate the movement of fluids. "Observation of the structural characteristics of the time series of the empirical data for these three performance categories led Losada to write a set of coupled differential equations to match each of the structural characteristics of the empirical time series," they wrote.

The theorists had crossed the electric fence between the physical and social sciences. Inanimate materials react uniformly and predictably; people do not. Pure water melts at 32 degrees Fahrenheit and boils at 212. The temperature at which an employee "melts" or "boils" depends on the circumstances and the person, never mind that the emotional terms are just metaphors. Like Frederick Winslow Taylor's *Principles of Scientific Management* a century before or the current software that reduces a unique individual to a single score, Fredrickson and Losada were practicing widgetry.

They plotted a beautiful butterfly-shaped graph of the ostensible relationship between P (positive information) and N (negative information). Underneath it, they explained: "The formula connecting P/N to emotional space is $P/N = (E - i)b^{-1}$, where E is emotional space, i is the initial value of positivity/negativity (equal to 16), and b^{-1} is the Lorenz inverse constant (equal to 0.375). $P/N = 1$ when $E = 18.66$."

And when the ratio of *P* to *N* crosses 2.9013, they asserted, something wonderful happens. "The trajectory in phase space shows a chaotic attractor." Or in English, the employee enters a mindset for high performance. "We call this dividing line the *Losada line*," wrote Losada. But if *P/N* gets too high, it creates a "disintegration of the complex dynamics of flourishing." That upper limit was calculated as 11.6346.[12]

People who wouldn't know an *i* from a b^{-1} latched on. The paper, "Positive Affect and the Complex Dynamics of Human Flourishing," garnered 322 scholarly citations in the subsequent years and 164,000 Internet mentions and worked its way into the general management bookshelves.[13] Fredrickson wrote a book anchored in what she called a "huge discovery." Its subtitle: "Top-Notch Research Reveals the 3-to-1 Ratio That Will Change Your Life." Losada brags that he "briefed Vice-President Al Gore and the president of MIT . . . on the interaction dynamics of high performance teams."[14] He started a business around his research. He called it Losada Line Consulting.

Then, in 2011, Losada and Fredrickson's paper was made assigned reading for Nicholas J. L. Brown, a 52-year-old, part-time positive psychology graduate student at the University of East London with little math education beyond high school. He found their claims fishy. He recruited physics professor Alan D. Sokal and psychology professor Harris L. Friedman to write a rebuttal. Their paper reads like Dr. Sheldon Cooper on *The Big Bang Theory* condescending to Penny.

The ratios of 2.9013 and 11.6346 are nonsense—"entirely unfounded," they said. "We find no theoretical or empirical justification" for using the math of fluid dynamics to describe recognition and criticism, they concluded. Losada made "numerous fundamental conceptual and mathematical errors." Their assumptions are "far-fetched."

"One can only marvel at the astonishing coincidence that human emotions should turn out to be governed by exactly the same set of equations that were derived in a celebrated article several decades ago as a deliberately simplified model of convection in fluids," the men snarked. Far more likely, they argued, the math behind 2.9013 and 11.6346 "has been contrived to demonstrate an imagined fit between some rather limited empirical data and the scientifically impressive world of nonlinear dynamics."

Brown, Sokal, and Friedman went on like this for more than 30 pages, saving some of their best sarcasm for Losada's use of physics terminology in his hypothesis that "high performance teams operated in a buoyant atmosphere created by the expansive emotional space in which they interacted" while low-performance teams are "stuck in a viscous atmosphere highly resistant to flow, created by the restrictive emotional space in which they operated."

If metaphors for human behavior could be translated into real equations, it would have "remarkable implications for the social sciences," wrote the trio. "One could describe a team's interactions as 'sparky' and confidently predict that their emotions would be subject to the same laws that govern the dielectric breakdown of air under the influence of an electric field. Alternatively, the interactions of a team of researchers whose journal articles are characterized by 'smoke and mirrors' could be modeled using the physics of airborne particulate combustion residues, combined in some way with classical optics."[15]

Whatever fame Fredrickson and Losada got from their paper for eight years, they paid for once the rebuttal hit the streets. They were "turning human beings into 2.9013," one blog smirked.[16] They suffered from "physics envy," one commentator observed. "At heart, all social scientists want to be natural scientists and so if natural scientists use differential equations to do cool stuff, they want to use them too," he wrote.[17]

"The Emperor's New Clothes analogy is horribly overused, but in this case, it seems apt—or at least, I hope so," wrote a columnist for *Discover* magazine. "The alternative is worse: that no one spoke out simply because no one in the field of positive psychology could see anything wrong with it."[18]

The balderdashing of Fredrickson and Losada's paper caused Losada to go silent. Asked for a response, he gave none, leaving Fredrickson alone to answer the critics. She distanced herself from her former collaborator. She would not defend the "complex dymanics" concepts or calculations; "Indeed," she wrote, "I have neither the expertise nor the insight to do so on my own." She took the highly unusual step of withdrawing the portions of the 2005 paper that depended on them.

But "rest assured," Fredrickson wrote in a new author's note to her book, "the scientific evidence for the value of computing your positivity ratio, and striving to raise it beyond 3-to-1, has grown stronger in the years since I wrote *Positivity*."[19]

In sticking to her 3-to-1 guns, Fredrickson missed one of the key points of the rebuttal. Just as the proportions of a real person vary substantially from those on da Vinci's drawing, the right ratio of positivity depends on that person's personality. Every person is different. Engagement is an individual and unique phenomenon. We are not widgets, nor do we conform to widget formulas.

For an employee, the right ratio of recognition to correction depends on his or her mindset, circumstances outside of work, and the challenge he or she is facing. Someone who was raised by an alcoholic parent or has suffered some serious tragedies may be hypersensitive to criticism; his best ratio of good to bad might be exceptionally high. Someone exceptionally confident and aggressive might, from those whose opinions she respects, want to be challenged more often; her ratio might be quite low. The best way a business can know the difference and act correctly on that information is through managers who are inside each of their employees' heads.

There is no Losada line. The whole exercise was silly. Even if there were some magical threshold of 2.9013, no one could apply it. Leaders and managers, being human, being far more likely to pounce on problems than on successes, struggle to recognize people on any regular basis. Forget the perfect ratio. Just give some real thought to what kind of reinforcement would mean the most to your people and dial it up.

A highly attentive manager knowing what kinds of recognition and what type of correction will be most effective is the only means to ensure the highest levels of motivation. Recognition is an exceptionally powerful tool in the hands of someone who knows an employee and wants to see her properly acknowledged for her best work.

This is the only real way to magnify her success.

THE TENTH RULE

Unite Them

On August 8, 2013, Brigham Young University's football players arrived at the locker room for the team's annual photo day to find a bad surprise. In place of their last names on the back of their jerseys were the words "Spirit" or "Honor" or "Tradition."

"We have identified these as the core principles of what the program is going to be," head football coach Bronco Mendenhall told the sports writers who showed up that day to get an early look at the team. "After eight years and the successes we have had to this point . . . and the vision I have for this program and what I see going forward, I intend that to be very visible for anyone who wants to know about our program and what it stands for, on the biggest stages."

With the team, it was a huge fumble. "Many players were stunned and incredulous as they filed into the indoor practice facility to get their pictures taken in their new jerseys," reported *The Salt Lake Tribune*.[1] At a school that emphasizes civility and deference to authority, the reaction was more muted than it would have been elsewhere. "Several players with negative things to say about the change refused to comment publicly," the newspaper reported. Those who spoke on the record were circumspect.

"I am not really sure how I feel about them yet," said All-America linebacker Kyle Van Noy. "One thing I have enjoyed about playing here at BYU is having the last names on the backs of the jerseys. . . . So it is going to be different. I don't know if it is for sure yet. I think they might be testing it out. I don't think anyone said it is going to be there all year."

For the university's many Polynesian players, having their family names on the back had always been a source of pride, defensive tackle Eathyn Manumaleuna told the newspaper. The new jerseys would take some getting used to.

"All of us wanted our names on our backs," Manumaleuna said. "We weren't expecting this. . . . But it is a good way to keep us unified and keep us as a team together, both offense and defense. It also lets people who are watching us know what we are about. We are about tradition, spirit and honor. So this is probably a pretty good way to do that."

Like employees of any boss, the football players weren't in a great position to tell Mendenhall to take a hike. Others were. The blunder quickly got hashtagged "Jerseygate" on Twitter.

"Just when I thought you couldn't possibly be any dumber, you go and do something like this," tweeted a fan of rival University of Utah. A BYU fan rushed to his NCAA rulebook to confirm that slogans are not allowed on a college jersey, and tweeted "Breathe easy" to his fellow supporters. "Absolutely the dumbest thing ever," tweeted former BYU linebacker Jordan Pendleton.

In an emergency meeting with the players several hours after the media left, the coach reversed his decision, tweeting that "Spirit," "Honor," and "Tradition" jerseys would be worn only for the homecoming game. "Talked to my team tonite," Mendenhall wrote. "They want to wear tradition spirit honor on jerseys for homecoming only. Last names for rest of the year. PERFECT!"

Tribune columnist Gordon Monson unleashed on the coach in the next day's paper.[2] "Mendenhall is not a complete idiot, but, like a lot of us, has an inner idiot that must be squelched. He's a good man and a good coach. Sometimes, he just loses his way and has a hard time finding the path back to . . . oh, I dunno . . . reality," wrote Monson. "It's just the latest example of a controlling Mendenhall driving a good idea—stressing solid values within his program—about five freeway exits past the best off-ramp."

"Individuality doesn't have to be obliterated to conjure togetherness," wrote the columnist. "In this case, the players knew that, the coach did not."

The Tenth New Rule is "Unite Them."

You could say it's about teamwork, because it is, but the words "team" and "teamwork" have been so overused and abused that they are often throwaway terms. Teamwork pablum is spewed everywhere. "None of us is as smart as all of us." "It takes two flints to make a fire." "Teamwork makes the dream work." "T.E.A.M. = Together Everyone Achieves More." "Sticks in a bundle are unbreakable." And the fingernails-on-the-chalkboard-worthy "There is no 'I' in 'Team.'"

In trivial cases, these Successories bromides can make a well-meaning but clumsy supervisor sound like manager Michael Scott in an episode of *The Office*. More seriously misplaced, they can deflate a real team, just as Mendenhall's attempted stripping of family names did to BYU's players. In the worst cases, commandments like "Be a team player" or "Take one for the team" reprehensibly try to create a sense of guilt when a widget is upset her wages are being frozen by an executive team whose annual pay packages have two more zeroes behind them.

Uniting a group of employees is a matter of creating the conditions under which collaboration naturally develops and increases. It is equally, however, a matter of not repeating the nonsense that so many leaders and managers spout and the missteps so many make in trying to build a team.

The roots of collaboration run deep. For our ancestors not so long ago, uniting in a common mission was a matter of life and death, so it got into our blood.

"When two tribes of primeval man, living in the same country, came into competition, if (other things being equal) the one tribe included a great number of courageous, sympathetic and faithful members, who were always ready to warn each other of danger, to aid and defend each other, this tribe would succeed better and conquer the other," wrote Charles Darwin. "The advantage which disciplined soldiers have over undisciplined hordes follows chiefly from the confidence which each man feels in his comrades. . . . Selfish and contentious people will not cohere, and without coherence nothing can be effected. A tribe rich in the above qualities would spread and be victorious over other tribes."[3]

Run that survival-of-the-most-united experiment for tens of thousands of years, tight tribes flourishing and fractured ones dying out, and you end up with a creature that is naturally cooperative, a being who actively looks for opportunities to collaborate, who generally will both trust others and prove trustworthy. Her blood pressure rises and falls based on who is nearby.[4] Her language changes to match the inflections and word choice of others.[5] How much she eats is influenced by how much she sees others eating.[6] She is 30 times more likely to laugh when with others than when alone.[7] She likes music because it's the reassuring sound of people working together.[8] She is a person who wants to be in the safety of a tribe, wants that tribe to prevail, and wants to do her part for the tribe.

There's just one catch.

Her company is not a tribe.

Some senior executives say their employees are like a tribe. They say they are like family. "You may call them employees, but we call them family. We're hiring vehicle service attendants in Minneapolis," Avis Budget Group tweeted in late 2014.[9] Get real. Tribes don't do layoffs. When families merge through marriage, the heads of the families don't go looking for which family members have now been "made redundant" so they can create "economies of scale" in the newly constituted family. Tribes don't put other members of the tribe in cubicles. Families don't incorporate in Delaware. Tribes and clans have lousy track records for diversity.

Tribes share what they grow and hunt much more equally than $10 million for the chief and minimum wage for the warriors. Tribes don't make new members sign papers acknowledging they are legally "at-will" members of the tribe. Tribal chiefs don't have to point out that the group is a tribe. Tribes don't compare themselves to corporations.

CEOs who use these terms are messing with their employees' heads. The same wiring that makes a person eager to be in a tribe makes an employee fairly easily manipulated by pep talks, sports metaphors, and pure guilt—guilt that in not sacrificing himself for the greater good, he is a "selfish and contentious" member of the "tribe."

Corporate leaders who use tribal metaphors are trying to trick the widgets. They are pulling powerful psychological triggers to get more for themselves. Check your wallet when you hear it. From a commercial enterprise, no employee can count on the reciprocal loyalty that came from being a member of a clan, especially today. It's business, after all, which is exactly what the company will say when it does the un-tribal things that a business has to do. "Never love a corporation," a former business editor of a major U.S. newspaper once wrote on Facebook to his former colleagues being laid off. "It will never love you back."

"Courageous, sympathetic and faithful" members of a tribe in Darwinian conditions would often sacrifice themselves because they could expect the same in return. Even if they died advancing the tribe's interests, which they sometimes did, their deaths served to make the survival of their family's genes in their children, siblings, and nieces and nephews more likely. "Die in battle," so to speak, for a firm, and the only thing you get is security walking you and your box of personal stuff to the door.

A company can't be a tribe. It can, however, be a team.

However mangled the metaphor, a team remains the best description for the complicated collaboration that motivates employees and synchronizes their work to accomplish a common goal they could not otherwise accomplish. Like a professional sports franchise, a company today is a group of unrelated individuals recruited to get things done, things that cannot be done alone. Each person has a role and gets paid for the importance of the role to the victory and how well he or she plays that position. Membership is temporary. Players can join the team and put on the jersey. They can be released or resign and leave the jersey behind. It's a business.

"Loyalty to any one sports team is pretty hard to justify, because the players are always changing, the team can move to another city," comedian Jerry Seinfeld once observed. "You're actually rooting for the clothes when you get right down to it. You are standing and cheering and yelling for your clothes to beat the clothes from another city. Fans will be so in love with a player, but if he goes to another team, they boo him. This is the same human being in a different shirt. They hate him now. "Boo! Different shirt! Booooo."[10]

But employees can switch loyalties like that. They generally play hard for their current team and find that others do the same. Large majorities of employees in the United States agree that there is a strong sense of teamwork at their jobs (70 percent), that they have many strong working relationships (81 percent), and that they get to work with a lot of talented people (77 percent). The degree to which people feel united with their colleagues does not vary much from one country to another. Yet employees' feelings of "a strong sense of teamwork" are highly predictive of their customer focus, obligation to the company, and retention. It is even modestly predictive of an employee's feeling that he is safe from accidents on the job.

It's not just teamwork, but its intensity, that drives the highest levels of performance. There is a direct relationship between the quantity and quality of collaboration and the degree to which employees say their job brings out their best ideas and how hard they intend to work. The strongest sense of obligation and giving one's best to customers triples between the two positive responses on the teamwork scale. The strongest forms of ingenuity jump by six times. In other words, "good enough" usually isn't, leaving a lot of performance, money, patents, and breakthroughs on the table. Senior leaders need to be quite deliberate in how they assemble and direct workgroups if they want the greatest benefit from them.

Working closely with people inevitably leads to friendships. It sometimes even leads to marriages. We are social creatures, and we make friends wherever we go, particularly when spending as much time together as we do with people at work. But organizations are created to accomplish their organizational goals. They are not fraternities or night clubs. Friendships are more the delightful consequence of strong collaboration than they are the cause.

Collaboration is more important than friendships to business results. In a head-to-head statistical matchup between the statements "I have good friends at my current job" and "I have many strong working relationships at my job," the second statement is substantially more powerful for employees' drive to work hard for the company, customer focus, desire and plans to stay, pride in working there, and their best ideas. It makes sense. Friendships do not need to accomplish anything more than make the friends happier for the connection, the mutual support, and the shared experiences. Collaborators, by definition, get something done.

The patterns in the data indicate most employees would say, "It's nice to have friends at work. It's important to have collaborators. It's crucial to have teamwork." Companies that agonize over whether someone has a "best friend at work" are building their collaborative foundation in the wrong spot.

Employees not having been born into a tribe, not being members of a fraternity, the central issue of collaboration is why anyone would surrender his or her own objectives for those of the team. The answer is as simple as it is so often muddied: because sharing in the team's accomplishment is worth more than what that employee could accomplish alone. Unless that condition is met, only a moron would sign on.

Yes, the team needs strong, capable, and inspiring leadership. Yes, the other members of the team need to be expert in their respective roles. Of course the group needs to have an insightful and compelling strategy. And someone has to keep a lid on the fear that can make people lock up under pressure. But each of these and many other components of a crew's success are secondary to the one core reason why anyone commits herself to a team: It's the best option for her.

"If a team is to reach its potential," University of Oklahoma and St. Louis Cardinals coach Bud Wilkinson once said, "each player must be willing to subordinate his personal goals to the good of the team." Nonsense. Even if a team goes all the way, a player who can't claim it as part of his own résumé won't care about the accomplishment.

Baltimore Ravens running back Damien Berry spent the 2012 football season on injured reserve while the rest of the team won the league championship. Regardless of being sidelined, as a member of the team, he was entitled to one of the most prized possessions in sports—a Super Bowl ring.

He sold it seven months later.[11]

The Ford Motor Company had a long list of problems when Alan Mulally became its CEO in 2006.

It was losing money on every car it sold.[12] It was bleeding cash, running a $17 billion deficit over the course of just that year.[13] Its union contracts bound it to high costs and inefficiencies. Just a few months earlier, it had been outsold by Toyota for the first time.

The company's resources were spread too thinly over the makes Lincoln, Mercury, Aston Martin, Jaguar, Land Rover, Volvo, and—of course—Ford. "You could argue if you put yourself back in that time that Ford was likely on the road to bankruptcy first (before GM and Chrysler)," said *The Detroit News* business columnist Daniel Howes.[14]

It was only five years removed from the end of its century-long relationship with Firestone Tire after mutual recriminations in the wake of tire failures and deadly collisions on Ford vehicles riding on Firestone tires.

Ford was still smarting from the exodus of experienced employees after Jacques Nasser, CEO until 2001, briefly instituted a program requiring that 10 percent of the company's managers be given a job-threatening grade of C on their performance.[15] They had learned the hard way that fear kills teamwork.

Executives who were not members of the Ford family, which held a controlling interest in the public company, were historically in a precarious position. "I just don't like you," Henry Ford II said when, in 1978, he fired Lee Iacocca, with whom he had a long-running feud.[16]

And Mulally was not even an automotive guy, having come from a long career at airline manufacturer Boeing.

At the center of all the problems was the fractured relationship between the people at the top, breaks that mimicked and magnified the ones throughout the company. If the new CEO did not unite the members of the executive team, any turnaround strategy was likely to fail.

Mulally was succeeding William Clay Ford Jr., who willingly stepped aside as CEO and remained as chairman. As chief executive, Ford "found himself unable to overcome an entrenched careerist culture that resisted all change and put individual advancement ahead of corporate success," wrote *The Detroit News* reporter Bryce Hoffman. "In their dark-paneled offices, executives plotted ways to undermine one another's efforts." There was, the journalist observed, "an enduring culture of intrigue and backstabbing among Ford's leadership."[17]

Southwest Airlines chairman and cofounder Herb Kelleher astutely pointed out at the time that Mulally's first job would be "winning the hearts and minds of the people at Ford."[18]

The company could not focus its efforts and resources, simplifying production and creating economies of scale, unless the executives stopped defending just their divisions and worked together. "That will be the enabler to get everything else done," Bill Ford told Mulally. "If you can't do that—if we can't get that—then we'll just be whistling past the graveyard."[19]

The new CEO lost two leaders before he got started. Although Anne Stevens and Mark Fields, chief operating officer and president of the Americas division, respectively, were held out as architects of some of the company's biggest initiatives, they were not collaborating well. "I was not part of Fields' inner circle, so I chose to retire," Stevens wrote years later.[20] A month later, she became chief executive of Carpenter Technology Corporation.[21]

Chief Marketing Officer Hans-Olov Olsson realized his plans for a large marketing campaign across all the Ford brands would collide with Mulally's plans for consolidation. And he missed Sweden. He became vice chairman of Volvo.

Fields wasn't exactly on the same page with Chief Financial Officer Don Leclair either. Emblematic of the tensions between leaders, Leclair had a memorable run-in before Mulally arrived when he told the Americas president he had to make further cuts to an already lean advertising budget.

"There's no other alternative," said the CFO. "You're going to do this."

"When you run the f------ business, you can do it," said Fields. "But you don't run it. You're the CFO. So, I'll take your counsel, but that's it."

"You're going to do this!" yelled Leclair.

Fields jumped up and screamed back, "I'm tired of this b---s---!"

"Cut it out!" Bill Ford intervened.[22]

Mulally's challenge was to get feuding executives in an eat-or-be-eaten culture to start working together, executives who reasonably doubted how long the new CEO himself would survive. He did so in part by convening his immediate team every Thursday morning for a "business plan review," or BPR, session around a ring-shaped table in the nondescript Thunderbird Room at headquarters in Dearborn, Michigan.

In the mandatory meeting, executives were expected to make their own presentations to their colleagues, rather than having lieutenants do it; to present hard facts and candid assessments, not polished face-saving numbers; to create "one plan" for the company; to "respect, listen, help, and appreciate each other"; and to "have fun . . . enjoy the journey and each other."

Mulally banned side conversations and people using their BlackBerrys during executive team sessions. "These regulations proved particularly onerous," wrote Hoffman in *American Icon*, his book about the turnaround. "At Ford, meetings were political theater; side discussions where the real business of the company was conducted. They were where deals were cut and truths too powerful to put in a PowerPoint presentation were shared."

The CEO also outlawed making fun of their fellow leaders. "Making jokes at the expense of others was a regular pastime at Ford—one some of the executives . . . had spent decades mastering," wrote Hoffman. "They had not gotten where they were just because they were the best and the brightest, but because they knew how to dish it out and how to take it. In a company like Ford, the weak went to the wall; only the strong survived. Now they were being told they were on the same team, and Mulally expected them to act like it."

At first, the executives resisted. Mark Schulz, head of the international division, fumbled through his first BPR presentation after Mulally refused to allow one of Schulz's subordinates to make it. After the meeting, Schulz told the new CEO that he would have trouble making all the BPRs because of his travels and the time needed to prepare those presentations. "That's okay. You don't have to come to the meetings," said Mulally. "I mean, you can't be part of the Ford team if you don't, but that's okay. It doesn't mean you're a bad person." Fields, too, petitioned to be excused from the meeting because of the demands on his time. He, too, was rebuffed.

Although the executives were attending the new meeting, they were not really collaborating. Despite the fact that Ford was on track to lose a record amount of money, color-coded status slides presented at the BPR uniformly showed green rather than yellow or red. In the past, telling the truth was treacherous.

"They've never worked together like this, they're scared to death," said Mulally. "'Is it safe? Can I really have a red up here and survive?'" Two months into the new job, Mulally had seen enough green. He called one of the meetings to a halt. "Team, we're going to lose $17 billion and all the charts are green," he said. "Is there anything that's not going well here?" Many of the executives looked at the floor. "So, we can't manage a secret, we've got to be honest with each other and it's going to be okay." They still didn't believe him.

At the next BPR, Mark Fields unenthusiastically brought a slide showing red because of a grinding noise in the suspension of the new Ford Edge. "We're having trouble with the lift-gate actuator on the back," said Fields. "We agreed we were only going to deliver these vehicles when they were absolutely perfect. I've got 2,000 of them sitting on the tundra."[23]

"When I showed that first red, there was a lot of tension in the room," Fields said years later.[24] Some around the circular table wondered if he had just signed his own death warrant.

Mulally started clapping. "That's great visibility," said the new leader of the team. "Is there anything we can do to help?" People began chiming in with ideas and resources. That moment, when someone was rewarded for telling the truth and his colleagues began offering help, is widely considered a turning point in the culture of Ford and the beginning of eight years under Mulally of a more direct and collaborative approach. "It was a breakthrough," said the CEO in an interview with *The Telegraph* of London. "It was the most exhilarating and terrifying thing, but at that point I knew it was going to be okay."[25]

As difficult as the company's troubles were when the new CEO arrived, the Ford executives had no idea what awaited them. In some ways, they got lucky. By arguably being first in line to go bankrupt, Ford completely mortgaged itself at the same time Mulally came on board. It borrowed $23.6 billion before the credit markets collapsed in the Great Recession. "Because of the money it borrowed nearly three years ago," *The New York Times* reported in 2009, "Ford is in far better shape than its two crosstown rivals. The loans have kept it independent and on a course to survive the worst new-vehicle market in nearly 30 years."[26]

The turnaround at Ford took more than having a united executive group. It required making massive cuts to costs and employees; closing more plants; absolving itself of half its retiree healthcare obligations with company stock; selling Volvo, Jaguar, Aston Martin, Hertz rental car company, and its stake in Mazda; and ending the Mercury brand. It required getting the entire company focused around Mulally's mantra of "One Ford—One Team, One Plan, One Goal," the kind of corporate boosterism that only means something to the degree that executives make it mean something.

A few on the executive team—most prominently Schulz, who chaffed at Mulally's directions—were forced out. Others bowed out over time. CFO Leclair left two years into the new CEO's term. The head of human resources, who had recruited Mulally, left in 2008 to become a corporate officer for Chevron. The vice president of communications was replaced about a year after the new CEO arrived. But many executives stayed, eventually persuaded that Mulally was not there to clean house of leaders who were willing to invest their careers in the resurgent Ford.

"It says something about Mulally, and the effectiveness of his style, that you could count on one hand the number of senior brass cashiered in his tenure," *The Detroit News* columnist Daniel Howes, originally a Mulally skeptic, wrote one week before the CEO stepped down in mid-2014. "He didn't clean house, to borrow the cliché, so much as rearrange the furniture to form a more efficient (and profitable) organization."[27]

By the end of the former Boeing leader's auto industry tenure, Ford's debt was back from junk status to investment grade. Ford regained control of the assets it pledged to borrow billions before the recession. It was still enjoying the reputation of being the one American automaker that did not go bankrupt or take a taxpayer bailout. It netted $7.2 billion in 2013.[28]

There is a temptation looking at stories of successful teamwork like that at Ford to assume the collaborators sacrificed for the good of the group. Mulally "took a sledgehammer to the silos that had divided the company into warring fiefdoms for generations," wrote Hoffman. "It was not easy, nor instantaneous, but in the middle of a truly existential crisis, Ford's executives finally stopped making decisions based on what was best for their own careers and started trying to figure out what was best for the company as a whole."

Except that they didn't.

What united the Ford executives who chose to stay was creating the conditions under which it was better for each of their careers to collaborate there than to go elsewhere. Where that criterion was not met, as it was not for Anne Stevens or Hans-Olov Olsson, people left.

By playing a subordinate role to Mulally during his tenure, Mark Fields inherited both the CEO job and a much stronger Ford than the mess his predecessor got. And he was making about $10 million a year along the way.[29] Despite not getting to be quarterback for a while, Fields continuing to wear the blue Ford jersey was hardly bad for his career stats.

The CEO himself was a brilliant strategist and unifier, but he was well compensated for his troubles. In his final calendar year at the head of Ford, Mulally was paid $23.2 million in salary and stock. He had accumulated 6.18 million shares of the company's stock, worth $95.5

million. The tens of thousands of people laid off by Ford during the recession are the ones who "took one for the team." The CEO and his crew did not.

While Mulally got most of the press and accolades, the executives that stayed for what the CEO called an "exhilarating . . . ride back up" got a piece of the victory. "The truth is that Mulally's years-long leadership clinic," wrote Howes, "is as much about the Ford veterans he led as it is about him."[30]

Such are the dividends for the members of a united team.

THE ELEVENTH RULE

Let Them Lead

THERE WAS NOTHING THE LEADERSHIP OF THE PRODUCTION PLANT IN the American Midwest could do to stop its closing.

Their industry was in decline. A digital alternative was chewing up market share faster than the traditional players could adjust. And so the announcement came from headquarters that of 60 plants operating around the United States, 40 would be closed.

"The decision regarding which plants to close wasn't performance-based, but rather was determined by the plants' proximity to large postal centers," said one of the plant's leaders, who asked his name not be used because he was speaking without clearance from his former employer. "Our plant wasn't located in a place that would make sense to keep it open."

There was another complication. The company set the closing for two years away. Rather than the traditional ambush shutdown, this one would allow time enough for the employees to look for new jobs and more deliberately plan for their futures. It was also, however, a long time to try to keep a team of employees motivated when they knew their ultimate reward would be the same: a severance check, a handshake, and one last drive back home.

"We knew we couldn't say, 'Let's try to save our plant with record performance,' or 'Let's ensure we deliver the best possible quality, service and profit as we go out.' Plant performance wouldn't influence the decision to close our location and we felt focusing on other stakeholders would ring hollow," said the leader.

On the other hand, the certainty of the closing might be liberating, a chance to do something they might not have tried otherwise. After all, if they pushed the boundaries, what was the worst that could happen? Risk having the plant closed and everyone sent packing? That was going to happen anyway.

The leadership of the plant met with the employees and laid out the problem. They had a radical proposition.

"We think our best option is to give the plant to you over the next two years," said the leaders. "That means you will be involved in all facets of running the facility. Our goal is that you will be supremely prepared to find a new job. We want you to be able to say during an interview in two years, 'I was a machine operator, but I also participated in quality improvement initiatives, covered for my manager at production meetings, was a member of interviewing teams, and helped monitor the production process.'"

And so they did. They painted "Always Learning All Ways" in large letters on the plant wall. They made business cards with that slogan on the front and the company values on the back. With their coaching, the managers turned over the plant to its employees. They let the employees lead.

"Our plant leadership team had always made focusing on employee development a priority, but now this philosophy was on steroids," said the leader. "About six months before the plant was to close, I was walking down the hall when a member of our maintenance team stopped me and said, 'I have to tell you. This is the most fun I've ever had in a job.' After a short conversation about how things were going, he turned and walked down the hall with a visual bounce in his step.

"As I watched him walk away, I thought to myself, 'There goes a guy who is about to lose his job in six months and he's smiling and as engaged in his job as he could be. This focusing on developing people is magic!'"

The plant still closed, of course. Many of the employees had to switch industries. It was almost as disruptive as these things usually are. By definition, endings in business are not happy. But on their way out, the employees got an experience they might not have gotten otherwise. And in the process, the plant broke all its previous performance records.

It made many of those who worked there wonder why it took the pending closure to give frontline employees a turn at the wheel.

THE ELEVENTH NEW RULE IS "LET THEM LEAD." IT TURNS THE VOLUME way up on a widely recognized imperative.

There is a large body of research on how important it is for employees to have a say in how their work is done. In the research journals, it's most often called employee "voice." Employees are more motivated in jobs where their opinions matter. People are more committed to doing things that are at least partly their own idea, rather than having their goals and the way they do their work dictated to them by the higher-ups.

This is hardly a novel or controversial idea today, but it once was, and in a few dark corners it still is. One in four Americans still can't say their ideas are taken seriously or that they are given the freedom to do their jobs in a way that works best for them. It's worse in the United Kingdom, Canada, Australia, and Brazil. "Show up, do exactly as you're told, collect your paycheck," one marketing manager summarized as his company's culture. The company has an "insulting, micromanaged environment," he continued. "It operates by a hierarchical caste system. There is no respect for employees: 'When I want your opinion, I'll ask the director what it is and then give it to you.'"[1] This kind of "voice aversion" is a symptom of an incompetence that evidences itself in managers feeling threatened by employees' insights and abilities, one study found.[2]

The roots of this dehumanizing philosophy rest with Frederick Winslow Taylor, a late nineteenth- and early twentieth-century American mechanical engineer who was arguably the father of modern widgetry. His time-and-motion studies were revolutionary in helping businesses make their processes more efficient. Six Sigma and Lean Management have their foundations in Taylorism. These process improvement strategies work elegantly for materials and machines. They cut waste. They save time. They make products better, less expensive, and less likely to fail.

They fail miserably when applied to people.

Taylor spent a lot of time studying how to get the most work out of laborers moving "pig iron" (a "pig" was a 92-pound block of the metal) at Bethlehem Iron Company in Pennsylvania. He obsessed over the mechanics of men lifting the pigs and carrying them onto railcars. He obsessed over what pay scheme would best drive the strong men who did the work. He obsessed over the perfect size of a shovel, big enough to maximize the material in each shovelful, small enough not to slow down the worker.

He did not obsess over what these workers thought about it.

"It would be possible to train an intelligent gorilla so as to become a more efficient pig-iron handler than any man could be," Taylor wrote in his *Principles of Scientific Management.* The project manager's calculations "replace the judgment of the individual workman," who was, in Taylor's opinion, "so stupid and so phlegmatic that he more nearly resembled . . . the ox than any other type."[3]

"Scientific management was degrading," wrote one Taylor biographer. "In reducing work to instructions and rules, it took away your knowledge and skill. In standing over you with a stopwatch, peering at you, measuring, rating you, it treated you like a side of beef. You weren't supposed to think. Whatever workmanly pride you might once have possessed must be sacrificed on the altar of efficiency, your role only to execute the will of other men paid to think for you. You were a drone, fit only for taking orders. Scientific management, then, worked people with scant regard not only for the limitations of their bodies but for the capacities of their minds."[4]

Taylor has been dead for a long time. His ghost lives on. It shows up in the tone of the questions asked on many employee engagement surveys. Most of the questions asked of employees to determine the volume of their "voice" today are patronizing or too weak. They ask for reactions to statements such as "I have an opportunity to participate in the goal-setting process,"[5] "My suggestions are given serious consideration,"[6] or "My ideas on work process and procedure improvements are valued."[7] One survey asks if employees feel their opinions "seem to count" on the job.[8] Another checks to see if "my manager listens to what I'm saying."[9]

"Giving serious consideration" to someone's ideas is a euphemism for blowing them off. So is "valuing someone's ideas" or granting them an "opportunity to participate." Your ideas "seem to count"? Well, do they or don't they? "And thanks for actually 'listening to what I'm saying,' Beloved Manager. You're such a humanitarian, doing all that listening and stuff."

At their heart, these statements remain rooted in Taylorism, the worker petitioning his overseers for a small say. That quiet undertone of employee voice is nowhere near as powerful for motivating an employee as providing legitimate options to actually take the lead on the job.

Among U.S. employees who do not supervise others, huge swings in intensity occur between those who strongly disagree and those who strongly agree they get the chance to lead. The proportion of people most committed to customer service increases from 7 to 57 percent. The proportion of those feeling the greatest obligation to work hard for the company jumps from 3 to 49 percent. And the number of those who say working at the company brings out their best ideas goes from a measly 3 percent to a large majority of 78 percent.

"This is a very uplifting, happy, and optimistic environment, even when business is tough," wrote one 24-year-old woman working at headquarters for a large American retailer. "I get learning opportunities in every experience, whether it is good or bad. The leadership is genuinely concerned about my development and growth."

"I make a drastic impact on team projects as a contributor and pseudo-lead member," wrote a 30-year-old employee of a Canadian industrial company.

The people who aren't given the reins once in a while aren't going to stick around to just take orders. Seventy-four percent of Americans deprived of a chance to lead wish they were working somewhere else.

Forty-six percent are actually making plans to get out. Turnover intentions are only one-fifth as common among those who feel the most entrusted by their employers.

Seeing a standard five-point scale on questions like those we asked about "Let Them Lead" (strongly disagree, disagree, neutral, agree, strongly agree), many executives believe that any response north of neutral is good enough. Yet much of the power of this rule is in people not just agreeing, but strongly agreeing, they get the chance to lead; not just agreeing, but strongly agreeing, their company trusts them with important decisions.

If the mothers of those executives were asked their level of agreement with the statement "I love my child" and chose "agree," those executives (depending on how they behaved in high school) would not comfort themselves with the answer being on the positive side. They would immediately question what they had done or failed to do that made Mom hedge her response. Mom would undoubtedly have her reasons.

It turns out that where it applies to an issue central to the employee's experiences at work, a single notch of reservation can be expensive. For example, the proportion of American nonsupervisors who strongly agree "I work because I love it, not because of the money" jumps from 10 to 27 percent depending on whether they have that bit of hesitation about whether they get the chance to lead. Companies are not shy about asking for an uncompromising level of intensity from their workers—focusing on the customer, being vigilant on safety or product defects, taking on the competition, giving their best thinking. In this rule, as with the others, employees willingly deliver that intensity if the organization is uncompromising in delivering for them. In today's workplace, it's imperative that managers let them lead.

More than most, this rule makes leaders and managers nervous. It doesn't help that articles in some respectable publications are asking for their heads. "Is it Time for Mutiny?" asked the headline in a recent *Harvard Business Review* blog.[10] "Is it Time to Abolish Middle Management?" asked an article in *Psychology Today*. "The new economy, technology and Gen Y make middle management unnecessary."

"Now technology itself has become the great general manager," one self-described futurist wrote in an *HBR* guest column. "It can monitor performance closely, provide instant feedback, even create reports and presentations."[11] It can ask you how your weekend was, see the best future opportunities for you, and coach you as you take on additional responsibilities.

Oh, wait. No, it can't.

There are several conclusions from the decades of research on employee engagement that are by now rock-solid, established facts. Fear kills creativity. Pay is relative more than absolute. Meaning is more important than money. What's recognized gets repeated. And the most widely accepted precept of them all: Managers matter.

One of the most important challenges for companies today is how best to balance the employees' need to take greater responsibility without depriving them of the structure, guidance, and coordination among business units that allows a business to accurately be termed an "organization."

"The productivity of work is not the responsibility of the worker, but of the manager," observed Peter Drucker. "Great managers are an organization's glue," wrote Tom Peters in 2001.[12] "The manager is the critical player in turning each employee's talent into performance," wrote Curt Coffman and Marcus Buckingham.[13]

The central role of managers has always been much easier for organizations to understand than to implement. Great managing is hard work. It's a specialist's role; few individuals have the inclination to invest so much of themselves in the success of others. Few know how to read individual motivations and match abilities with responsibilities. Less commonly appreciated, great managing on the front lines requires a cascading chain of effective one-to-one working relationships from the CEO to chief-whatever to EVP to SVP to VP to director to manager. The pattern shows up in an organization's engagement levels as clearly as voltage being transmitted or dropping off from a power generating station depending on the quality of the lines that lead from it.

Grand plans for powerful coaching cultures routinely fall victim to a change in ownership or leadership, a market collapse, quarter-to-quarter pressure from Wall Street, sneak attacks by competitors, or the company's entrenched patterns of promoting to management people who have no business being in charge of another human. Rather than work these issues down the field, some companies just punt.

Online shoe retailer Zappos decided to defy some of those laws of human nature in 2014 when it adopted an untested philosophy called "Holacracy." Other companies will owe Zappos thanks for risking its own culture to teach lessons to everyone about the best balance of power between managers and employees.

Zappos is an unconventional place to work, and generally a better one for it. Unlike most call centers that put a widget-watching timer on its representatives from the second they answer a call, Zappos encourages its employees to talk with a customer as long as the buyer wants, for the better part of the day, if needed.[14] Consistent with the evidence on motivation, it believes happy employees make for happy customers. For several years, it published a thick, annual *Culture Book*—part yearbook, part collection of employee comments. Anyone outside the company could get one for free just by asking.

Everyone goes through the same training as those who work in the Customer Loyalty Center. At the end of training, the new recruits are told the company will pay them for their time and travel, plus a $2,000 bonus, to quit. Zappos figures it's cheaper to pay people to leave than have them stay if their hearts are not in it.[15]

Zappos is known for its party atmosphere. "Create Fun and a Little Weirdness" is one of its "core values."[16] For most, it's a cool place to work. Employees in 2013 got a bonus of stock worth 20 percent of their annual pay.[17] Zappos does well on external measures of employee engagement. *Fortune* named it one of the "100 Best Companies to Work For" six years running.[18]

CEO Tony Hsieh came to Zappos first through his $500,000 venture capital play, then decided to take a leadership role.[19] He told *The New Yorker* in 2009, the same year Amazon purchased the company for $1.2 billion, that he was on a mission to spread Zappiness—the Zappos version of happiness. He wrote a book about it. "Eventually, we'll figure out a way of spreading that knowledge to the world in general, and that has nothing to do with selling shoes online," he told the magazine.[20]

The Holacracy philosophy Zappos adopted is the 2007 brainchild of software engineer Brian Robertson, who was inspired by the 1967 book *The Ghost in the Machine* by the late Hungarian-British intellectual Arthur Koestler. *Ghost* includes Koestler's theory that the human brain is composed of "holons," circles that are—and this is the simplest definition—at once complete by themselves and part of something larger. It's gobbledygook.

"Holacracy is a comprehensive practice for structuring, governing, and running an organization," says the Holacracy website. "It replaces today's top-down predict-and-control paradigm with a new way of achieving control by distributing power. It is a new 'operating system' that instills rapid evolution in the core processes of an organization."[21]

When Zappos announced it was going to become a holacracy, some of the business press, undoubtedly impressed by what Zappos had accomplished so far and underwhelmed with the traditional bureaucracies, greeted the news positively. "Zappos Says Goodbye to Bosses," sang a headline in *The Washington Post*.[22] "Shoe Firm Zappos Gets a Reboot—with No Managers and No Job Titles," announced *The Independent* in Great Britain.[23] "No Managers Required: How Zappos Ditched the Old Corporate Structure for Something New," blurted out *Fast Company*. "Once again," concluded the magazine's report, "Tony Hsieh has proven to be an avant-garde business person, unafraid to take risks and try new things. And if he and his 1,499 Zappos partners (organized into 400 circles) pull off this holacratic experiment, next on your reading list just may be the Holacracy Constitution."[24]

No, it won't.

Version 4.0 of that "constitution" is a 30-page brain-suck that makes Robert's Rules of Order read like a ski resort pamphlet. It's torturous enough that a parallel "plain English" version had to be written. Clause 2.6.3, "Removal of Sub-Circles," goes like this:

"A Circle may remove, through its due governance process, any Sub-Circle contained within such Circle at any time, by (a) removing such Sub-Circle entirely, in which case all of such Sub-Circle's Roles, including further Sub-Circles, recursively, shall also be terminated, however any Policies defined for such Sub-Circle's Domain shall be retained by such Circle unless otherwise specified through such Circle's governance process; or (b) collapsing such Sub-Circle back into a Role that is not authorized to serve as a Circle, in which case all of such Sub-Circle's Roles shall be automatically terminated, including any further Sub-Circles, recursively, but such Role so collapsing shall itself be retained, as shall any Policies defined for such Role's Domain; or (c) dissolving the Sub-Circle's boundary without removing its contents, in which case such Sub-Circle shall be removed, however all Policies and Roles within such Sub-Circle, including further Sub-Circles, shall be retained within the Circle so dissolving such boundary."

The Holacracy Constitution raises death by paper cut to a fine art.

Initially inspired as it was by Koestler, once a member of the German Communist Party before he became disillusioned with Stalinism, Holacracy is especially ironic in claiming to give more power to people while it does just the opposite. "Holacracy is hierarchy on steroids: the hierarchy is spelled out in more detail than in any conventional organization you have ever seen," warned a commentator in *Forbes*.[25] The *Economist* magazine caught the central internal contradiction of the philosophy: "There are no bosses here, because I say so."[26]

"Holocracy is a peculiar business philosophy that even Hsieh's followers have trouble explaining," wrote one confused reporter who spent three weeks around the Zappos people. "From what I gather, Holacracy is what the office would be if nerds took over."[27]

Holacratic or not, Zappos still has plenty of nonnegotiables. Hsieh isn't any more flexible than Yahoo CEO Marissa Mayer on the issue of working remotely. "We really wanted to build the company around culture, company culture being the number one priority," he told *Fast Company* in 2010. "And it's much easier to build a culture when it's actually in person versus remotely by email."[28]

Some of his employees complain his moving the company's headquarters into the deserted former Las Vegas city hall made them into guinea pigs in his personal grand vision.[29] "The new location downtown isn't very convenient or safe," one employee wrote. "Downtown Las Vegas still has a steady supply of homeless people and shady areas. I have had more than a few incidents with the 'local inhabitants.'"[30] Requiring employees to show up in person for work is Hsieh's prerogative. The weirdness is in making a show of removing titles and then exercising the authority that goes with having the title he supposedly no longer holds.

By the middle of 2014, as the initiative was still being rolled out, the cracks began appearing. Hsieh and his team "tend to bite off a bigger piece of the cookie than they can chew," one employee observed. "Their approach to rolling out 'Holacracy' is interesting. It was almost as if the right leg doesn't know what the left leg is doing and the employees are almost feeling paralyzed. . . . It's hard for anyone to speak up and give an opinion. If you don't ride the boat, the only choice is to get off it. Leadership and Tony himself are missing in action since he is focused on other projects within the city. It's almost like he assumes the company can run itself."[31]

Far from wanting to run everything themselves, employees were missing the guidance that all the evidence shows can come from someone more experienced with a broader jurisdiction. "My experience was with a manager who was so hands-off that we'd sit next to each other all day and he wouldn't utter a word to me. Being new to the workforce, I needed leadership, training, communication, and a sense of progress. I got none of this," wrote the Zappos employee. "The shift to Holacracy, while an interesting idea, is incredibly experimental and most questions about the process are answered with, 'We're still figuring that out.'"[32]

The danger of fouling up with an experiment like Holacracy is that all an employee needs to do to get out of the Skinner box is resign. Only the company has to live with the legacy of a bad idea. "Some senior managers and directors have no idea what they are doing. Others are good," wrote a former Zappos employee. "I personally left because I was teaching my boss more than he was teaching me."[33]

What Holacracy was teaching Zappos and everyone watching the experiment is that letting employees lead changes the role of managers, but it by no means eliminates it. Managers matter. The solution to poor managers has always been great managers, not the elimination or parceling out of the job itself. If we didn't already have individual supervisors of individual employees, we'd think it was the most incredible management idea anyone could conceive—because it is. A single, highly qualified and caring manager, someone who gets inside the employee's head and delivers uniquely for that person on the implicit social contract, would be revolutionary. It would be astounding because the evidence would show that it works, because the evidence shows that it does work.

Counterintuitive as it may seem, letting people lead increases the importance of managers. They become more involved in knowing the abilities of their people. They have to know when to give a person more responsibility and when too much responsibility would be setting him or her up to fail. They spend less time directing, but more time coaching. They must become even better at reducing ambiguity and confusion, more astute at helping their people navigate organizational politics. They spend more time championing the introverts on their team, better at seeing each person's future. They have even greater accountability for their people's success.

In short, letting them lead is the kind of strategy that would have given Frederick Winslow Taylor indigestion.

But he deserved it.

THE TWELFTH RULE

Take It to Extremes

"LET'S DO THIS!" SAID THE E-MAIL TO DAVE HARRIS FROM ONE OF HIS best friends.

It was early 2010. Harris's friend had learned about an endurance event coming in a few months to Bear Creek Ski Resort near Allentown, Pennsylvania. Seven miles. Military-style obstacles. Slogging through mud pits. Scaling walls. Running through fire.

To Harris, who calls himself "Dave The Harris" Braveheart-style on the blog where he chronicles his athletic adventures, the answer was a no-brainer. "As a man, if your friend suggests doing something like this, it's not a question. To answer 'No' would question your manhood," he wrote.[1] Harris's dad signed up as well.

The three men didn't know at the time they were in the vanguard of a movement. The organizers called their event the "Tough Mudder."

Tough Mudder was started by Harvard MBA and former British counterterrorism analyst Will Dean. "I noticed that people were bored with marathons and triathlons," Dean said in 2013. "Running's a bit boring. In what other sport do you have to listen to music to make it passable? I wanted to make something that was Ironman-meets-Burning Man, a test of all-around fitness, but in this fun, slightly quirky environment."[2]

Dean recruited attorney and fellow Brit Guy Livingstone as his cofounder. "I said it looked fun and exciting and I was up for it," Livingstone once remarked. "Had I spent any longer as a corporate lawyer, my appetite for risk would have been completely bashed out of me."[3]

Dean's design for the endurance event was a semifinalist in Harvard's annual business plan competition. But his professors thought his projection of 500 entrants was too high. The general manager of the ski resort where the first one was held thought "they'd be lucky to get 300 people." Even the event's organizers didn't realize how many Dave The Harrises there were out there.

Tough Mudder fired up a website and spent $8,300 on Facebook ads in February 2010. Two days later, a couple of registrations came in. Two days after that, another couple came in. In the first few days, "I'd say, 'Guy, pretty awesome day, we got 10 people,'" Dean told *The New York Times*. "Then, not a week later, we'd say, 'Not a bad day: 200.' And the day before the price went from $80 to $90, we got 400 in two hours. That's the day I got really excited. I couldn't sleep that night."[4]

E-mails and calls saying "Let's do this!" were apparently flying around the Northeast. Tough Mudder hit a nerve with people stuck in the widget factory. "I have been looking for something like this my entire life," one guy e-mailed the organizers. "I have never climbed Everest, never swam the English Channel, never did an Ironman, but now I don't even want to. I want to race in the Tough Mudder Run! . . . How do I qualify for the race? I am in good shape, but I am well aware that this is a level of fitness no one really understands until they actually go through it. . . . Thank you! You have given me a reason to struggle through my miserable work days."

Four thousand five hundred people signed up. Roughly one-fifth were women. They came from 37 states. Forty-six Pennsylvania state troopers signed up together to run in honor of an officer killed the previous year.

"The registration process . . . entailed signing a death waiver," Harris reported. "Yes, a death waiver! The rest of the registration process seemed insignificant compared to the fact that you could die on the course." Some of the initial Mudders came in kilts or with Braveheart face paint. One team came painted like blue Avatars from the previous year's hit movie. A few ran in loincloths. But most just came in regular running clothes and hit the course.

They ran between burning hay bales, through mud pits, and through the woods carrying logs on their shoulders. They walked over a two-rope bridge through a muddy pond. They slid face-first down a steep, tarp-covered hillside into water at the base. "We made people sign a pledge when doing their event," said Dean on a promotional video for the first run. "They pledge that they won't leave anyone behind."[5]

The first event was a victim of its own success. "As the race progressed, more and more people started to get backed up at the obstacles," wrote Harris. "At one of the last obstacles, I got stuck in a line that was over 45 minutes long. By the time I got to the front, they closed it because it was getting dangerous." Harris's dad took a wrong turn and missed "Suicide Hill," so he doubled back. "In the end, he almost ran the course twice—toughest Mudder there by far."[6]

"This race jump-started my athletic drive," the "husband, dad, and now triathelete" wrote. "I perhaps even over-trained for the race, if there is such a thing. Either way it turned out to be a great race and got me back on the map."[7]

Four years later, Tough Mudder had gotten tougher: 10 to 12 miles long with a couple dozen obstacles, most of them more intimidating than the originals. The course stops one out of four runners from finishing. The challenges included a head-to-toe plunge into ice and water, slippery monkey bars over more cold water, rope climbs over two-story walls, a high dive, claustrophobia-inducing underground or partially submerged tubes, and two obstacles where wet and muddy runners are hit with jolts from 10,000-volt dangling wires.

"The idea was to crawl, commando style, through the mud-water, while suffering the electric shocks," wrote a woman from *The*

New Yorker who completed the event. "I looked back at my teammates, who nodded enthusiastically. I got down onto my stomach and began clambering. After a second, I felt a shock: it *really* hurt. I could feel my limbs buckle, and I heard myself screaming, 'Yow!' I kept wriggling through the water, screaming, and getting shocked."[8]

Making the Tough Mudder tougher only accelerated its growth. Four years on, it had also become, in the words of *The Telegraph* of London, "a new global phenomenon."[9] Tough Mudder was on track to hit 2 million entrants, each paying in 2014 from $130 to $200 to be abused and endangered. An estimated 3,000 had tattooed the logo on themselves.

Going to extremes like this is not new. Sport parachuting dates back to the end of World War II, when there was a surplus of military parachutes and a relative abundance of former soldiers who knew how to use them.[10] The Iditarod Trail Dog Sled Race has been in existence since 1973, if you had the sled, the dogs, and the ability to get to Alaska. The modern version of bungee jumping has been around since 1979. Since 1950, diehard skiers were watching each year's new Warren Miller ski film in preparation for risking their own necks trying to imitate a trick in one of them. "Hang on tight, 'cause here we go!" Miller narrates in his 1984 release. "We're going to ski where there's no lift lines, and no bad snow either."[11]

But there were no helmet-mounted GoPro cameras back then to record a first-person perspective of the mountain bike ride through the wilderness or the kayak run through whitewater. A 5K race was just a race—just running, as fast as you could. Then stop. No one threw fluorescent corn starch at you. Zombies did not chase you. Medals went to the top finishers; there were no "participant medals." Few people had "bucket lists" like the ones they make today. Most important, there was no Facebook or Twitter or Instagram on which to post the photos or video to a thousand friends or followers making them feel like slugs for not having done something similarly intense.

In the past, extreme events were largely reserved for the athletically elite. Today they are part of a burgeoning industry open to anyone willing to sign the death waiver. Now there is the Spartan Beast, the Warrior

Dash, the Muddy Buddy, the Mud Run, Rebel Run, Rugged Maniac, and dozens of lesser-known events. There is a similar extreme trend in nearly every weekend endeavor.

These events are zealously democratic. One of Harris's fellow Mudders in that inaugural event was captured in a photo hanging onto one rope and walking on another as he muscled his way out of the water. The guy had the kind of midsection lots of guys get sitting too long at the office. "Don't worry, buddy. If you fall in, that belly will keep you afloat," some guy commented on Facebook. Others quickly came to the man's defense. "Wow! All I see is a guy working his ass off!" one wrote in response. "You don't have to have a flat belly to be able to kick someone's or something's ass. Do the race yourself and see what you say after."

While the percentage of those who enter an extreme event will probably always be small, nearly every office has a couple of Mudders or Spartans or Warriors or Muddy Buddies. They represent a larger cultural trend for everyone to be the stars of their own adventures, whether they are physical or artistic or professional, to be not just Dave Harris, but Dave The Harris.

The trend has powerful implications for the workforce. All those weekend warriors go to work on Monday wanting to do something incredible at their job as well. They are more easily bored by "miserable work days," more at risk in a good economy of being lured away to a more exciting place to work, and more likely to be up for the right challenge. They are simply expressing in their sometimes muddy method the pinnacle of human motivation.

"When you read books of people who climb mountains, are those books full of moments of joy and happiness?" asked Duke University economics professor Dan Ariely in a widely circulated 2012 speech. "No, they are full of misery. In fact, it's all about frostbite and difficulty walking and difficulty breathing—cold, challenging circumstances. If people were just trying to be happy, the moment they get to the top, they would say, 'This was a terrible mistake. I will never do it again. Let me sit on a beach and drink mojitos.'"

"Instead," Ariely continued, "after they go down and they recover, they go up again. If you think about mountain-climbing as an example, it suggests that we care about reaching the end, the peak. It suggests we care about the fight, about the challenge."[12]

THE LAST OF THE NEW RULES, THE TWELFTH RULE, IS "TAKE IT TO Extremes." It's the culminating imperative for a reason. Each of the preceding rules lays the groundwork for the final one, and the ultimate question of an engagement strategy is how well it helps an enterprise and the people who work there reach their potential.

For decades, it has been drilled into the heads of MBA students, the people who often become the executives who run companies, that the ultimate goal of a business is to "maximize shareholder value." "There is one and only one social responsibility of business," wrote Nobel Prize-winning economist Milton Friedman in what came to be an influential 1970 *The New York Times Magazine* article, "to use its resources and engage in activities designed to increase its profits so long as it stays within the rules of the game, which is to say, engages in open and free competition without deception or fraud."[13]

It's not a law, but executives treat it like it is. It is the underlying assumption of the questions with which executives are peppered each quarter when they get on the conference call with Wall Street analysts: What are you doing to make sure the firm makes as much money as it can? How will you maximize the stock price? Nearly every publicly held company is expected to take its metrics to extremes.

Organizations are not shy about asking their employees to do something incredible for the enterprise. They set "stretch" revenue and profitability goals. They want to "crush the competition" by capturing market share. They want to invent new medicines. Or bring a cool new product to market. Or be the one thing people at the industry trade show are talking about. Or go public. "The only way you can achieve something that big is an absolutely obsessed, monomaniacal, overwhelming intensity and focus that starts today and goes tomorrow and the next day and the next day and the next day for 365 days and then for

3,650 days," said leadership expert Jim Collins in 2010.[14] Talk like that makes CFOs drool.

There's just one problem: Who cares? How can a company create intensity when Collins's 1994 phrase "big, hairy audacious goal" now makes people laugh their lunchroom milk through their nose?

In the past, the answer was taken for granted. Investing oneself in the objectives of one's employer was the mark of a professional. "It's like baseball," a company president told William Whyte for his 1956 bestseller, *The Organization Man*. "A good player doesn't think of the contract when he is up to bat. He drives for the fences."

Right or wrong, people of a generation or two ago were more likely to subordinate their individual ambitions to those of their employer. "They have an implicit faith," wrote Whyte a half century ago, "that The Organization will be as interested in making use of their best qualities as they are themselves, and thus, with equanimity, they can entrust the resolution of their destiny to The Organization."[15] It was nice while it lasted.

Being well past the days when most employees will "entrust" their sense of achievement to wherever they work, there are two reasons why people will deliver the focused intensity most enterprises crave.

First, the evidence is clear an employee will help the company pursue its big dreams if his leaders and managers have so invested in his experience at the firm that they triggered his natural reflex of reciprocity. Forty-nine percent of workers in the United States agree they "enjoy being challenged to push my limits at work," and another 28 percent strongly agree. Where an employee lands on that question is determined by how well the firm built the job around his abilities, made him fearless, paid him well, kept him from burning out, made it a cool place to work, spoke plainly, made the work meaningful, paved the way to a promising future, recognized his best work, put him on the right team, and let him lead.

When a company is delivering on its end of the bargain, an employee will push through the metaphorical mud, cold water, and electrical wires. She will feel she owes it to her employer, because in a world where so few have that experience, she does. It's as close to a law of human nature as you'll find. You can challenge people to push their limits for the benefit of the firm because, the research shows, you've earned the right.

The second reason why people push themselves to extremes is for their own sense of accomplishment. Few statements are more powerful to determine the intensity of an employee than this one: "I believe I can accomplish more at my current organization than I could somewhere else." In the United States, 37 percent of workers agree with that statement, and another 21 percent strongly agree. The proportions of workers who believe they are in the right place are higher in Latin America, China, and India. Among the Americans who most forcefully agree they are in the right place to demonstrate their potential, a staggering 93 percent say they feel an obligation to work as hard as they can for their company. Only 8 percent are thinking about working somewhere else, and only 4 percent are planning to do anything about it.

The pattern is reversed among those who strongly disagree they are in the right company to optimize themselves; 86 percent wish they were working at that certain "somewhere else," and 56 percent are making plans to get out in the coming year. Few things suck the life out of a person more than stagnation. There are "no growth and learning opportunities" at his company, one employee complained. "What you're doing now is what you'll be doing 5 years from now."[16]

It's in this second area—reaching the organization's goals through the combined accomplishments of each person—that companies too often fall short. If the stores double their revenue over seven years, what will each store manager personally have accomplished? If the company gets its new product to market on time, how will that achievement have built the career of each member on the development team? And if Tough Mudder, for example, becomes the leading brand in the obstacle run industry, what will employees of Tough Mudder get from it. Ironically, as it grew exponentially, the company that makes such a big deal of its customers pushing their boundaries was facing the question of whether it could afford its employees the same opportunity.

"When the company first began there was also a lot of opportunity to develop myself professionally and try new challenges, although this is no longer really true," one former Tough Mudder employee reported.[17]

"I do not recommend dedicating the long days and nights, sweat and tears to this company—for it will demand it—as there is no agenda to return the dedication, unless you can cut the budget even further, which is much more likely to be their reciprocated response," wrote another.[18]

One employee reported the company pushed its people to write good online reviews, and when it laid off some employees, required them to sign nondisparagement agreements in return for severance payments. The scheme seems to have backfired. "In my time at Tough Mudder, nearly every person I've admired, looked up to, or enjoyed working with has quit," one person tattled. "Anyone with good future prospects or a decent sense of self-worth knows they could be doing better, and leaves after a year or two, tops."[19]

Perhaps it's more difficult to create a real sense of accomplishment on the job than it is to spend one afternoon plowing through the mud.

WHEN AN OFFICER OR SAILOR ARRIVES FOR THE BEGINNING OF HIS duty aboard a U.S. Navy submarine, he is referred to as a "non-qual." It means he's not qualified. Sometimes he's called a "nub." It stands for "non-useful body." Or "no use to the boat."

These are rough designations to give to a man (or, since 2010, woman) who volunteered to serve his country, who scored high on the Navy's aptitude test, who made it through the rigorous Nuclear Power School, who qualifies for the clearances needed to handle classified information, and who, in the case of officers, is often a graduate of the Naval Academy. They are hardly slouches.

Yet they will not get much respect—they will remain non-quals— until they prove themselves in six to nine months of intensive training, deprived of sleep, fresh air, space, sunlight, and fresh fruit and vegetables. "A non-qual's first day onboard any Navy sub is intimidating, to say the least," wrote one submariner. "Upon a new man's arrival, he becomes the most junior and most inexperienced member of a very highly trained crew."[20]

The crew members will be locked in a workplace they cannot leave for months on end. They will have little or no contact with their friends and family on land. They will be subject to bosses they can neither disobey nor avoid. "You take a small city, put it inside a thermos, send it halfway around the world, and have it be away from any external support for months at a time," said former attack sub commander Brad McDonald.[21]

There is no better example of what it takes to get a large group of people to take it to extremes than a U.S. Navy submarine. At any time, roughly 1,100 officers and 9,100 enlisted men and women are serving aboard U.S. Navy submarines. They are underwater in 70 vessels spread around the globe, patrolling, spying, following other adversaries' subs and ships, protecting American aircraft carriers, and sneaking Navy SEALs to hostile coastlines. Fourteen are solely dedicated to carrying nuclear ballistic missiles to deter North Korea, Russia, or China from using their nukes. Their locations are highly classified.

What's often obscured in the seriousness and the secrecy is that each submarine is a submerged workplace. Each officer is a manager. Each torpedoman, nuclear machinist, cook, and electrical technician is an employee. Human nature is human nature; it's just under more pressure.

Few environments create a more challenging environment for a leader to motivate his team. Depending on the abilities of the commander and his subordinate officers, the time under way sequestered with his team can create camaraderie or hostility, safety or injury, missions accomplished or missions botched. Because of these pressures, submarines have proved a unique lab for leadership, human psychology and physiology, and workplace safety. When those who plan space expeditions want to understand the stresses astronauts will have during long periods in orbit, they look to subs.

While some aspects of life aboard a submarine are right out of a Tom Clancy novel, "being in submarines, is not anything like the books that I had read," discovered one sailor inspired as a teenager by *The Hunt for Red October*. A sub is no normal workplace. The Navy obsesses over the mental profile that differentiates between those who excel under the sea and those who opt out. Claustrophobics need not apply.[22]

"Among the challenges presented by a submarine deployment are a paucity of personal space, long periods with no sunlight, an unusual day/night schedule, and extended periods of separation from friends and loved ones with minimal communication," states a 2009 report on psychological assessments of submariners. "When we combine these with a very cognitively demanding workload, a requirement for extremely high levels of job/task proficiency, a rigid military hierarchy, and no psychiatric support underway, it becomes evident that the psychological resilience of the crew needs to be greater than that required for most jobs."[23]

The abilities of the officers under those conditions also need to be greater than those required for most leadership roles. Under that kind of pressure, the effect of any leadership deficit is likely to be magnified. The effect of strong leadership abilities and investment is so much more appreciated and respected.

Each of the aspects of an engaging work environment emerges with greater force in the stories of submariners and research on their performance. There is a higher premium on empathetic officers. Ruling by intimidation is more terrifying. "The absolute authority bestowed on commanding officers by regulation could conceivably breed toxic leadership traits and cruelty," a U.S. Navy captain warned in a 2012 analysis of commander misconduct in the *Naval War College Review*.[24]

Pay needs to be a non-issue under these hardships; submariners get premium pay.[25] Keeping submariners healthy is a challenge. Good meals, one of the few luxuries on board, are served four times a day, while exercise might mean squeezing onto a stationary bike in the sonar equipment space. Eighteen-hour work cycles mess with people's natural rhythms.[26] Nubs are under exceptional pressure, having to work their regular shifts and complete an extensive list of "qualifications" during their "off" hours on every aspect of the boat: propulsion, navigation, electronics, air, leaks, fire suppression, and weapons.

"Heaven forbid you should be caught on the mess decks watching a movie, because you should be studying," a torpedoman on the *USS Virginia* told a documentary filmmaker during his qualification period. "You don't watch movies. You don't read books. You don't play video games. You don't hang out. You study. You learn. You study. You learn.

And then if you've got a little bit of time, you catch some sleep and then you better be studying again. My family thinks I'm crazy."[27]

Operational security notwithstanding, just like every other enterprise, the modern Navy is a more transparent place, putting more pressure on commanders that their every act passes greater scrutiny. "Commanding officers who violate the trust bestowed on them can expect technology to allow them to be caught and held accountable, often in the public eye," observed the *Naval War College Review* article.[28]

It goes without saying that protecting their country is a huge motivator for submariners to make the sacrifices they do. But they also serve in hopes that their hard work is building their own futures. Because most of what a submariner does is either invisible outside the Navy or classified, recognition within the service is that much more important than it would be in the rest of the working world.

Teamwork may be optional on land; in a sub, it's a life-or-death issue. "While other military organizations share something similar, we are the only group—outside of maybe astronauts—who exist continually surrounded by an environment that can kill us in an instant if someone makes a mistake, 24 hours a day, seven days a week, when out at sea," wrote one retired sub officer. "Submariners must trust their shipmates, and their ships, literally with our lives."[29]

And although the military gets stereotyped as the ultimate top-down organization, the evidence indicates that the Navy gets the most from its submariners when the crew members get greater opportunities to make decisions rather than simply executing the orders of their superiors. When commanding the fast attack nuclear submarine *USS Santa Fe*, then-Commander David Marquet discovered the ship ran better, his people performed better, and he reenlisted more of the crew when he encouraged them to come to him with a solution rather than a question.

"Captain, I intend to submerge the ship. We are in water we own, water depth has been checked and is four hundred feet, all men are below, the ship is rigged for dive, and I've certified my watch team," a member of his crew once announced in the kind of assumption of leadership Marquet promoted.

"Very well," the commander replied.

"Eventually," Marquet recalled, "we turned everything upside down. Instead of one captain giving orders to 134 men, we would have 135 independent, energetic, emotionally committed and engaged men thinking about what we needed to do and ways to do it right."[30]

The consequences of combining all the right aspects of leadership, or failing to do so, could not be starker. Some sailors will surface after a tour to report it was a workplace hell "living in a dank metal tube," reporting to a "micro-managing, narcissist," and slowly going crazy.[31] Others will come up pumped up. "You will never work with better, more dedicated people," reported an electronics technician who trumpeted the "lifelong personal and professional relationships" during his "exceptional" experiences in the submarine service.[32]

What non-quals learn, beyond how to run the ship, is that with the right leadership, they can accomplish more than they realized. "I am a very junior, nub officer on a Virginia-class boat," wrote one. "I just got home from a 2330 (11:30 p.m.) work night on a non-duty Friday. . . . I find very little time for my wife, who I love very much. Yet, at the end of the day, I love it!"[33]

And when they finally earn the submarine warfare insignia—their "dolphins"—they'll carry not only the highly respected designation on their uniform, but the date when and ship where they earned it in their memories forever.[34] It's a very exclusive club.

What submarine commanders learn is a concentrated form of what every effective leader comes to know—that the most important things they accomplish are through the support of their crews. "I came into the Navy because I wanted to be war hero. I wanted to sink Russian submarines. I wanted to have medals on my chest, to have movies made about me," said Captain McDonald. "Once I'd been here, what I found out was that I'm sheriff and judge to these men. I'm their mother and their father, their brother, their priest, their marriage counselor, their financial advisor, their doctor. You have to take care of these guys. I learned that if I take care of these sailors, they'll take care of the ship."[35]

When things go as they should, combining all the right aspects of motivation and support in a submarine gets the Navy what it needs to defend the country and gives the sailors accomplishments they can bank on. "I never got my degree, but when it came time to transition, I had several offers before I even had my [authorization to leave the Navy] written up. I got a great job, and have since been promoted ahead of others with more time in the company and with bachelor's degrees in electrical engineering," wrote a former nuclear electrician's mate on a San Diego–based submarine. "Not so much that I will use my military knowledge on the outside, but the fact that I trained on, operated, and eventually supervised the operation of the nuclear propulsion plants of two different classes of submarines in the space of a few years demonstrates to any employer that no matter what I'm thrown into, I will not only succeed, but I will excel."[36]

If the average workplace were sealed up and plunged into the ocean for a few months, chances are when it was raised to the surface, inside would be a circus. Assuming there hadn't been a mutiny, no one would want to hear another word from the CEO or the rest of the leadership. Colleagues would be at each other's throats. No one would sign on for another stint under those conditions. Little would have been accomplished.

But the Navy submarine fleet creates exceptional levels of accomplishment under trying conditions. Where they succeed, they do it not because they recruit super-humans, not ultimately through military compulsion, not because they have some trick to suspend the laws of human nature, but because a long history of failures and successes taught them how to combine the elements of leadership and support that gets non-quals their dolphins and makes serving undersea an invigorating experience. We could all take a lesson from it. Under the right conditions, it's quite amazing what people can do, and just how much they can take it to extremes.

Handling
the Truth

AROUND 2009, SOME PEOPLE WHO KNEW A LOT ABOUT COMPUTERS and apparently had a lot of resources at their disposal set loose a computer virus to disable Iran's nuclear facilities.

The malware eventually came to be known as "Stuxnet." *The New York Times* dubbed it "the most sophisticated cyberweapon ever deployed."

Whoever wrote the code isn't talking—one of those if-we-told-you-we'd-have-to-kill-you things. But the nonspies who followed its trail say Stuxnet carried two ingenious digital "warheads." First, it made the computer-controlled centrifuges Iran was using to enrich uranium spin wildly out of control. Second, "the computer program also secretly recorded what normal operations at the nuclear plant looked like," reported the *Times*, "then played those readings back to plant operators, like a pre-recorded security tape in a bank heist, so that it would appear that everything was operating normally while the centrifuges were actually tearing themselves apart."[1]

By destroying the machines' performance while generating reassuring reports that everything was fine, the virus reportedly destroyed one-fifth of Iran's uranium centrifuges and set back its nuclear program several years.[2]

If it's aimed at a rogue nuclear weapons program, that kind of mischief and misdirection is a good thing. If it ends up happening inside a law-abiding company upon which many employees, customers, and stockholders depend, it's a bad thing. Soon after one is unleashed, an old-school employee engagement initiative has a similar effect on an organization's culture as Stuxnet has on uranium centrifuges. It messes with the morale of the people in the company. But the scores on the reports will say everything's much better than it really is.

Many large companies do engagement surveys. It's become a kind of corporate hygiene, like issuing an annual report or reenrolling everyone in the insurance program.

It takes about half a year to prepare a typical engagement survey for a company. There's a lot of agonizing over when to "freeze" the employee list and send it to the survey firm. Company leaders prefer dates when everything is quiet: after emergence from bankruptcy, before the merger is announced, or—for retailers—well away from the holiday shopping season when most of the profits are made and when it's most likely a customer will interact with an employee. "Surveys should not be administered to employees during times surrounding particularly traumatic organizational events—for example, when a restructuring, planned down-sizing or a salary freeze has been announced," two practitioners for a major consulting company wrote in 2012.[3] Before the survey even starts, the results are suspect for being gathered at an artificially tranquil time.

There's also a lot of hand-wringing about what questions to ask. Many consultancies carry in their briefcases poll statements that are a couple of decades out of date, some even stamped with 1990s copyright dates to vouch for their antiquity. Other survey questions do a double backflip trying to stay positive. "Our survey said, 'If I were offered a job with similar pay, I would not consider leaving,'" one employee said. "I had to stop for a second and think, 'So, does "Agree" mean I'm quitting or I'm staying?'" It's much cleaner to state, "I'd quit if I could find a job that pays the same," but companies don't want to plant ideas of quitting in people's heads.

Legal sometimes weighs in to veto certain inquiries. No asking about pay, they might say, or no asking the union members about job security, even though both of those are kind of big deals. The virus is beginning to take shape.

About a month before the survey opens, Internal Communications fires up e-mails, posters, cafeteria table tents, and a series of other reminders that will tell people to take the survey. Managers see this train coming. Bad supervisors start acting like good ones with their widgets. Employees who hadn't seen any recognition in months get congratulated for breathing. Pizza and doughnuts appear. Babies are kissed. Election season is under way.

When the survey opens, the first of a series of all-company e-mails starts begging people to participate. It's a big event. We really want your opinion, they say. Your responses are confidential, they assure. Sometimes there's a contest to see which departments can get the highest "response rate." After 11½ months of not asking people's opinions about their jobs, it is suddenly imperative each employee answer the questions. Now!

"Why haven't you taken the survey yet?" one manager asked his subordinate.

"How did you know?" she replied.

"I didn't," he said. "But now I do."[4]

In these days of surprise layoffs and executives who see discontent as disloyalty, there are serious doubts about how candid people are going to be. "Here's the thing for HR managers everywhere," said Kai Ryssdal, host of the public radio show *Marketplace*, "we all lie on those surveys."

"Exactly," said *Freakonomics* coauthor Stephen J. Dubner, "we lie on most surveys, but especially [to the question], 'How happy are you? And I'm the person who pays you and I need you to tell me how happy you are.'"[5] Given the amount of leverage companies have over their employees and the arm-twisting to get them on the record, many people will inflate their scores, telling leadership precisely what it wants to hear.

One administrative assistant told her colleagues she'd been warned that lots of special attention would be given to groups who scored low. Get a high enough score, and you will be left alone, she was told. "Just circle five to survive, Baby," she told her team. "Mark five to survive!"[6]

Cooking the books reaches a full boil when managers are paid bonuses based on ostensibly high engagement. A little forensic analysis of the responses at one large U.S. retailer found that a large proportion of the employee surveys for one store were completed within minutes of each other . . . around midnight . . . from an Internet address traced to the store manager's house. He was canned. But many other managers, eager for the bonus tagged to high scores, get away with less clumsy forms of gaming. The perverse incentives were captured best in a 2004 *Dilbert* cartoon that circulated to knowing laughs among the engagement consultants.

"Our bonuses will depend on the results of the employee attitude survey. If we boost our morale rank, we'll get bigger bonuses," says the boss. "Get it? All you have to do is say you're happy and you get money." He winks.

"You want us to lie?" asks Dilbert.

"No-o-o-o! Heaven forbid. Absolutely no lying. But if you did lie, imagine the things you could buy with that money," the boss responds. "I'll hand out the surveys and you can let your conscience guide you."

"Is 'Paradise' too over the top?" Dilbert asks his colleagues as he marks his responses.

Wally says, "I'm going to lie me up a new couch."[7]

The engagement industry doesn't know how much answers are inflated by employees' fears of being exposed or punished, but practitioners admit in their professional journals to suspicions there is a problem. When some employees are afraid to even take the survey, "the consequences are biased," warned one academic paper.[8] Even when using an outside firm that keeps the individual-level data locked up, "employees may still be concerned about openly sharing their views on an identified survey on sensitive topics such as manager effectiveness and intention to stay at the company, knowing that their data could ultimately be identified to them," wrote two professors in a late 2011 edition of a journal for industrial and organizational psychologists. "Research from other areas of psychology suggests that assurances of data confidentiality may not reduce concerns about data privacy."[9]

One analyst who matched employees' demographic responses on engagement surveys against the true information in their personnel files found that people gave fictional answers one-fourth of the time. "What if I told you that 26 percent of your employees either blatantly lie or inadvertently misidentify demographic questions on employee surveys?" wrote the analyst. "If you're like most managers we work with, you'll immediately distrust the survey process and its reported data—and that's completely fair."[10]

Assuming an employee decides to answer forthrightly, she doesn't get anything in return. When she responds to the last question and hits "Submit," her answers disappear into the ether. She just shared incredibly sensitive information that says a lot about her mindset. The survey people, if they stopped at her line in the massive spreadsheet, could see how her answers compared with national or industry benchmarks. But she sees only a generic final screen: "Thank you for participating in the survey." She's supposed to passively wait for whatever comes next.

And then the survey closes. From the measurement standpoint, it's dead quiet. The company, of course, continues to change. Nothing was ever truly frozen in place. New people join the company; their opinions won't count for almost a year. Some people who were there when the survey was taken resign, retire, are fired or laid off; their answers live on at the company. Managers come and go. Departments are reorganized. Sales go up or down. CEOs step down or are forced out by a grumpy board. Sometimes the whole place gets acquired or merged. The engagement of each employee changes from day to day. But in the master file at the measurement company, the data are fossilized. The engagement archaeologists move in.

It can take a couple of months for the results to come back. Depending on what the consultants report, the executive team might take another month trying to decide what to share, how to spin the news, and what they plan to do with the information. One consumer packaged goods company that took its survey in November had yet to distribute the reports in April, at which point the company should have just thrown them out.

Sometimes, the leaders get their briefing and dismiss the whole thing. "Well, we're better off than I thought we were," one CEO said. His minions got the hint. The company's "Your Voice Matters" initiative died on the spot. The employees' voices didn't matter that much.

At most organizations, however, the results in some form eventually reach the people who participated. Now the real fun begins. It's called "Team Feedback and Action Planning." It's part Alcoholics Anonymous meeting, part religious revival, part crisis intervention, part Chinese Cultural Revolution reeducation camp.

Each employee gets a copy of the engagement scorecard for the team. People search their memories for what was happening when they responded. "Did we take this before or after the merger?" "Were we in the middle of union negotiations at that time?" "Was this before the product recall?" "Wasn't that the week we had the big snowstorm?" people ask on a sunny spring day. "I forgot what answer I gave to that question." They struggle to make sense of information that's gone stale.

The company and its consultancy promised that individual answers would be confidential. Looking at their first scorecard, many newbies are in for a shock. In a report that combines the answers of as few as four or five people, it's just not that tough to guess which guy dropped a few ones or twos into the group's composite. It was nice knowing him.

It's bad enough at the companies that commission a survey. It can be worse at those that sell them. One of the leading firms in the engagement space is "completely closed to feedback and criticism," an employee tattled on Glassdoor. "If you indicate you are anything less than fully 'engaged' or criticize in any way, then look out." A senior consultant at another name-brand survey house wrote that "the company preaches a value system that other employers should embody to improve employee engagement, morale, and productivity and does absolutely none of it with its own employees."[11]

Team feedback sessions can take various forms, most of them designed to get people to divulge information to help improve engagement—but that might later be used against them. One consultancy recommends a "fishbowl technique." Four volunteers or draftees are made to sit on chairs in the middle of the group and are peppered with questions on some topic of engagement. The rest of the team is forbidden to talk while the manager interrogates. Employees take turns in the fishbowl. "This exercise forces everyone to truly hear perspectives of others, which will then serve as the platform for dialogue," the company claims.[12]

Employees should be reminded just how good they have it, one firm advises. "In a non-defensive tone, the management team carefully pointed out the positive efforts already in place, including training seminars, career development initiatives, staff promotions and other employee-focused initiatives," one consultancy reported.[13] It's a best practice.

Because of these tactics, it's likely that much of the increase that a company sees in its engagement scores from a traditional survey are from managers reinterpreting the questions, gaming, and intimidating, and from employees fearing their answers will be revealed. Managers at some organizations tie themselves in knots explaining to employees why they really do have "a best friend at work." The results get a little BFF'ed up. "My best friends are from grade 9 and grade 12, even though I am in my mid-50s," wrote one engagement expert. "My best friendships are not based on people I work with. If your best friend is at work, perhaps you are working too much."[14]

In the early years of an engagement initiative, the well-meaning executives who commissioned the survey are pleased. They feel they are methodically looking out for their people. It's no longer supposition; they have data—real data—on where the company needs to focus its efforts. HR is happy because it can go stat-to-stat with accounting and operations and marketing. The centrifuges look to be spinning just fine.

Then hints start coming in that something's not working right. Engagement scores go up, but they do so only fractionally. People scratch their heads when some of the most notoriously abusive managers turn out to have gotten high scores and the bonuses that go with them. Turnover doesn't get any better. Sometimes it gets a lot worse. So many other aspects have to be factored out to find the effects of engagement that it raises questions about just how much the whole employee attitude thing matters.

The worst problem with most engagement interventions is that they are based on industrial assumptions. They treat people like cogs in an occasional realignment of the machinery.

These tune-ups work great on assembly lines. If a company wanted to improve a process like making doughnuts, for example, it would evaluate the ingredients in the dough, the proximity and speed of the machines, the temperature of the oil, and the viscosity of the glaze. After analyzing the glitches, it would adjust the production line and fire up the machines again. Chances are the problems would be fixed and would stay fixed for a long time. Inanimate machines and ingredients react predictably to consistent processes.

The whole measure-analyze-adjust-resume cycle does not work on people. Six Sigma, Lean Management, Total Quality Management, and the rest of the strategies for improving manufacturing processes fall flat when copied and pasted onto employees as "Team Feedback and Action Planning." They are not machines. They are not widgets. Each individual is unique, and none responds predictably like uniform ingredients, equipment, or chemical processes.

Executives justifiably ask, "Why is engagement going up while our performance is going down?" The consultants have a couple of responses. "Engagement isn't everything. Some aspects of company performance are outside the control of your people." (Which is true.) "If engagement had not gone up, it would have been even worse." (Kind of a sorry response, but occasionally true.) What they never say, which is more likely true than either of the official answers, is that engagement may not, in fact, be going up at all. Many companies have the same problem with engagement that Ford had with operations when Alan Mulally became CEO: everyone knows things are broken, but indicators on the PowerPoint slides all show green.

"No one believes our engagement scores," said one insider at a large corporation. "We teach to the test." The organization now has a double problem: morale did not improve as intended, maybe even decreased, and the means of determining the true level have been contaminated.

The virus's work is complete.

BEFORE HE PASSED AWAY TOO EARLY IN LIFE, PROFESSOR BRUCE F. Baird taught future MBAs at the University of Utah Graduate School of Business how to determine the value of an expert's advice.

Say you drove your old Porsche from the Rocky Mountains to San Diego in 110-degree heat, but on arriving at the Pacific, you think the engine sounds strange. A friend believes one of your pistons is "slapping" inside the engine and needs to be replaced immediately. Another friend believes it's just the richer, more humid air at sea level, and the car will return to normal when it returns to a higher altitude.

Before making the drive back east, you take the car to a German mechanic named Hans, who will charge you to look at the vehicle. Hans's advice may help you to avoid either the cost and delay of an unnecessary repair or the much greater cost and delay of getting stuck in the desert, having to be towed into Baker or Barstow, and having to make a more complicated repair in a place with fewer Porsche mechanics. (Dr. Baird got the exercise from being in exactly that predicament.)

What is the value of Hans's advice if he's right 100 percent of the time? What about 90 percent? Eighty? Seventy?

What the grad student discovers when he runs the numbers is that the value of Hans's guidance decreases as the correctness of the mechanic goes down. This makes sense. When the probability that the mechanic is right reaches 50 percent, his advice is worth nothing. You might as well flip a coin.

The point of the exercise, however, is for the future executive to understand how the value of the mechanic actually goes back up as his advice becomes predictably bad. In fact, if you know that a mechanic is wrong 90 percent of the time, he's as valuable as one that is right 90 percent of the time, as long as you know he's that bad. Have him look at the car. Get his recommendations. Then do exactly the opposite.[15]

This is the state of employee engagement today. It's gotten so bad that the term "engagement" itself may lose credibility, if it hasn't already. It's become, in too may quarters, a check-the-box exercise, a waste of time, a fiction, or—worst of all—a process the employees end up feeling was a trick to get themselves fired or to work harder with no reciprocal investment from the company. Engagement strategies, such as they are, have become so gummed up and contaminated by unintended consequences, so rife with bad advice, that they now make powerful cautionary tales. Think twice before you get in that car and head for the Rockies. Take nearly everything that's become the standard way of addressing employee engagement...

...and do the opposite.

Take, for example, the idea that the morale of "disengaged" people is their fault. "What we've seen is that you're not going to move the Reds," wrote one advisor who separates employees into wonderful Greens, redeemable Yellows, and damnable Reds. When "interpreting" a "Best Places to Work" survey, he advised, "The best thing to do with the disengaged folks is to help move them out of the organization. Help them find a place where they're going to be more happy."[16]

Of course some people bring a lousy attitude to work. Of course some people are just in the wrong job. But what if—and it's almost always true—many of the people who are frustrated or demoralized are simply responding as anyone would to managerial neglect, intimidation, uncompetitive pay, exhaustion, or the company's failure to deliver on one of the other elements that make a great job? In that case, demonizing the "disengaged" is like assigning a warehouse worker to move boxes in the freezer without a coat and then blaming him for shivering. Pushing out the employee only creates a false sense of having addressed the issue while the conditions that make people "Red" remain firmly in place, if not worse.

The goal of most engagement strategies is to see scores go up. In a company where people have been conditioned to tell management what it wants to hear, the goal in the short term might be to just get people comfortable telling the truth, which means scores will come in lower to match the actual level of engagement. No score on a piece of paper ever improved an organization's performance. Only the true morale of the employees does that.

Engagement programs typically measure once a year, perhaps with a few "pulse" checks in between. No company keeps tabs on its other crucial indicators—sales, foot traffic, oil prices, interest rates, call volume, brand impressions—so haphazardly. If the commitment and intensity of employees is central to performance, as all the evidence says it is, then attitudes should be measured continually, each employee getting to voice his or her opinion at least several times a year. (HR departments say this causes "survey fatigue," but there is no evidence for the alleged phenomenon. What wears people out is giving their honest opinion and having nothing substantial done about it.) Everyone in the company should understand how every major influence on the organization, from a change in CEOs to a merger to the back-to-school sales season, sparks employees' energy or saps their strength. Otherwise, rumor and conjecture rule while the firm flies blind.

Most of the pressure in an engagement initiative is traditionally placed on the frontline managers. With the greater transparency forced on companies, the increasing skepticism among workers, and the underappreciated fact that the managers' morale is ultimately determined by the quality of their leadership, it's inescapable that the CEO and his or her team be as accountable for the experience of the people at the firm as are the supervisors.

In this age, it's patronizing, rude, and just a little creepy to ask as many personal questions as most engagement surveys do and then tell the person nothing about what her answers just revealed. The implicit message is, "Stand by and wait for the Team Feedback and Action Planning in a few months." "Submit survey" into pure silence sends the unintended but still unavoidable message that the worker deserves no individual guidance and therefore has little responsibility for his or her own engagement, even if behind the scenes she is being labeled "Red" and targeted to be "helped out of the organization." In this situation, the savviest of the frustrated or demoralized employees will lie like a broken watch.

But when people are given regular access to a confidential self-assessment, cool things start happening. Some people share their ups and downs, like the healthcare leader who, directed with everyone else in the building to move to a different work space, said her engagement was at the fifty-third percentile and was singing 1960s songs to get through a tough day. Isn't that what a leader wants—people who can admit they have taxing times and grind through them anyway? Isn't that real employee loyalty? Empowering people with the truth, nearly everyone starts to chill out about the previous Orwellian pressure to declare every day a perfect day in the Workers' Paradise. Managers give their people credit for acting like grown-ups. Conversations become candid. Problems get fixed.

One of the dumbest ideas in the engagement business is paying bonuses to managers for high scores. It guarantees gaming and inflated numbers. It poisons conversations between supervisors and their teams. How is a worker supposed to know whether her boss is paying her attention because he genuinely cares about her experience or if he just wants to use her and her colleagues to make a few thousand more in cash? Even the most earnest of managers becomes suspect.

The remedy is a strategy from the CEO down that gives managers plenty of information about team morale but puts the focus on team performance. Take away the reasons to game the results, and the manager has every incentive to know the truth and create the real experiences at work that employees reciprocate with their best work.

Each of these ideas individually is a substantial revision of the playbook now used by leaders and managers. Together, they constitute a comprehensive rethinking of the strategies for attracting, retaining, and motivating people on the job.

The means of improving people's commitment to their companies and intensity in their work must be continual rather than event-based, less logical and more responsive to their emotions, less calculated and more reciprocal, less uniform and more individual. These conclusions come shouting out of any decent analysis of the research on so-called engagement, or any meaningful conversation with a person about his or her job.

It will be too much for many, maybe most, enterprises until forces outside those companies give them no other choice. It is nonetheless inevitable. It's now apparent the mechanics that organizations have been consulting in the last decade give predictably bad advice. Too many organizations got on the engagement bus hoping to reach the Rockies—and instead ended up broken down in Barstow.

The Profitable Pursuit
of Happiness

ONE OF THE BEST THINGS YOU CAN DO FOR YOUR BUSINESS IS TO MAKE your employees happy.

Those who have not been following the engagement industry for the last two decades might be puzzled that this simple, self-evident declaration is controversial. Over the years, many of the consultants who advise executives on how best to motivate their people developed an allergy to happiness.

Equating engagement and happiness "makes my ears ring and my mouth twitch," wrote one *Forbes* contributor. "There's no proof that happy employees will do anything great for your company."[1]

"Someone can be happy at work, but not 'engaged,'" opined one author of several engagement books. "They might be happy because they are lazy and it's a job with not much to do. They might be happy talking to all their work-friends and enjoying the free cafeteria food. They might be happy to have a free company car. They might just be a happy person.

But just because they're happy doesn't mean they are working hard on behalf of the company. They can be happy and unproductive."[2]

When one well-intentioned advisor asserted that "Job happiness is the oil in the gears of performance," he was roundly criticized for questioning the engagement orthodoxy. "Why are employee engagementologists so angry with me?" he asked on LinkedIn. Maybe it was his observation that engagement initiatives had "turned a basic principle into a nightmarish bundle of theoretical gobbledygook."[3]

At the center of the war on worker happiness are some disdainful assumptions about human nature and the maturity of a company's workers. According to this line of thinking, rather than being responsible grown-ups, your employees are more like children at risk of being spoiled.

"The idea of trying to make people happy at work is terrible," said the CEO of one old-school consultancy.[4] He compares employees to bears in Yellowstone National Park whose "natural instincts" are fouled up if they get a taste of human food. "Once the bears taste a peanut butter and jelly sandwich, they quit digging for roots and catching deer," he wrote. "Don't feed the bears."

"If you're measuring the effectiveness of your culture by your workforce's 'satisfaction,' you're doing it all wrong," he declared (which was ironic, given that satisfaction has been the first question on his company's survey forever). "Fortune 1000 executives often come up to me and say, 'Our company culture is robust—our employees have an 85 percent satisfaction rate.' Good for you. You have ruined your workplace. Ask any employee, 'What will satisfy you?' and the answer is easy: free lunches, more vacation time, latte machines—and don't forget a ping pong table."[5]

This is nothing more than the Theory X thinking that Douglas McGregor nuked with Theory Y in the 1960s. It's the "sit on a beach and drink mojitos" view that Dan Ariely mocks as failing to explain human striving. It's John Stuart Mill's discredited *Homo economicus* premise wrapped in a Yogi Bear cartoon. And it's demonstrably wrong.

Researchers often don't call it happiness. They prefer to label it "personal well-being," "psychological well-being," or "subjective well-being." It's still happiness. Not only do they find there's nothing wrong with it; most conclude that without happiness, the *quid pro quo* version of employee engagement runs out of gas. "Attempts to enhance employee engagement will achieve only limited success if they focus narrowly on commitment and citizenship without seeking to nurture employee psychological well-being," concluded one 2010 research paper.[6]

"Research in the applied sciences is increasingly demonstrating the significant role of employee psychological well-being in issues involving *both* employee *and* organizational health and betterment," states the *Oxford Handbook of Positive Psychology and Work.*[7]

Companies usually hire people with drive. Those people often bring to their jobs a strong combination of graduate degrees, academic honors, glowing recommendations from past employers, high scores on your timed IQ test, distinguished military service, patents in their names, presentations at industry trade shows, and massive LinkedIn networks with whom they have strong reputations for hard work and accomplishment. Most come to an organization excited about what it does and the unique way it does it. Most want to show what they can do so they can get an even better job. And increasingly, as *The Wall Street Journal* reported, pay-for-performance bonuses are being given instead of raises in order to "push workers to deliver results."[8]

How concerned should executives be that making employees happy will metamorphose them into slugs? That they won't reciprocate that the company helped to make their lives better? That they'll play Ping-Pong, sip lattes, take too much vacation, and miss the performance thresholds for their bonuses? For many reasons, the "wipe-that-smile-off-your-face" strategy doesn't make sense.

Maybe too many engagementologists don't understand what happiness is for most employees. "Most people will readily accept that an unrelenting series of what are initially pleasurable experiences will gradually become less enjoyable and fail to produce the same positive emotional experience," wrote two British professors. "For example, sitting on a yacht in the Mediterranean with unlimited sun, food, and drink would certainly make most people happy for a while—but day after day, week after week—and year after year, it would surely begin to seem pointless and would challenge the happiness of even the most determined hedonist. In fact, most people will also accept that living a life that involves moving from one positive experience to another will not be particularly enjoyable—unless the experiences have a point—or lead towards achieving a worthwhile goal of some kind."[9]

One of the biggest threats to employee engagement, if that's even what we're going to call it in the future, is the parsimonious "Don't Feed the Bears" philosophy. Employees are becoming much savvier about their alternatives and their own motivations. Life on the job and life outside of work are blending. Companies are demanding more of their people. It's really going to fall apart if the implicit message behind cultural initiatives remains, "I only want to improve your experience here to the degree it makes you work harder for this company." In that form, employee engagement is a trick, one that some employees may have fallen for in the past but that fewer and fewer will in the future.

Employees are already, and will increasingly be, better informed, more skeptical, more demanding, conditionally loyal, thrill seeking, hungry for recognition, focused on their own accomplishments, and setting their own limits to protect their quality of life. They will interview their prospective manager as much as he or she interviews them. They'll become fearless, not because their jobs are secure, but because they'll keep their options open.

They'll measure their engagement when they want, not when the company says. They'll know a potential employer's culture before they apply, not after they're hired. They'll know their market worth, and they'll switch jobs to get it. They'll go where they can get incredible recognition and where they can get the chance to lead. They'll go where the work is meaningful and leave when the company squashes that purpose. Most of all, they will work where they can be not just "engaged," but truly happy.

They will not be unreasonable or calculating or selfish. They will just be wiser and more mature. With the death of the paternalistic organization, it's only natural that its former "kids" grew up to have their own opinions, ways of life, and goals. They will require not just saying the right things or checking the employee engagement boxes, but a more robust and genuine compact between them and their company.

The cool thing about reciprocity is how enthusiastically people will step up in return for leaders and managers who are investing themselves in their employees' happiness and success. There are few conversations more invigorating than talking to someone who loves his or her job.

What comes through powerfully in our analyses, the comments of those the team behind this book interviewed, and what people post online about their jobs is that making people happy is good for employees and good for business. Once in a while, you will hear someone say he's "engaged" or "disengaged" at work. Not often. Even after two decades of HR using it, it's not part of the natural vocabulary among employees, and it's now safe to say, it never will be. When people talk about where they work hardest, they talk about happiness.

When people have managers who get inside their heads, they appreciate and reciprocate the individual attention. "I have a good manager," wrote a subject-matter expert at a software firm in India. "I can talk to my manager like how I talk to my friend, about anything, and my manager also understands me." The company, the employee posted, is "a great place to learn, grow, and be happy."[10]

Nothing kills happiness and makes people want to escape more than fear. Making employees fearless allows them to focus on the task at hand without distractions. "I work with amazing people," wrote an online analytics employee in San Francisco. "I went to a top-tier university, but I'm more impressed by the people I work with now. Everyone is so super smart, and they're all fantastic people with diverse backgrounds and experiences. Our culture is why I love it here; we're transparent, hard-working, fearless, passionate people. I couldn't be any happier."[11]

When the organization worries as much about its employees' financial future as it does about its own, it gains incredible loyalty. "I am very happy in this organization. They are paying me a handsome salary," said one man. "I've had good opportunities in this job," said a woman who works for a consulting firm in India. "I'm able to earn good money and I bought a car recently. I am happy."

Everyone knows many companies today are pushing their employees to their limits. Those that instead create balance in their workers' lives create happiness that translates into commitment. "It's a challenging position where I get to create some of my own work," said a woman who works at the Hospital for Sick Children in Toronto. "I have autonomy and amazing work/life balance. I work for an amazing employer."

The business case for the Fifth Rule—"Be Cool"—is all about happiness, that the more people enjoy the time they spend at work, the more they will invest themselves in the work itself. "It's just all so interesting," said a man working for Pharmaprix in Canada. "Not having a science background and now working as a pharmacist's technician, it's pretty cool, and I never thought I'd be good at it as well."

Transparency tells people you trust them and you can be trusted. "This is a collaborative, transparent, wonderful place to work," wrote a salesperson in San Francisco. "Yeah, it has the start-up perks like ping pong, kegs, x box, etc., but it also has a culture of getting your work done and delivering results."[12] What a professional and well-fed bear.

Nothing makes the case for happiness at work more than employees' need for meaning in it. The two are not the same, but they overlap heavily. "The work is inherently valuable and meaningful to me," wrote one schoolteacher. "I feel like my job has purpose. My job is fun," said a person working for the city of Moncton, New Brunswick.

Happiness is not just about the present. It's heavily influenced by someone's view of the future, the same view that our research shows is a crucial motivator on the job. "The firm has various niches which give the staff the opportunity to practice different types of accounting, tax, and auditing work," wrote a staff accountant at an Atlanta firm. "The firm pays for CPA exam study material and days off to sit for exam. We're a happy staff with an optimistic future."[13]

When recognition is common, employees develop resilience against adversity. "There are creative, brilliant people on my cross-functional team. All our work is appreciated," said one invigorated person in the survey. "It's a very uplifting, happy, and optimistic environment, even when business is tough. There are learning opportunities in every experience, whether it is good or bad. The leadership here is genuinely concerned about my development and growth."

When leaders design incentives to make collaboration the optimal choice for each person in the group, and reduce the reasons to go it alone, teamwork flourishes. It, too, makes people happy. "The best part about my job is a job well done and being part of a happy and motivated team," said one woman we interviewed. Is there anything on the job that dampens your enthusiasm? we asked. "Nothing comes to mind."

"This is an encouraging environment," said a woman working for a construction company. "We're happy for each other's successes."

Giving people the opportunity to take responsibility motivates them to rise to the occasion. "My work area is a very sophisticated place, consisting of lots of advanced automated machinery," said an employee of an engineering college in India. "This place is a training platform. It makes me happy to be able to train students and many others."

Far from wishing they could avoid the hardest conditions or challenges, those whose leaders and managers invest in their people have employees who enjoy the climb. "My job is very stressful, but very good," said a worker at a construction firm. "I love this job. I'm happy with all the company has given me for so many years."

It's obvious from these comments how dangerous the whole happiness thing could be to an organization.

One of the coolest things that pop out when searching the word "happy" among the responses in the New Rules research is how it's most frequently used to refer to customers. "The best thing about this job is working with customers to make them happy," said one employee of a bakery whose comment is representative of hundreds of others in every industry. "It's the personal pride, wanting to do the best at anything I do. And it's my coworkers, enjoying being part of this particular team."

Happy employees create happy customers. It's been said enough that it seems trite. To watch it happen is actually quite profound. People are emotional creatures. Emotions are contagious. Happiness is an exceptionally powerful force. The executive who understands it, and genuinely wants to create it in his or her business, is substantially more effective than those who worry about spoiling their employees.

"We tend to make things overly complex," said the blogger taken to task by the engagementologists. "The fact is, life is really not that complicated. Human nature is human nature, and it plays out the same in almost every culture and epoch of history. At the core of human nature is a desire to be happy. Humans are wired to embrace things that are pleasant and to resist things that are not. . . . While there is some variance in what makes people happy on an individual level, one thing is certain: Having a bad job is bad."[14]

The measure of one's life, according to many philosophies, whether religious or not, is how you treat other people while you're on this planet. None of those creeds includes the opt-out clause "except when you're at work."

Get inside their heads. Make them fearless. Make money a non-issue. Help them thrive. Be cool. Be boldly transparent. Don't kill the meaning. See their future. Magnify their success. Unite them. Let them lead. Take it to extremes.

And go ahead—just make them happy. Trust in the power of human reciprocity. Feed some bears. Do some great things for your employees just because it feels great to make the day of someone who chose to join your organization. Chill out for a while about the return on investment, because it will be there. Make them smile. Give them a great story to tell about you when they get home tonight. Sleep better knowing you did not do just the most profitable thing but also the right thing.

Your people are not your greatest assets. They're not yours, and they're not assets. They are someone's son or daughter, brother or sister, mom or dad. They're people—people for whom you have a crucial stewardship and with whom you are building a personal legacy that will last long after you have retired. Do right by them, make them happy, and they will be the major force behind the success you share with them, and the best part of being privileged to be a leader.

The Science Behind the New Rules— Engineering a Better Vehicle

By Brenda Kowske, Ph.D.*

COMPANIES AND AUTHORS OFTEN SUCCUMB TO THE TEMPTATION TO claim their engagement models were handed down from Olympus.

Ours came from Minneapolis.

As midwesterners, we're not given to hyperbole. When it gets as cold as it does in Minnesota, one does not need to exaggerate; just reporting the facts makes enough of an impression.

This book makes many bold assertions. To the degree that we make strong claims, we believe they should be backed by strong research, and questioning and testing of our own conclusions before we publish them.

---

* Dr. Kowske was the principal researcher on the New Rules studies during 2013 and 2014. The New Rules of Engagement℠ and the New Rules index℠ are registered service marks of BI WORLDWIDE. The New Rules index and its associated metrics detailed in the Appendix are copyright protected by BI WORLDWIDE, 2014, and are used here with permission of the company. They cannot be reproduced without permission.

Widgets is backed not only by many years of experience, but by hard behavioral science. Two-and-a-half years of investment and investigation into the current state of employees' opinions around the world culminated in the New Rules. We took a linear, scientifically rigorous approach, following industry standards for assessment creation. This appendix describes how we created the survey questions, chose the employees to survey, collected their information, and analyzed the data. Our goal was to identify the survey statements that best strengthen employee motivation in our current work environment.

We sought to tell the true tale of people's work lives, the story they would tell their leaders if they were completely honest. Finding powerful connections in their numerical answers, punctuated by their candid comments, it was our privilege to see the incredibly complex mixture of experiences that make people eagerly anticipate or sadly dread going to work. Having done our homework, we believe we are in a unique position to help improve life on the job today and the performance of those companies that understand its importance.

Researching Employee Engagement

BMW endeavors to build "the ultimate driving machine." We sought to build a survey instrument that measured the ultimate employee experience. There's a reason why we test-drive before buying a car. All cars are going to run. All cars will get you from A to B. But does the car respond when you need to merge quickly? Does it smoothly handle a quick turn made to avoid a pothole? Does it hydroplane in rain? Most important, does the cup holder put the morning coffee easily within reach?

Intuitively, we know when a car "fits." We feel safe and secure. Everything we need is at hand. Driving feels effortless. The workplace, when it fits, feels that way too. To measure that phenomenon, we needed a survey that captured the kind of job, manager, and leader that employees see as "ultimate" and that they reciprocate with their hardest work.

It's not an easy task. The workplace is complex, with a million moving parts. Not only are those parts in motion, but—not being widgets—they think, feel, and act on their own volition. Consider all the reasons people like working. They might be driven by the sense of accomplishment, the opportunity to create, the camaraderie, and—yes—the paycheck. For these and for countless other reasons, they go to work every day, each playing a part in the combined work of the organization. Strong and synchronized, employees' motivations help the company reach its goals.

Their company might get from A to B, but will employees look forward to the trip? Will they stay with that vehicle, or trade it in for one that drives better?

What we've come to call "employee engagement" can be measured through a variety of ways: observation, interviews, focus groups, and the like. Each of these data-gathering techniques can play an important role in understanding employees and their opinions. Organizational surveys, however, are the most cost-effective and accessible method for learning the levels and drivers of employee engagement, so we focused our energies there.

Step 1. Creating Survey Statements

To develop a survey, we first needed to write statements with which employees could agree or disagree. Based on our substantial experience in the field, we began an extensive list of every reason employees work. We voraciously reviewed the academic literature and tapped topics such as employee motivation, job design, leadership and manager traits and styles, performance management, learning and development, and work-life balance, to name a few. Then we reflected on our practice—what do employees complain about? How about leaders, managers, and HR? And why do employees leave their job?

In 2012, we had conducted the pilot study of New Rules statements in the United States, and shortly thereafter replicated the study in Australia. We gathered those statements together, compared our notes with the research, and started writing. Everything from career possibilities to customer focus to work-life balance to the work itself—you name it, we wrote a statement about it. Specifically, employees could indicate if they strongly agreed with, agreed with, felt neutral about, disagreed with, or strongly disagreed with statements like "My manager understands me" and "I get the chance to lead at my job." The team sat for hours—nay, days—creating, wordsmithing, and editing survey statements. We wrestled over the use of the words "company" versus "organization." We argued the finer points of punctuation use. We considered buying stock in Caribou Coffee (where much of this book was written). And at the end of our labor of love, the survey had 80 statements employees could use to describe their work and the organization, its culture, and its environment.

We also measured engagement itself, or the extent to which people wanted to stay at their organization and were motivated to do their best at their jobs. We scoured the academic literature and were, of course, aware of how various consulting firms were seeking to untangle the engagement issue. Leaving no stone unturned, we brought these documents together to examine each model's similarities and differences. By tying our measure to research done in the past, we ensured our measure had, in technical terms, "content-related validity"—which means our survey instrument was designed to measure the broad concept of engagement. We took the common and unique model elements and tested them in our survey using 14 statements designed to measure levels of employee engagement directly.[1]

Finally, survey results lack insight unless you know who said what, not by individual employees, but by employee groups. We added demographic questions asking employees to tell us their gender, age, income, union and expat status, highest level of education, and work location country, and we asked them to categorize their job. We asked about their organization as well: how big it is; what industry it's in; if it's nonprofit, multinational, private, or public; and whether anyone's been laid off lately. By asking employees to characterize themselves and their organizations, we were ready, if needed, to report on the engagement of women leaders, people who work in high tech, or call center employees in India. We could also make powerful comparisons between groups, telling chief human resources officers all about the differences they might expect, say, between senior leaders, frontline managers, and their rank and file. Nineteen statements enabled analyses such as these, bringing the total number of statements and questions in the survey to 113.

Part of building this survey included translating statements for our international audience. We used a process of translation and back translation. Native speakers translated the survey into, for example, Brazilian Portuguese. Then, another, independent translator translated the Portuguese version of the survey back into English. The original and back-translated English survey versions were then compared. Where discrepancies existed, the translators and the research team discussed the item's intended meaning and decided on the final wording. By putting the statements through such a rigorous process, we ensured that employees were asked the same question in each of our study's countries or regions.

Step 2. Choosing Survey Respondents

With the survey in order, our next task was to send it out to the people we wanted to hear from: employees. We pegged our goal at 1,000 employees per country. Why 1,000? Because 1,000 responses allowed us to "generalize" to the population of the country, meaning our sample of 1,000 is statistically big enough to represent the opinions of everybody who works.

But choosing respondents is not just about size; it's about how well the employees who answered the survey represent the population at large. We didn't want to talk only to 1,000 production workers, or women, or employees younger than 30. We needed this 1,000 to represent the working population in our target countries.

We could have used company data, like other research done on the subject. But people bring their biases to company-administered surveys. At work, they might pad their responses, answering diminutively for fear of repercussions. Or they might "yell" in the hopes they will be heard, and state their case more strongly. There are motivations at play when employees take a survey at work. We avoided the issue by going straight to the employees, bypassing the company and its influence.

We partnered with a premiere global market research firm that maintains a repository of 12 million people around the world willing to take surveys. The list is called a "panel," and consists of people who volunteer to take surveys online for nominal compensation. Panel members fill out a profile, allowing the research firm to select people who meet certain criteria as required by the various research studies they serve. The firm carefully verifies identities by way of postal address comparisons, and it near-religiously monitors and excludes panel members who answer irresponsibly. We targeted those that were 18 years or older and working:

- 30 hours per week or more
- In Brazil, Canada, China, India, the United Kingdom, the United States, or within the Latin American region outside of Brazil
- At an organization employing more than 500 people

This book, therefore, talks about the engagement of adult, full-time or nearly full-time employees of larger organizations, those most likely to have HR departments, policy manuals, multiple levels and divisions, and the constant streams of people joining and leaving. For simplicity, *Widgets* cites statistics for the United States most frequently, then mentions important differences for the other regions where they exist. In our sample, employees in a wide variety of industries were surveyed, including high tech, retail, manufacturing, healthcare, and the financial sectors. Organizations varied widely in size as well, from companies with 500 employees to those that employed numbers exceeding the population of Luxembourg. Employees held the gambit of job titles, with management well represented. Overall, the demographic characteristics of the sample and their organizations were widely varied and representative of a diverse economy.

Step 3. Collecting Information

Data collection began on October 30, 2013. By December 5, we had collected sufficient data to begin the analyses. During data collection, the research team monitored daily the proportions of gender, age groups, and industries so as to avoid hearing from a select group. When it came to age and gender, we were particularly vigilant. We compared proportions with national labor statistics, and when we needed more of a certain type of employee—say, women in Latin America—we stopped collecting information from men and continued to survey women in that region. See Table A-1 for the number of surveys received, valid surveys retained after data cleaning (more on that in Step 4's "Cleaning the Data" section), the maximum margin of error, and incidence rates for each country.

TABLE A-1   RESPONSE STATISTICS

Country	Surveys Received	Surveys Retained for Study Inclusion	Incidence Rate*	Maximum Margin-of-Error (95% C.I.)†
US¶	1,009	990	68%	1.6%
UK	1,009	1003	62%	1.5%
Canada	1,007	993	41%	1.6%
Brazil	1,006	1004	64%	1.5%
Latin America	1,022	1016	57%	1.5%
China	1,008	971	85%	1.6%
India	1,007	969	73%	1.6%

* Incidence rate = number of surveys completed/(total invites sent – number of ineligible respondents)

† Maximum margin-of-error = $(1.96)\sqrt{[p(1-p)/n]}$, where p = the sample proportion, which for maximum MOE is set at 0.50 and n = country sample size.

¶ In the United States, 225 additional surveys were collected for research purposes beyond the scope of this book. Those surveys have been omitted from U.S. counts.

Step 4. Analyzing the Data

We followed a rigorous methodological model- and assessment-building protocol that is well accepted in academic circles. After cleaning the data, we sorted the statements into themes. These themes represented how employees categorized unique aspects of work. We interpreted these themes and gave them names. These themes became the New Rules.

We made sure the statements would measure workplaces similarly, whether deployed now or months from now. We looked across countries to see if the themes changed. And we built the standard New Rules survey by selecting the items that not only best predicted employee engagement but also were action-oriented, equipping clients to improve their policies and practices.

It seems deceptively simple.

Cleaning the Data

The point of data cleaning is to eliminate errors in the data. The accuracy of all research studies is threatened by error. In *in situ* social science research, the accuracy suffers more so since rarely can we set up double-blind, medical-type experiments in naturally occurring situations like the workplace.

We therefore do our best to eliminate error going into data collection, as we did when we watched proportions in the sample—and we scrub the data again when all the data are in.

First we double-checked surveys for signs that employees weren't giving thoughtful answers. We looked for contradiction in answer sets. Some statements in the survey are negatively worded, and others, positively worded. If the employees agreed with both, we knew they weren't reading carefully. For example, it's unlikely that you would agree with the statement "My job is boring" and also say that "I love my job."

We also looked for employees that "straight-lined"—those that clicked the same response for all the statements—or those that used some kind of pattern to their answers, such as answering all statements "strongly agree" on one screen, then all "strongly disagree" on another.

If an employee straight-lined to the midpoint of the survey, the market research firm terminated the survey and deleted the straight-lined responses from the data set. If she or he straight-lined in every group of statements both negatively and positively worded, her or his responses were deleted. If an employee completed the survey in less than five minutes—an amount of time that through testing we determined to be far too short to have carefully read and considered the 113 questions, we deleted her or his responses.

We looked for "sampling error" as well, ensuring our group of employees was not in some way systematically dissimilar than the group of employees they are supposed to represent. To curb sampling error, we again compared our sample's characteristics with the characteristics of the working population in each of our target countries. We used national statistics from the U.S. Bureau of Labor Statistics and the Organization for Economic Co-operation and Development for our comparisons.[2]

Most sample and population demographic proportions matched well. However, in four of the seven countries/regions (China, Brazil, India, and Latin America), the sample was quite a bit younger than the working population we were emulating. We found minor age differences in the remaining countries. We attributed the differences to delivering the survey online; in some countries, older generations are not as plugged in. Additionally, in countries with a larger proportion of smaller businesses, younger employees may be drawn to larger companies.[3] Since we only allowed those working in organizations larger than 500 employees to participate in the study, this may have further affected the age mix.

To fix the issue, we proportionally weighted the data. Simply put, we multiplied results by the proportion of the population to our sample. For example, in Canada, 24 percent of the adult working population is aged between 25 and 34. However, in our sample, the percentage is 30. To equalize our sample, we multiplied results of this age group by 24 percent/30 percent, or 0.78. Contrariwise, the sample came up short in the 55-to-64 age category; population and sample percentages were 15 and 11 percent, respectively. This age group's responses were multiplied by 15 percent/11 percent, or 1.42.

In short, so that we didn't overrepresent younger workers' opinions in our results, we equalized our findings according to country- or region-specific workforce statistics. By deleting careless answers and weighting the data, our data set contained thoughtful answers from a group of employees who most closely represented the opinions we would expect to hear if we asked our questions of every employee in each country or region.

Defining and Measuring Employee Engagement

We had data on employees' day-to-day experiences, opinions, and attitudes. It was employees' raw material: the equivalent of a car's steel, rubber, and whatever that plastic is that disintegrates on impact. We had a lot of good stuff, but looking at it all strewn about in piles and vats, we thought, "That doesn't much look like employee engagement." The material was pretty useless in its raw form. It needed to be transformed into parts we could use to describe employees' ultimate workplace—and to build the New Rules. In scientific terms, we needed "factors."[4]

Factors are themes that emerge from the data. They are composed of survey statements that form natural clusters because employees respond to certain related statements in similar ways. For example, when they rate one item high, they consistently rate certain others high as well; the same is true for low-rated statements. The research team looked for these rating patterns, seeking groups of statements scored consistently similarly within countries' or regions' samples. In short, we ran a statistical test called a "principal component analysis," or PCA,[5] on each of our study country's or region's data.

One of the PCA's results is a "component matrix," which shows how statements are related or not related to each other. By looking at those statements highly related to each other, themes emerged. The themes were remarkably similar across countries and regions, although notable differences emerged as well.

We used this approach to reconceptualize "employee engagement." Engagement has historically been defined as a mix of motivation, the expenditure of extra effort at work, high performance, happiness or satisfaction on the job, commitment to the company, excitement or enthusiasm, goal alignment, advocacy of the company, and feelings of fulfillment.[6] There's also a flavor of "extraordinary" to engagement. Employees devote extra effort, hit stretch goals, and feel not just satisfied but overtly enthusiastic.[7] Between consultancies, no two models are alike, indicating confusion in the field.

When we ran a PCA on items that measured the outcomes of work—the eventual, overarching attitudes or intentions of employees—we found results diverging from the traditional views on employee engagement. Our empirical investigation yielded two factors: organizational commitment and employee performance. Thus, the PCA performed on the measure of engagement formed our standard engagement metrics—one measuring intensity of commitment and the other, intensity of performance (Table A-2). These two metrics include elements of organizational pride, advocacy, and commitment, as well as high performance in the arenas of customer service, work improvement, and innovation, respectively.

TABLE A-2   THE NEW RULES STANDARD EMPLOYEE
ENGAGEMENT METRICS AND THEIR STATEMENTS

Intensity of Commitment	Intensity of Performance
I am proud to work at my organization.	I feel an obligation to work as hard as I can for my organization.
I would recommend this organization as a great place to work.	I am willing to work especially hard for my organization's customers.
I wish I were working somewhere else.	I actively look for ways to improve the way I work.
I am planning to leave this organization within the next 12 months.	I've often been recognized as a top performer at my organization.
	Working here brings out my best ideas.

Creating the New Rules

After defining the measures for employee engagement, we turned our attention to measuring the workplace. In casting a wide net over the entirety of the work experience, our goal was to find the elements of work that matter most to employee engagement. We used a PCA to find the themes or factors of the work experience, and then we looked at the strongest relationships between these elements and engagement.

A quick note on our goal for this exercise: We've heard time and time again HR leaders lament about the rote nature of their employee surveys. HR professionals can't tell what to fix after they get the results. Managers complain about lack of payoff from their time spent answering question after question. Leaders wonder why in the world they are spending hundreds of thousands of dollars when *nothing happens*— turnover is still 20 percent. For this and other reasons discussed in the "Handling the Truth" chapter of this book, we believe the old system is broken. It might have worked when engagement was a new concept, but it certainly does not work today.

So we set out to rehab engagement. Since recovering from the Great Recession, we wanted to discover the real story of employee engagement as it exists today, not 15 years ago when many of the consultancies in the market first defined it. We wanted to give engagement agency, action, and impact. From reading the rules, we wanted our audience to understand what they and their company needed to do to improve the working relationship between the employee and his or her company. We sought to discover the "new."

We started with the U.S. employees' responses. The U.S. PCA gave us 13 factors, 12 of which were interpretable.[8] We then looked at those statements that "hung together"—groups of statements that were related to each other and not as related to other statements. We looked at each group of statements as a whole, looked for a theme, and defined the factor. To find the theme, we used the primary output of the PCA, the "factor loadings." Loadings are numbers from –1 to 1 that represent the degree to which each of the statements correlates with each of the factors. The higher the loading, the more that statement correlates with the factor compiled by the PCA. In other words, the statements with the highest loadings are the most representative of the factor, or rule. For example, the following statements all had a loading of 0.6 or above on one factor and low loadings on the others:

- I have too much work at my job to maintain a healthy lifestyle.

- My family and friends worry about my stress at work.

- I am burned out from my job.

- I am concerned I will have an accident at work.

- My job is stressful.

- Sometimes I feel like I can't do anything right at work.

It was the research team's task to define what this rule *is*, given that these statements measured it. It doesn't take a rocket scientist to realize that all these statements measure something related to health or stress. Thus, these statements were sorted into those assigned to the rule we eventually called "Help Them Thrive"—a rule advising leaders to support employees' physical and emotional health rather than contributing to the problem with long hours and workplace stress.

Not all of the factors were as straightforward. This is typical; social scientists know that the interpretation of factors is a combination of art (the art of interpreting data based on your professional understanding of the world) and science (the statistical outputs). Let's look at how we determined each rule in turn.

The First Rule: Get Inside Their Heads

It came as no surprise that one of our factors spoke of the person who sits between the employee and the company, who connects with the employee nearly every day if not several times a day, the person who can make an employee's work life heaven or hell: the person's manager. It's a role foundational to employee engagement, and that's why it's rule *Numero Uno*.

The statements composing this rule spoke of an explicit understanding between manager and employee. Employees described a manager who sought out information, knew each employee's motivations, and assigned work deftly. She is manager extraordinaire.

There was another aspect to this factor.[9] The statements refer not only to how well managers know their employees but also to how they recognize them for the work they do. We separated out this latter sub-category, because while certainly a manager is expected to give employees a pat on the back here and there, it is not the sole characteristic of a great manager. A manager can't recognize effectively without *knowing* employees. We targeted the First Rule on understanding employees, and we captured recognition elsewhere in the rules (discussed under the Ninth Rule, "Magnify Their Success").

The Second Rule: Make Them Fearless

Employees grouped together statements about stress and its two primary causes at work: a work-life imbalance and fear. A fear-inducing event, say, an announcement of soon-to-be-revealed "cost-cutting measures," evokes a choice for each employee: should I stay and hold my ground or flee the scene? Before an employee chooses between "fight" and "flight" lies a moment in which rational, logical behavior stalls. Survival is their only concern, as decisions are routed first through the limbic system, the emotional center of the brain. Unable to think clearly, solve problems, or take action, a fearful employee is of little use to the organization unless leaders want him or her to simply follow instructions, like a widget.

The Great Recession imparted a legacy of cost-cutting measures, the most damaging of which was layoffs, at least to employee engagement. Call it a fancy name like "reduction in force," the more pedestrian "downsizing," or the somewhat-sneaky "right-sizing"; it doesn't matter. Layoffs hurt employee morale. Fear of layoffs was a hallmark of this rule.

It reflects a culture of fear as well. Public humiliation, idle (or so not idle) threats of termination, stomping around like a red-faced toddler—believe it or not, there are organizations that not only allow leaders to act this way but use it to motivate employees. Faced with such aggressive, unstable behavior, employees caught in such an organization are fearful. We measured the fear factor with the rule "Make Them Fearless."

We felt health, stress, and work-life balance were topics that should be handled and improved differently than leaders' attempts at moving from a culture of fear and intimidation to collaboration and interdependence. Of course, fear induces stress, but stress is not only caused by fear. The health, stress, and imbalance rule, "Help Them Thrive," is discussed in the Fourth Rule below.

The Third Rule: Make Money a Non-Issue

Not surprising, money came up. People work for money, so one might think it's kind of a "well, duh" sort of rule. Actually, this factor had a basket of statements that told a more compelling story. Employee concerns did not focus on raw dollar amounts, but rather their perceptions of pay fairness. It's a function of social referencing. Compensation and benefits professionals and the managers they advise need to provide employees with not only market-rate compensation but also information that proves the packages' fairness.

Traditionally, we also think that concerns about money are about cash in hand: if a person's wage today is enough to support his or her lifestyle. Not so. Employees took the long view when it came to their compensation, focusing more on their income forecast. Employees expected their income to increase as their organization grew. Coupling this factor with the smaller factor that contained statements about health benefits and paid time off, we termed this rule "Make Money a Nonissue." Compensation won't be a cause for consternation as long as a company follows the mantra "Keep it competitive and keep up."

The Fourth Rule: Help Them Thrive

Employee health is a top concern for all leaders, whether motivated by altruism or cost containment. An employee can't put his best foot forward if he's sick, tired, or both, so a healthy employee is fundamental. It's a condition that must be met before we can even consider his engagement.

We partially discussed this factor already above in our example. Employees thought about job stress, fear, and work-life balance together, but for practical purposes we separated out issues of balance and fear, as featured in the Second Rule. To relieve an overworked, burned-out workforce, executives might change policies and the cultural expectations for working late. Fear caused by a caustic manager or looming layoffs requires completely different fixes. Therefore, these two rules emerged from one factor. The rule measuring stress and work-life balance is dubbed "Help Them Thrive."

The Fifth Rule: Be Cool

What's cool? James Dean? The latest tech device? It's setting the trend, not following it. It's irreverently changing the norm. It's speaking up no matter what, regardless of popular opinion. It's spitting in the old guard's face—metaphorically speaking, of course.

One factor contained statements about creative, exciting organizations that embrace differences of opinions—very cool places to work. Another subcategory was included: one about leader honesty and organizational transparency. Both these themes were about top leaders and the organizations they manage, but practically speaking, HR practitioners, managers, and leaders need to measure and act upon these themes separately. Hence, the Fifth Rule, "Be Cool," was born. The Sixth Rule encapsulates leader honesty and transparency.

The Sixth Rule: Be Boldly Transparent

Speaking of cool, leaders who either lie or just don't share much information are decidedly uncool, and employees said as much. Employees need to be able to trust their leaders, like they need to be able to trust their car's guidance system. Without a map, there's no process for getting from A to B—or even knowing where B is.

Employees expect their leaders to have a compelling vision for the company and share it with everyone. Implicitly, employees need to be able to trust their leaders' ability to get them there. Employees bank on leaders to support their livelihood, so trust in leaders and in their version of the future is a must.

We live in a time when this rule is enforced by technology. The Internet and social media make available plenty of unofficial information about a company. It's therefore that much more important that official communications are regularly filled with accurate information.

We called this rule "Be Boldly Transparent."

The Seventh Rule: Don't Kill the Meaning

Another factor had everything to do with employees' jobs. In it, we saw statements about the everyday aspect of just feeling darn good about a job well done and also statements about doing exemplary, unparalleled work and attaining not just stretch goals but life goals. Two levels of job performance were teased out in the rules, "Don't Kill the Meaning" and "Take It to Extremes."

Don't Kill the Meaning is about loving work and understanding why a personal contribution makes a difference. Employees who give meaning to their jobs know the work is important and impacts the goals of the organization. They work for reasons beyond the paycheck. It is the antithesis of boring, but rather enlivening, engaging, and purposeful.

The Eighth Rule: See Their Future

People prefer to invest with confidence, a confidence that was shaken by the Great Recession. When thinking about where to contribute professionally, they'll choose a company with a bright future because opportunities for employees follow company success.

But it's not enough for the company to be on the road to something great. Employees need to know what that future means for them. The translation of company goals to personal, professional success—that's what drives employee engagement. Simply, employees are looking for a promising career. Employees have one eye on the horizon, and it's up to their managers and leaders to translate employees' visions into their job or career at the organization. This factor became the rule "See Their Future."

The Ninth Rule: Magnify Their Success

Since the days of B. F. Skinner and John Watson, we've know that rewards (and punishment) alter behavior in animals—and in humans. For leaders, rewarding the right actions and behaviors is a very powerful tool in creating a high-performing workforce.

It's a tool for leaders, but people expect it. In fact, at work as in the rest of life, people naturally crave the brain chemical released by a reward, dopamine. They will pointedly look for the levers to push and pull in order to get the reward, whether it is a pat on the back, a trophy, or an on-the-spot award. Hand in glove with other aspects of management, one factor called out an important aspect of managing: recognizing members of the team. We called this subcategory within the factor, "Magnify Their Success" (the other category being the First Rule).

The Tenth Rule: Unite Them

Another factor contained statements about relationships, period. We all know it's fine to have close professional relationships at work, and sometimes those evolve into personal friendships. But it's not about having a best friend at work as such.

It is about working with talented people, a network of colleagues and coworkers that you trust to do their jobs—and have fun while doing them, preferably. Employees want a strong team backing them up. We call this factor, "Unite Them."

The Eleventh Rule: Let Them Lead

In the spirit of de-widgetizing the workforce, one factor called out the importance of letting employees *think*. People, being the willful, big-brained entities that they are, are naturally predisposed to wanting to solve problems and take action. Frankly, it makes their job easier in the long run if they're able to continually improve their work process. Unfortunately, perhaps in large part due to our roots in Frederick Taylor's experiments, leaders have traditionally been compelled to dehumanize work, leaving employees with robotic roles.

Job autonomy and what's known in the literature as a "participatory work environment" formed a factor dubbed "Let Them Lead." These statements talk about employees' authority to make on-the-job decisions. When employees lead, they wholeheartedly and unabashedly contribute ideas. Leaders expand their scope of influence by offering their employees opportunities to lead. It's a win-win: employees feel a sense of contribution and agency, and the company reaps the benefit of many minds solving—and overcoming—the company's obstacles to success.

The Twelfth Rule: Take It to Extremes

Employees don't want any job; they want *the* job—perhaps even the ultimate job, the job that lets them meet a life goal, where an employee not only accomplishes a goal but does something incredible. The employees are pushed to their limits and loving every minute of it.

In this factor, employees expressed how challenging work contributed to its meaningfulness. Yes, it's great to have a job that contributes to something bigger, but in the same breath, employees want work to build, not only the company's competence, but their own. To grow and develop and to establish a sense of confidence that can only be achieved by surmounting a huge challenge and emerging victorious—that's what employees are looking for in the rule "Take It to Extremes."

APPENDIX

The Remainders

While most factors were included in the New Rules, a few were not. One factor was about customer orientation, quality focus, and learning—statements that reflect readiness to perform and job performance. We thought of this factor as more of the outcome of engagement, rather than a precursor to engagement as are the other rules. It's also not "new"—companies have long sought to create and support a high-performance culture. Another factor reflected employees' perceptions of their opportunities outside the organization—an aspect of engagement outside the control of leaders and therefore not as helpful, practically speaking. It is unavoidable that an employees' commitment to a company depends on his or her alternatives; companies will always have to work harder to retain those who get calls from other companies' recruiters. Yet another factor contained more avant-garde test statements concerning intrusiveness in the arenas of well-being program practices and peer-based performance reviews. Since these practices are rarely used and therefore irrelevant to many organizations, the factors were withheld from the New Rules.

International Differences

We started this journey in the United States, with U.S. data. Therefore, the descriptions above apply to the United States. The New Rules studies were also conducted in various places around the world. We used these studies to investigate the consistency of the engagement patterns across cultures. We ran and interpreted PCAs for each study country and region.[10] We didn't anticipate that these rules would be universal. Rather, we sought to identify the similarities and differences. China and, to a lesser extent, India were the most different in factor structure. The countries and regions in the Americas were much more similar, as was the United Kingdom. See Table A-3 for the mapping of New Rules internationally.

TABLE A-3 COUNTRY/REGION PRINCIPLE COMPONENTS ANALYSES MAP*

	U.S.	U.K.	Canada	Brazil	LatAm	China	India
1. Get Inside Their Heads	✓	✓	✓	✓	✓	✓	✓
2. Make Them Fearless	✓	✓	✓	✓	✓	✓	✓
3. Make Money a Nonissue	✓	✓	✓	✓	✓		
4. Help Them Thrive	✓	✓	✓	✓	✓	✓	✓
5. Be Cool	✓	✓	✓	✓	✓		
6. Be Boldly Transparent	✓	✓	✓	✓	✓		
7. Don't Kill the Meaning	✓	✓	✓	✓	✓	✓	✓
8. See Their Future	✓	✓	✓	Combined with Rule 3	Combined with Rule 3		
9. Magnify Their Success	✓	✓	✓	✓	✓	✓	✓
10. Unite Them	✓	✓	✓	✓	✓	✓	✓
11. Let Them Lead	✓	✓	✓	✓	✓	Combined with Rule 7	Combined with Rule 1
12. Take It to Extremes	✓	✓		✓	✓	Combined with Rule 7	Combined with Rule 11
Learning and Development (not included in the New Rules)				✓	✓	✓	Combined with Rule 7

* This table compares our study countries' or region's PCAs. A check mark indicates the rule was represented in a factor that emerged from that country's or region's data. Some rules combined in a single factor consistently for all areas and, where applicable, this has been noted in the rule-specific text in Step Four. Blank cells in this matrix denote that the rules' statements cross-loaded or were found in factors that were not interpretable.

Step 5. Measuring the New Rules of Engagement

Although we tested 113 statements, we certainly weren't going to recommend to clients that they spend valuable employee time answering such a long survey in which many of the statements essentially asked the same thing but in different ways. We needed to identify the statements *most important to engagement* that *best measured the rule.*

We set about choosing three statements that measured each rule well. The number three is important. We expect items measuring the same rule to be consistently scored—they should all be high or low, relatively speaking. This is called "internal consistency reliability." Had we measured a rule with only one statement, we wouldn't have been able to measure internal consistency; there would have been no other items with which to compare responses. Two items offer only one reference point. Three items, however, allow us to triangulate scores and assess internal consistency. Multiple statements stabilize the factor's score[11] and make it a more reliable measure of the rule.[12]

But which statements to choose?

Returning to our analogy of a car, our measure needed to not only measure parts of the "machine" but diagnose the cause of sluggish operations, misfiring spark plugs, and misaligned wheels. Again, two criteria dictated item selection: one was the extent to which the item best represented the rule, and the other was the strength of its relationship to employee commitment and work intensity. To evaluate the first criterion, we used the factor loadings in the component matrix. The statements with the highest loadings are the most representative of the factor, or rule.

For the second, we ran a series of relative weights analyses, or RWA. RWA is a fancy regression, and regression is a fancy correlation, which at its core is simply a measure of how related two things are to each other. As it turns out, statements in a survey are often related to each other, as well as what they are trying to predict—in this case, employee engagement. This is a big problem for survey researchers, because we want to know how, for example, the item "My job is boring" is related to employee engagement, not how "I love my job" is related to "My job is boring" *and* employee engagement. It's a phenomenon called "multicollinearity," and it is the bane of survey researchers.

We wanted none of that. In this part of our research, we needed to isolate the *unique* relationship of one item within a factor to employee engagement. That's exactly what RWA does; in scientific terms, it transforms predictors (the rules) into a new set of uncorrelated, or "orthogonal," predictors that are maximally related to the original, correlated predictors. Then it uses both uncorrelated and correlated predictors to produce importance estimates, or "weights" on an outcome, in this case, engagement.[13] RWA was designed specifically to tackle the issue of multicollinearity.

So we did an RWA for each bank of statements which factored together against our two employee engagement measures: intensity of commitment and intensity of performance. The "weights" that RWA generates are scores that basically say how important or uniquely related each item is to engagement. Sort the statements high to low by weight, and you have a list of statements, within a factor, by order of their importance to engagement.

Armed with these pieces of information, we had a lengthy, heated discussion over the final choice of the three statements that would measure the rules. Coffees, lunches, and peanut M&Ms were consumed. In sum, a grand ol' time was had by all of the stats-minded members of the research team. We looked at the factor loadings and relative weights side by side: Where the top-loaded statements and highest weights coincided, we chose those statements. When they didn't, we let practicality be our guide. What statements, together, most holistically measured the rule and therefore would be the most useful to the people who made decisions about employee's lives at work? Which statements were the most action-oriented? With these questions guiding our choices, the standard New Rules survey was created: a practical, short, 36-item assessment that gives leaders clear direction for improvement.

Summary

We started with raw materials, then crafted parts—each rule akin to the transmission, chassis, tires, and, yes, that all-important cup holder. Each piece has a unique and important part to play, and without one, no one's getting anywhere.

Assembling them in a standard way gives us a vehicle, and only that. It's not going to feel custom-fit, and it's likely not going to meet particular needs, whether they are riding in six inches of mud, racing in a car club's road rally, handling curves despite slick conditions, or getting the family and its gear to the cabin for the weekend.

To make the New Rules hum, leaders and professionals need to align the company's goals and strategy with specific rules. We need to take note of what the company is doing well and diagnose failing areas to strengthen the weaker parts. Whether a whole-hog overhaul or incremental, targeted improvements to the organization, we retool, reaching "the ultimate employee experience" through the New Rules. But make no mistake—employees are not simply "assets" or "resources"; they are most certainly, collectively, in control of the future. They are in the driver's seat, and the New Rules attend to them accordingly.

Notes

THE STRUCTURE OF THIS BOOK AND THE KEY STATISTICS IN IT ARE from analyses of New Rules studies conducted in 2012 and late 2013. Interviewed for those studies were representative samples of people working for large companies in the United States in 2012, in Australia in late 2012, and in the United States, Canada, Brazil, the rest of Latin America, the United Kingdom, China, and India in late 2013. The studies are described in detail in the Appendix of this book.

As additional New Rules studies are conducted, information about them will be posted on WidgetsTheBook.com. On first reference in a chapter of this book, statistics from the studies are typically attributed. For ease of reading, further statistics or results from New Rules analyses are typically unattributed. Results from other research sources are attributed in the text and appear as an endnote to that chapter in these notes.

"Human Resources"

1. Taylor, Frederick W. *The Principles of Scientific Management.* New York: Harper & Brothers, 1911.
2. Gueutal, Hal G., and Dianna L. Stone, eds. *The Brave New World of eHR: Human Resources Management in the Digital Age.* San Francisco: Jossey-Bass, 2005.
3. Wessel, David. "Software Raises Bar for Hiring." *Wall Street Journal,* May 31, 2012.
4. *Marketplace Money.* American Public Media, January 3, 2014. Hosted by Carmen Wong Ulrich. Accessed April 14, 2014, http://www.marketplace.org/shows/marketplace-money/marketplace-money-friday-january-03-2014.

5. "Gallup." Glassdoor.com summary of employee reviews of Gallup. Accessed October 13, 2013, http://www.glassdoor.com/Reviews/Gallup-Reviews-E7246.htm.
6. Anonymous former employee. "Between What Is, and What Should Be Is Measured in Light Years at Gallup." Glassdoor.com employee review of Gallup, October 18, 2013. Accessed November 11, 2013, http://www.glassdoor.com/Reviews/Employee-Review-Gallup-RVW3197952.htm.
7. "Our Unique Culture." Gallup.com (corporate website). Accessed November 11, 2013, http://www.gallup.com/careers/108169/our-unique-culture.aspx.
8. "Right Management." Glassdoor.com employee reviews of Right Management. Accessed June 15, 2014, http://www.glassdoor.com/Reviews/Right-Management-Reviews-E1833.htm.
9. Anonymous current employee. "You Think It Can't Get Any Worse . . . Until It Does." Glassdoor.com review of Right Management, October 17, 2013. Accessed November 11, 2013, http://www.glassdoor.com/Reviews/Employee-Review-Right-Management-RVW3197282.
10. "Company Values." Right.com (Right Management corporate website). Accessed June 1, 2014, http://www.right.com/about-us/company-values/default.aspx.

The Reciprocal Employee

1. Svoboda, Elizabeth. "Hard-Wired for Giving." *Wall Street Journal*, August 31, 2013. Accessed October 13, 2013, http://online.wsj.com/news/articles/SB10001424127887324009304579041231971683854.
2. Carlin, George. *Brain Droppings*. New York: Hyperion, 1998.
3. Pinsker, Joe. "41 Percent of American Workers Let Paid Vacation Days Go to Waste." *The Atlantic*, August 22, 2014. Accessed August 28, 2014, http://m.theatlantic.com/business/archive/2014/08/41-percent-of-american-workers-let-their-paid-vacation-go-to-waste/378950/.
4. "Conversations with History—Richard H. Thaler." YouTube video, 51:06. Uploaded by "UC Berkeley Events," November 1, 2010, https://www.youtube.com/watch?v=tWQ8sBFxtwo.
5. Cosmides, Leda, and John Tooby. "Evolutionary Psychology: A Primer." Center for Evolutionary Psychology, updated January 13, 1997. Accessed November 11, 2013, http://www.cep.ucsb.edu/primer.html.
6. Tripp, Thomas M., Robert J. Bies, and Karl Aquino. "Poetic Justice or Petty Jealousy? The Aesthetics of Revenge." *Organizational Behavior and Human Decision Processes* 89, no. 1 (2002): 966–984. Accessed November 19, 2014. http://EconPapers.repec.org/RePEc:eee:jobhdp:v:89:y:2002:i:1:p:966-984.
7. Dubner, Stephen. "Should Tipping Be Banned?" *Freakonomics* (podcast), June 3, 2013. Accessed August 5, 2013, http://freakonomics.com/2013/06/03/should-tipping-be-banned-a-new-freakonomics-radio-podcast/.
8. "Man: I Bought Every Pie at Burger King to Spite Noisy Child." Fox10Phoenix.com, updated August 7, 2014. Accessed August 21, 2014, http://www.fox10phoenix.com/story/26216837/man-i-bought-every-pie-at-burger-king-to-spite-noisy-child.

9. Warren, Frank. "Half a Million Secrets." *TED Talk*, February 2012. Accessed August 21, 2013, http://www.ted.com/talks/frank_warren_half_a_million_secrets.

10. Spigel, Alex. "Give and Take: How the Rule of Reciprocation Binds Us." *Morning Edition*, November 26, 2012. Accessed November 26, 2012, http://www.npr.org/blogs/health/2012/11/26/165570502/give-and-take-how-the-rule-of-reciprocation-binds-us.

11. "What's the Human Body Good For?" *RadioWest* (podcast). Hosted by Doug Fabrizio, September 30, 2013. Accessed October 13, 2013, http://radiowest.kuer.org/post/whats-human-body-good.

12. U.S. Bureau of Labor Statistics. "Job Openings and Labor Turnover Survey Highlights, July 2014." Accessed August 18, 2014, http://www.bls.gov/web/jolts/jlt_labstatgraphs.pdf.

13. "The Battle for Brainpower." *Economist,* October 5, 2006. Accessed July 12, 2014, http://www.economist.com/node/7961894.

14. Chen, Brian X. "Star Witness in Apple Lawsuit Is Still Steve Jobs." *New York Times*, November, 30, 2014. Accessed December 1, 2014, http://www.nytimes.com/2014/12/01/technology/star-witness-in-apple-suit-is-steve-jobs.html?ref=technology&_r=1.

15. U.S. Bureau of Labor Statistics. "Job Openings and Labor Turnover Survey Highlights, July 2014." Accessed August 18, 2014, http://www.bls.gov/web/jolts/jlt_labstatgraphs.pdf.

16. Williams, G. Chambers. "Trucking Industry Faces Uphill Battle to Recruit Drivers." *Tennessean*, August 25, 2014. Accessed August 26, 2014, http://www.tennessean.com/story/money/industries/2014/08/24/trucking-industry-faces-uphill-battle-recruit-drivers/14457611/.

17. Reindl, J. C. "Builders Now Hurting for Skilled Workers." *Detroit Free Press*, June 9, 2013. Accessed August 5, 2013, http://www.freep.com/article/20130609/BUSINESS06/306090070/Skilled-builders-construction-carpenters-michigan.

18. Barrett, Rick. "Employers Plan Modest Wage Increases." *Journal Sentinel*, June 7, 2013. Accessed March 21, 2014, http://www.jsonline.com/business/employers-plan-modest-wage-increases-b9928807z1-210669171.html.

19. Goodman, Cindy Krischer. "Top Workplace Trends in 2012 and What to Look for in 2013." *Miami Herald,* 2012. Accessed March 22, 2014, http://miamiherald.typepad.com/worklifebalancingact/2012/12/top-workplace-trends-in-2012-and-what-to-look-for-in-2013.html.

20. "This May Be the Coolest Way Ever to Quit Your Job." *Huffington Post*, September 30, 2013. Accessed January 13, 2014, http://www.huffingtonpost.com/2013/09/29/quit-your-job-kayne-dance_n_4013902.html#slide=more292236.

21. "Everything Is Obvious, Once You Know the Answer." *RadioWest* (podcast). Hosted by Doug Fabrizio, March 5, 2012, http://radiowest.kuer.org/post/3512-everything-obvious-once-you-know-answer.

22. "The Hidden Side of Keeping Employee Morale High." *Freakonomics Radio.* Hosted by Kai Ryssdal, *Marketplace*, February 22, 2012. Accessed September 28,

2013, http://www.marketplace.org/topics/life/freakonomics-radio/hidden-side
-keeping-employee-morale-high.

23. Stern, Stefan. "How to Live Long and Prosper." *Financial Times,* March 12, 2012. Accessed at http://www.ft.com/intl/cms/s/0/02682732-6855-11e1-a6cc-00144 feabdc0.html#axzz2gZv39YU2.

24. Sorenson, Susan, and Keri Garman. "How to Tackle U.S. Employees' Stagnating Engagement." *Gallup Business Journal* (2013), http://businessjournal.gallup.com/ content/162953/tackle-employees-stagnating-engagement.aspx.

25. Jacobsen, Darcy. "5 Famously Disengaged Employees and the Lessons They Can Teach Us." *Globoforce* (blog), June 5, 2012, http://www.globoforce.com/gfblog/ 2012/5-famously-disengaged-employees-and-the-lessons-they-can-teach-us/.

26. Dunn, Kris. "Everything You Need to Know About Employee Engagement—in 3 Sentences and a Snappy Video . . . ." (*the hr capitali$t*) (blog), *Workforce Management*, September 6, 2013, http://www.hrcapitalist.com/2013/09/engagement.html.

27. "Our Mission." CIA.gov (Central Intelligence Agency website), undated. Accessed April 15, 2014, https://www.cia.gov/index.html.

28. Anonymous former intelligence analyst in Washington, D.C. "A Fun Place to Be, but Don't Make It a Career." Glassdoor.com review of Central Intelligence Agency, December 3, 2008. Accessed January 29, 2014, http://www.glassdoor.com/ Reviews/Employee-Review-CIA-RVW127361.htm.

29. Former analyst student trainee in Washington, D.C. "Interesting, but You Can't Tell Anyone About It." Glassdoor.com review of Central Intelligence Agency, January 8, 2012. Accessed February 20, 2014, http://www.glassdoor.com/Reviews/Employee
-Review-CIA-RVW1271685.htm.

The First Rule: Get Inside Their Heads

1. "David McCullough, Wellesley High School English Teacher, Tells Graduates: 'You're Not Special.'" *Huffington Post*, June 7, 2013. Accessed April 20, 2014, http:// www.huffingtonpost.com/2012/06/06/david-mccullough-wellesle_n_1575402 .html.

2. Suhay, Lisa. "'You're Not Special' Graduation Speech: David McCullough Spins It into a Book." *Culture* (blog), *The Christian Science Monitor*, June 14, 2013, http:// www.csmonitor.com/The-Culture/Family/Modern-Parenthood/2013/0614/ You-re-not-special-graduation-speech-David-McCullough-spins-it-into-a-book.

3. "You Are Not Special Commencement Speech from Wellesley High School." YouTube video, 12:45. Uploaded by "WellesleyChannelTV," June 7, 2012, http:// www.youtube.com/watch?v=_lfxYhtf8o4.

4. McCullough, David. *You Are Not Special: . . . and Other Encouragements*. New York: HarperCollins Publishers, 2014.

5. McCullough, David. "David McCullough: My Turn on the 'You're Not Special' Speech." *Newsweek*, June 17, 2012. Accessed April 20, 2014, http://www.newsweek .com/david-mccullough-my-turn-youre-not-special-speech-65243.

6. Fernandes, Deirdre. "After 'You're Not Special' Speech, a Quiet Season for Wellesley Teacher." *Boston Globe*, May 9, 2013. Accessed February 12, 2014, http://www.bostonglobe.com/metro/regionals/west/2013/05/08/after-memorable-you-not-special-speech-quiet-graduation-season-for-wellesley-high-teacher/QCX0uz3r766QSfybdZfhyL/story.html.

7. Matchar, Emily. "How Those Spoiled Millennials Will Make the Workplace Better for Everyone." *Washington Post*, August 16, 2012. Accessed March 26, 2014, http://www.washingtonpost.com/opinions/how-those-spoiled-millennials-will-make-the-workplace-better-for-everyone/2012/08/16/814af692-d5d8-11e1-a0cc-8954acd5f90c_story.html.

8. Wolfe, Tom. "The 'Me' Decade and the Third Great Awakening." *New York*, August 23, 1976. Accessed April 29, 2014, http://nymag.com/news/features/45938/.

9. Narula, Svati Kirsten. "The Complete Guide to Instagramming Your Thanksgiving Dinner." *Quartz* (online publication). November 26, 2014. Accessed November 26, 2014. http://qz.com/300662/the-complete-guide-to-instagramming-your-thanksgiving-dinner/.

10. Berfield, Susan. "Memo to Target Managers: Hispanics Don't All Wear Sombreros." *Bloomberg Businessweek*, July 11, 2013. Accessed March 27, 2014, http://www.businessweek.com/articles/2013-07-11/memo-to-target-managers-hispanics-dont-all-wear-sombreros.

11. Funderburg, Lise. "The Changing Face of America: We've become a country where race is no longer so black or white." *National Geographic*, October 2013. Accessed December 5, 2014, http://ngm.nationalgeographic.com/2013/10/changing-faces/funderburg-text?rptregcta=reg_free_np&rptregcampaign=20131016_rw_membership_r1p_us_se_w.

12. Grant, Adam M., Justin Berg, and Dan Cable. "Job Titles as Identity Badges: How Self-Reflective Titles Can Reduce Emotional Exhaustion." *Academy of Management Journal* 57, no. 4 (2014): 1201–1225. Accessed August 21, 2014, doi: 10.5465/amj.2012.0338.

13. Gino, Francesca. *Sidetracked: Why Our Decisions Get Derailed, and How We Can Stick to the Plan.* Boston: Harvard Business School Press, 2013. Cable, Daniel M., and Francesca Gino. "Reinventing Employee Onboarding." *MITSloan Management Review*, March 19, 2013. Accessed November 12, 2013, http://sloanreview.mit.edu/article/reinventing-employee-onboarding/.

14. Hogeveen, Jeremy, Michael Inzlicht, and Sukhvinder S. Obhi. "Power Changes How the Brain Responds to Others." *Journal of Experimental Psychology* 143, no. 2 (April 2014): 755–762. Accessed May 6, 2014, doi: 10.1037/a0033477.

15. Benderev, Chris. "When Power Goes to Your Head, It May Shut Out Your Heart." National Public Radio, August 10, 2013, http://www.npr.org/2013/08/10/210686255/a-sense-of-power-can-do-a-number-on-your-brain.

The Second Rule: Make Them Fearless

1. Malone, Michael S. *Bill & Dave: How Hewlett and Packard Built the World's Greatest Company.* New York: Portfolio, 2007.
2. "From Hoarding to Hiring." *Economist,* October 7, 2010. Accessed February 2, 2014, http://www.economist.com/node/17173957.
3. Krugman, Paul. "Productivity over the Business Cycle (Wonkish)." *New York Times,* January 17, 2011, http://krugman.blogs.nytimes.com/2011/01/17/productivity-over-the-business-cycle-wonkish/?_php=true&_type=blogs&_r=0.
4. Associated Press. "Temporary Jobs Becoming a Permanent Fixture in U.S." *Daily Herald,* July 8, 2013. Accessed May 20, 2014, http://www.dailyherald.com/article/20130707/business/707079900/.
5. Gordon, Robert J. "The Demise of Okun's Law and of Procyclical Fluctuations in Conventional and Unconventional Measures of Productivity." Paper delivered at the 2010 National Bureau of Economic Research Summer Institute meetings. Accessed December 15, 2013, http://faculty-web.at.northwestern.edu/economics/gordon/The%20Demise%20of%20Okun's%20Law_NBER.pdf.
6. Safdar, Khadeeja. "Vast Majority of Americans Wrongly Say Economy in Recession: Survey." *Huffington Post*, September 3, 2014. Accessed September 3, 2014, http://www.huffingtonpost.com/2012/04/10/americans-recession_n_1414984.html.
7. Bailey, James R., and Johathan Raelin. "Employees See Death When You Change Their Routines." *HBR Blog Network* (blog), *Harvard Business Review*, November 23, 2010, http://blogs.hbr.org/2010/11/employees-see-death-when-you-c/.
8. Pychyl, Timothy A. "Don't Delay." *Psychology Today*, February 13, 2009. Accessed January 31, 2014, http://www.psychologytoday.com/blog/dont-delay/200902/fear-failure.
9. Welch, Jack. "Jack Welch: 'Rank-and-Yank'? That's Not How It's Done." Online.wsj.com (*Wall Street Journal* website), November 14, 2013. Accessed September 15, 2014, http://online.wsj.com/news/articles/SB10001424052702303789604579198281053673534.
10. Rock, David, Josh Davis, and Beth Jones. "Kill Your Performance Ratings: Neuroscience Shows Why Numbers-Based HR Management Is Obsolete." *Strategy+Business* (magazine website), August 8, 2014. Accessed September 15, 2014, http://www.strategy-business.com/article/00275?pg=all.
11. Kouchaki, Maryam, and Sreedhari D. Desai. "Anxious, Threatened, and Also Unethical: How Anxiety Makes Individuals Feel Threatened and Commit Unethical Acts." *Journal of Applied Psychology*. Published online before print September 22, 2014. Accessed October 21, 2014, doi: http://dx.doi.org/10.1037/a0037796.
12. Wurtzel, Alan. *Good to Great to Gone: The 60 Year Rise and Fall of Circuit City.* New York: Diversion, 2012.
13. Collins, Jim. *Good to Great: Why Some Companies Make the Leap . . . and Others Don't.* New York: HarperCollins, 2001.

14. Scott, Julia M. "Paid Too Much." *Los Angeles Daily News*, March 28, 2007. Accessed May 15, 2014, http://www.dailynews.com/general-news/20070329/paid-too-much.

15. Goldman, Abigail, and Molly Selvin. "For Circuit City Staff, Good Pay Is a Bad Thing." *Los Angeles Times*, March 29, 2007. Accessed May 10, 2014, http://articles.latimes.com/2007/mar/29/business/fi-circuit29.

16. Becker, David. "Circuit City Shields Customers from Too-Smart Sales Clerks." *Wired*, March 29, 2007. Accessed May 12, 2014, http://www.wired.com/2007/03/circuit_city_sh/.

17. "Circuit City's Harsh Layoffs Give Glimpse of a New World." *USA Today*, April 2, 2007. Accessed June 22, 2013, http://usatoday30.usatoday.com/news/opinion/2007-04-02-edit_N.htm.

18. Joyce, Amy. "Circuit City's Job Cuts Backfiring, Analysts Say." *Washington Post*, May 2, 2007. Accessed May 12, 2014, http://www.washingtonpost.com/wp-dyn/content/article/2007/05/01/AR2007050101623.html.

19. Bhasin, Kim. "Circuit City Scion Tears into a Former CEO for Systematically Destroying the Company." *Business Insider*, October 22, 2012. Accessed February 2, 2014, http://www.businessinsider.com/circuit-city-former-ceo-schoonover-2012-10.

20. "The Best (and Worst) Managers of 2008." *Bloomberg Businessweek*, January 7, 2009. Accessed January 7, 2014, http://images.businessweek.com/ss/09/01/0108_best_worst/index.htm.

21. "Workplace Challenges: Managing Layoffs, and Motivating Those Left Behind." *Knowledge@Wharton* (podcast). Wharton University of Pennsylvania, November 24, 2009. Accessed July 23, 2013, http://knowledge.wharton.upenn.edu/article/workplace-challenges-managing-layoffs-and-motivating-those-left-behind/.

22. Ibid.

23. Bialik,Carl. "Seven Careers in a Lifetime? Think Twice, Researchers Say." *Wall Street Journal*, September 4, 2010. Accessed May 5, 2014, http://online.wsj.com/news/articles/SB10001424052748704206804575468162805877990.

24. Hoffman, Reid, Ben Casnocha, and Chris Yeh. "Tours of Duty: The New Employer-Employee Compact." *Harvard Business Review*, June 2013. Accessed July 22, 2013, http://hbr.org/2013/06/tours-of-duty-the-new-employer-employee-compact.

The Third Rule: Make Money a Non-Issue

1. Briers, B., M. Pandelaere, S. Dewitte, and L. Warlop. "Hungry for Money: The Desire for Caloric Resources Increases the Desire for Financial Resources and Vice Versa." *Psychology Science* 17, no. 11 (2006): 939–943, http://www.ncbi.nlm.nih.gov/pubmed/17176423.

2. Becchio, Cristina, Joshua Skewes, Torben E. Lund, Uta Frith, Chris Frith, and Andreas Roepstorff. "How the Brain Responds to the Destruction of Money." *Journal of Neuroscience, Psychology, and Economics* 4, no. 1 (2011): 1–10. Accessed November 3, 2013, http://psycnet.apa.org/journals/npe/4/1/1/.

3. Lea, S. E., and P. Webley. "Money as Tool, Money as Drug: The Biological Psychology of a Strong Incentive." *Behavior Brain Science* 29, no. 2 (2006):

176–209. Accessed November 3, 2013, http://www.ncbi.nlm.nih.gov/pubmed/16606498.

4. Becchio et al. "How the Brain Responds to the Destruction of Money."

5. "EURion Constellation." *Wikipedia*, July 2010. Accessed November 3, 2013, http://en.wikipedia.org/wiki/EURion_constellation.

6. "Episode 54: The Colour of Money." *99% Invisible*. Written and hosted by Roman Mars, May 16, 2012. Accessed August 12, 2013, http://99percentinvisible.org/episode/episode-54-the-colour-of-money/.

7. Hill, Adriene. "Money: The Myth We All Believe In." *Marketplace* (podcast), July 12, 2013. Accessed August 20, 2013, http://www.marketplace.org/topics/your-money/money-myth-we-all-believe.

8. Locke, E. A., D. B. Feren, V. M. McCaleb, K. N. Shaw, and A. T. Denny. "The Relative Effectiveness of Four Methods of Motivating Employee Performance." In K. D. Duncan, M. M. Gruneburg, and D. Wallis, eds., *Changes in Working Life*. New York: Wiley, 1980.

9. McGregor, Jena. "Why Slackers Still Get Bonuses." *Washington Post*, August 16, 2013. Accessed June 5, 2014, http://www.washingtonpost.com/blogs/on-leadership/wp/2013/08/16/why-slackers-still-get-bonuses/.

10. Judge, Timothy A., Ronald F. Piccolo, Nathan P. Podsakoff, John C. Shaw, and Bruce L. Rich. "The Relationship Between Pay and Job Satisfaction: A Meta-analysis of the Literature." *Journal of Vocational Behavior* 77, no. 2 (2010): 157–167, http://www.sciencedirect.com/science/article/pii/S0001879110000722.

11. Leddy, Chuck. "When 3 + 1 Is More Than 4." *HARVARDgazette*, October 24, 2013. Accessed January 18, 2014, http://news.harvard.edu/gazette/story/2013/10/when-31-is-more-than-4/.

12. Solnicka, Sara. J., and David Hemenway. "Is More Always Better? A Survey on Positional Concerns." *Journal of Economic Behavior & Organization* 37 (1998): 373–383. Accessed November 3, 2013, http://isites.harvard.edu/fs/docs/icb.topic212792.files/Indices_of_Wellbeing/HSPH.pdf.

13. Adams, Scott. *Dilbert*. October 29, 2005.

14. Shuck, Brad, and Kevin Rose. "Reframing Employee Engagement Within the Context of Meaning and Purpose: Implications for HRD." *Advances in Developing Human Resources* 15, no. 4 (2013): 341–355. Accessed July 10, 2014, doi: 10.1177/1523422313503235.

15. Keng, Cameron. "Employees Who Stay in Companies Longer Than Two Years Get Paid 50% Less." *Forbes,* June 22, 2014. Accessed June 23, 2014, http://www.forbes.com/sites/cameronkeng/2014/06/22/employees-that-stay-in-companies-longer-than-2-years-get-paid-50-less/.

16. Cooper, Charles. "Nadella Can't Escape 'Karma-Gate' Remarks." Forbes.com, October 20, 2014. Accessed December 7, 2014, http://www.forbes.com/sites/charlescooper/2014/10/20/nadella-cant-escape-karma-gate-remarks/.

17. Waller, Nikki. "What Satya Nadella Got Right About Raises." WSJ.com, October 10, 2014. Accessed December 7, 2014, http://blogs.wsj.com/atwork/2014/10/10/what-satya-nadella-got-right-about-raises/.

18. Partington, Richard. "The No-Raises Recovery: U.S. Workers' Wages Stagnate, But Rich Get Richer." *Financial Post*, August 19, 2014. Accessed September 4, 2014, http://business.financialpost.com/2014/08/19/us-recovery-wages/?__federated=1.

19. Ovide, Shira. "Microsoft Values CEO Satya Nadella's Pay at $84 Million." WSJ.com, October 20, 2014. Accessed December 7, 2014, http://blogs.wsj.com/digits/2014/10/20/microsoft-values-ceo-satya-nadellas-pay-at-84-million/.

20. Peele, Thomas. "Judge Tells Oakland to Disclose Worker Pay." *Contra Costa Times*, November 9, 2004. Accessed March 4, 2014, http://www.freerepublic.com/focus/f-news/1275361/posts.

21. International Federation of Professional and Technical Engineers, Local 21, et al. v. The Superior Court of Alameda County, 42 Cal. 4 319 (2007).

22. Brancaccio, David. "How Much You Earn—the Last Taboo." *Marketplace* (podcast), August 20, 2012. Accessed December 2, 2013, http://www.marketplace.org/topics/wealth-poverty/pay-day/how-much-you-earn-last-taboo.

23. Card, David, Alexandre Mas, Enrico Moretti, and Emmanuel Saez. "Inequality at Work: The Effect of Peer Salaries on Job Satisfaction." *American Economic Review* 102, no. 6 (October 2012): 2981–3003. Accessed November 3, 2013, doi: 10.1257/aer.102.6.2981.

24. Dreisback, Tom. "'Pay Secrecy' Policies at Work: Often Illegal, and Misunderstood." *All Things Considered*, National Public Radio, April 13, 2014. Accessed December 4, 2014, http://www.npr.org/2014/04/13/301989789/pay-secrecy-policies-at-work-often-illegal-and-misunderstood.

25. Weber, Lauren, and Rachel Emma Silverman. "Workers Share Their Salary Secrets." *Wall Street Journal*, April 16, 2013. Accessed April 14, 2014, http://online.wsj.com/news/articles/SB10001424127887324345804578426744168583824.

26. Lawler, Edward. "Pay Secrecy: Why Bother?" *Forbes*, September 12, 2012. Accessed January 25, 2014, http://www.forbes.com/sites/edwardlawler/2012/09/12/pay-secrecy-why-bother/.

The Fourth Rule: Help Them Thrive

1. Felton, Nicholas. "Nicholas Felton." Feltron.com (personal blog and website). Accessed December 5, 2013, http://www.feltron.com.

2. Felton, Nicholas. "2012 Annual Report." Feltron.com (personal blog and website). Accessed December 5, 2013, http://feltron.com/FAR12.html.

3. Bilton, Nick. "An Annual Report on One Man's Life." *New York Times*, February 9, 2010. Accessed March 14, 2014, http://bits.blogs.nytimes.com/2010/02/09/an-annual-report-on-one-mans-life/?_php=true&_type=blogs&_r=0.

4. Comstock, Jonah. "Survey: 32 Percent of Mobile Device Owners Use Fitness Apps." MobileHealthNews.com, January 29, 2014. Accessed October 23, 2014, http://mobihealthnews.com/29358/survey-32-percent-of-mobile-device-owners-use-fitness-apps/.

5. Wolf, Gary. "The Quantified Self." TED presentation, June 2010. Accessed January 3, 2014, http://www.ted.com/talks/gary_wolf_the_quantified_self.

6. Swithers, Susan E. "Artificial Sweeteners Produce the Counterintuitive Effect of Inducing Metabolic Derangements." *Trends in Endocrinology & Metabolism* 24, no. 9 (September 2013): 431–441. Accessed October 13, 2013, doi: 10.1016/j.tem.2013.05.005.

7. Sullivan, Bob. "Are You 'Binge Working?' The Question Is Deadly Serious." Accessed January 30, 2014, http://www.nbcnews.com/business/careers/are-you-binge-working-question-deadly-serious-n15016. *NBC Nightly News.* Hosted by Brian Williams, January 29, 2014.

8. Schachter, Harvey. "Burnout: The Topic Your Boss Doesn't Want to Talk About." *Globe and Mail*, September 10, 2012. Accessed April 2, 2014, http://www.theglobeandmail.com/report-on-business/careers/career-advice/burnout-the-topic-your-boss-doesnt-want-to-talk-about/article536067/.

9. Various studies are cited and well summarized in Knudsen, Hannah, Lori J. Ducharme, and Paul M. Roman, "Job Stress and Poor Sleep Quality: Data from an American Sample of Full-Time Workers." *Social Science & Medicine* 64, no. 10 (2007): 1997–2007. Accessed January 1, 2014, http://www.ncbi.nlm.nih.gov/pmc/articles/PMC1933584/#!po=2.17391.

10. Jaffe, Eric. "Workers in Windowless Offices Lose 46 Minutes of Sleep a Night." FastCoDesign.com. August 5, 2014. Accessed October 23, 2014, http://www.fastcodesign.com/3033998/evidence/workers-in-windowless-offices-lose-46-minutes-of-sleep-a-night.

11. Shannonhouse, Rebecca. "Is Your Boss Making You Sick?" WashingtonPost.com (*The Washington Post* website), October 20, 2014. Accessed October 23, 2014, http://www.washingtonpost.com/national/health-science/is-your-boss-making-you-sick/2014/10/20/60cd5d44-2953-11e4-8593-da634b334390_story.html.

12. Kunz-Ebrecht, Sabine R., Clemens Kirschbaum, Michael Marmot, and Andrew Steptoe. "Differences in Cortisol Awakening Response on Work Days and Weekends in Women and Men from the Whitehall II Cohort." *Psychoneuroendocrinology* 29, no. 4 (2004): 516–528, http://www.sciencedirect.com/science/article/pii/S0306453003000726.

13. Lindholm, Harri, Jari Ahlberg, Juha Sinisalo, Christer Hublin, Ari Hirvonen, Markku Partinen, Seppo Sarna, and Aslak Savolainen. "Morning Cortisol Levels and Perceived Stress in Irregular Shift Workers Compared with Regular Daytime Workers." *Sleep Disorders* 2012, Article ID 789274 (2012): 5 pages. Accessed January 1, 2014, http://www.hindawi.com/journals/sd/2012/789274/.

14. Ebrecht, Marcel, Justine Hextall, Lauren-Grace Kirtley, Alice Taylor, Mary Dyson, and John Weinman. "Perceived Stress and Cortisol Levels Predict Speed of Wound Healing in Healthy Male Adults." *Psychoneuroendocrinology* 29, no. 6 (2004): 798–809. Accessed January 2, 2014, http://www.sciencedirect.com/science/article/pii/S0306453003001446.

15. Berkowitz, Bonnie, and Clark Patterson. "The Health Hazards of Sitting." *Washington Post*, January 20, 2014. Accessed February 5, 2014, http://apps.washingtonpost.com/g/page/national/the-health-hazards-of-sitting/750/.

16. Pincker, Joe. "41 Percent of American Workers Let Paid Vacation Days Go to Waste." *Atlantic*, August 22, 2014. Accessed August 23, 2014, http://m.theatlantic .com/business/archive/2014/08/41-percent-of-american-workers-let-their-paid -vacation-go-to-waste/378950/.

17. Mohn, Tanya. "U.S. the Only Advanced Economy That Does Not Require Employers to Provide Paid Vacation Time, Report Says." *Forbes*, August 13, 2013. Accessed August 15, 2014, http://www.forbes.com/sites/tanyamohn/2013/08/13/ paid-time-off-forget-about-it-a-report-looks-at-how-the-u-s-compares-to-other -countries/.

18. Robinson, Sara. "Bring Back the 40-Hour Work Week." *Salon*, March 14, 2012. Accessed April 22, 2014, http://www.salon.com/2012/03/14/bring_back_the_40_ hour_work_week/.

19. Stewart, Janet Kidd. "Slalom Consulting." *Chicago Tribune*, November 15, 2011. Accessed March 12, 2014, http://articles.chicagotribune.com/2011-11-15/ business/ct-biz-1115-workplaces-slalom-20111115_1_consulting-companies -vacation-firm.

20. Schulte, Brigit. "A company that profits as it pampers workers." WashingtonPost .com (*The Washington Post* website), October 25, 2014. Accessed November 2, 2014, http://www.washingtonpost.com/business/a-company-that-profits-as-it -pampers-workers/2014/10/22/d3321b34-4818-11e4-b72e-d60a9229cc10_story .html.

21. Andersen, Erika. "Want to Succeed? Don't Check Your Email—and Work Out at Lunch." *Forbes*, December 23, 2013. Accessed February 11, 2014, http://www .forbes.com/sites/erikaandersen/2013/12/23/want-to-succeed-dont-check-your -email-and-work-out-at-lunch/.

22. Newcomb, Alyssa, "Boss Gives Employees $7,500 for Vacations." *Nation* (blog), *ABC News*, July 14, 2012, http://abcnews.go.com/blogs/headlines/2012/07/ boss-gives-employees-7500-for-vacations/. Lorang, Bart. "Paid Vacation? That's Not Cool. You Know What's Cool? Paid, PAID Vacation." *FullContact* (company blog), FullContact.com, undated. Accessed March 15, 2014, http://www.fullcontact .com/2012/07/10/paid-paid-vacation/.

23. "SAS Institute CEO Jim Goodnight on Building Strong Companies—and a More Competitive U.S. Workforce."*Knowledge@Wharton* (podcast), Wharton University of Pennsylvania, January 5, 2011. Accessed April 30, 2014, http://knowledge .wharton.upenn.edu/article/sas-institute-ceo-jim-goodnight-on-building-strong -companies-and-a-more-competitive-u-s-workforce/.

24. "100 Best Companies to Work For." *Fortune*, 2014. Accessed March 1, 2014, http:// archive.fortune.com/magazines/fortune/best-companies/2014/list/.

25. Lohr, Steve. "At a Software Powerhouse, the Good Life Is Under Siege." *New York Times*, November 21, 2009. Accessed March 22, 2014, http://www.nytimes.com/ 2009/11/22/business/22sas.html?pagewanted=all&_r=1&.

26. Smith, Jacquelyn. "The Top 25 Companies for Work-Life Balance." *Forbes*, July 19, 2013. Accessed August 21, 2013, http://www.forbes.com/sites/jacquelynsmith/ 2013/07/19/top-companies-for-work-life-balance/.

27. Crowley, Mark C. "How SAS Became the World's Best Place to Work." *Fast Company*, January 22, 2013. Accessed November 13, 2013, http://www.fastcompany .com/3004953/how-sas-became-worlds-best-place-work.

28. Fishman, Charles. "Sanity Inc." *Fast Company*, December 31, 1998. Accessed September 12, 2013, http://www.fastcompany.com/36173/sanity-inc.

29. "*TODAY* Visits 'One of the Best Places to Work.'" Hosted by Kerry Sanders, NBC, January 16, 2014, http://www.today.com/video/today/54086868#54086868.

30. Fishman, Charles. "Sanity Inc." *Fast Company*, December 31, 1998. Accessed September 12, 2013, http://www.fastcompany.com/36173/sanity-inc.

31. "Best Companies 2014." *Fortune*, 2014. Accessed May 11, 2014, http://fortune.com/ best-companies/.

32. Lohr. "At a Software Powerhouse, the Good Life Is Under Siege."

33. Richard Florida and Jim Goodnight. "Managing for Creativity." *Harvard Business Review*, June 2005.

34. Crowley. "How SAS Became the World's Best Place to Work."

35. Florida and Goodnight. "Managing for Creativity."

36. Dolan, Kerry A., and Luisa Kroll. "The World's Billionaires." *Forbes*, 2014. Accessed March 3, 2014, http://www.forbes.com/profile/james-goodnight/.

37. Florida and Goodnight. "Managing for Creativity."

38. "SAS Institute CEO Jim Goodnight on Building Strong Companies—and a More Competitive U.S. Workforce."

39. Pfeffer, Jeffrey. "Wouldn't It Be Nice If It Weren't Always About—and Only About—the Money?" *Bloomberg Businessweek*, January 2, 2013. Accessed December 13, 2014, http://www.businessweek.com/articles/2013-01-02/ wouldnt-it-be-nice-if-it-werent-always-and-just-about-the-money.

40. Troeh, Eve. "Employers Embrace Wellness Plans." *Marketplace* (podcast), September 17, 2012. Accessed November 14, 2014, http://www.marketplace.org/ topics/life/health-care/employers-embrace-wellness-plans.

41. Schiffman, Lizzie. "Trek Bicycle Head John Burke Says Obese, Unhealthy Workers Bad for Business." *DNAinfo Chicago*, February 27, 2014. Accessed March 23, 2014, http://www.dnainfo.com/chicago/20140227/loop/trek-bicycle-head-john-burke -says-obese-unhealthy-workers-bad-for-business.

42. Mihelich, Max, "Wellness Programs Should Offer Alternative to Exercise." *Workforce* (blog), March 4, 2014, http://www.workforce.com/blogs/10-humane -resources/post/20290-wellness-programs-should-offer-alternative-to-exercise ?utm_content=buffere8db1&utm_medium=social&utm_source=linkedin.com &utm_campaign=buffer.

43. Singer, Natasha. "On Campus, a Faculty Uprising over Personal Data." *New York Times*, September 14, 2013. Accessed October 11, 2014, http://www.nytimes.com/ 2013/09/15/business/on-campus-a-faculty-uprising-over-personal-data.html.

44. Lewis, Al, Vik Khanna, and Shana Montrose. "Workplace Wellness Produces No Savings." *HealthAffairs Blog*, November 25, 2014. Accessed December 5, 2014, http:// healthaffairs.org/blog/2014/11/25/workplace-wellness-produces-no-savings/.

45. Singer, Natasha. "Health Plan Penalty Ends at Penn State." *New York Times*, September 18, 2013. Accessed January 9, 2014, http://www.nytimes.com/2013/09/19/business/after-uproar-penn-state-suspends-penalty-fee-in-wellness-plan.html.

46. Tom Emerick and Al Lewis, "The Danger of Wellness Programs: Don't Become the Next Penn State." *HBR Blog Network* (blog), *Harvard Business Review*, August 20, 2013, http://blogs.hbr.org/2013/08/attention-human-resources-exec/.

The Fifth Rule: Be Cool

1. Dar-Nimrod, Ilan. "Who, Me? The Birth of Cool." *Psychology Today*, June 13, 2012, http://www.psychologytoday.com/blog/who-me/201206/the-birth-cool-research.

2. Ogilvie, Jessica P. "What Defines 'Cool.'" *Los Angeles Times*, November 10, 2012. Accessed February 23, 2014, http://articles.latimes.com/2012/nov/10/health/la-he-whats-cool-20121110.

3. Singal, Jesse. "The New Cool: Can Coolness Be Studied Like a Science?" *Daily Beast*, June 18, 2012. Accessed January 17, 2014, http://www.thedailybeast.com/articles/2012/06/18/the-new-cool-can-coolness-be-studied-like-a-science.html.

4. Gayford, Martin. "Man Who Coined the Word Cool." *Telegraph*, July 19, 2007. Accessed April 15, 2014, http://www.telegraph.co.uk/culture/music/rockandjazzmusic/3666662/Man-who-coined-the-word-cool.html.

5. Wilson, Carl. "What Does 'Cool' Even Mean in 2013?" Slate.com, September 30, 2013. Accessed July 21, 2014, http://www.slate.com/articles/life/cool_story/2013/09/the_history_and_future_of_cool_what_does_the_term_mean_in_2013.

6. Dar-Nimrod, Ian, Travis Proulx, Darrin R. Lehman, Paul R. Duberstein, and Benjamin P. Chapman. "Coolness: An Empirical Investigation." *Journal of Individual Differences* 33, no. 3 (2012): 175–185. Accessed January 21, 2014, doi: 10.1027/1614-0001/a000088.

7. "Red Forman on Work." *That 70's Show* (season 6, episode 3). Directed by David Trainer, FOX, 2003, http://www.youtube.com/watch?v=aXrwjLahUdw.

8. Ryan, Liz. "That's Why They Call It Work?" *Bloomberg Businessweek*, December 30, 2011. Accessed January 8, 2014, http://www.businessweek.com/management/thats-why-they-call-it-work-12302011.html.

9. Burkeman, Oliver. "Who Goes to Work to Have Fun?" *New York Times*, December 11, 2013. Accessed January 8, 2014, http://www.nytimes.com/2013/12/12/opinion/burkeman-are-we-having-fun-yet.html?_r=0.

10. Silverman, Rachel Emma. "In Demand: Ninjas, Jedis and Gurus." *At Work* (blog), *Wall Street Journal*, May 18, 2012. Accessed January 29, 2014, http://blogs.wsj.com/atwork/2012/05/18/in-demand-ninjas-jedis-and-gurus/.

11. Burress, Jim. "Can Southwest Learn Anything from AirTran?" *Marketplace* (podcast), March 25, 2011. Accessed February 3, 2014, http://www.marketplace.org/topics/business/can-southwest-learn-anything-airtran.

12. Bailey, Jeff. "Southwest. Way Southwest." *New York Times*, February 13, 2008. Accessed November 12, 2014, http://www.nytimes.com/2008/02/13/business/13southwest.html?pagewanted=all&_r=1&.

13. Burress. "Can Southwest Learn Anything from AirTran?"
14. Bailey. "Southwest. Way Southwest."
15. Southwest Airlines. "Southwest Airlines Reports Record Fourth Quarter and Full Year Profit; 41st Consecutive Year of Profitability." Southwest Investor Relations. Accessed December 14, 2014, http://southwest.investorroom.com/2014-01-23 -Southwest-Airlines-Reports-Record-Fourth-Quarter-And-Full-Year-Profit-41st -Consecutive-Year-Of-Profitability.
16. "By Acquiring AirTran, Will Southwest Continue to Spread the LUV?" *Knowledge@Wharton*, Wharton University of Pennsylvania, October 13, 2010, http://knowledge.wharton.upenn.edu/article/by-acquiring-airtran-will-southwest -continue-to-spread-the-luv/.
17. Anonymous pilot (current employee) in Atlanta. "Great Co-Workers, Poor Upper Management." Glassdoor review of AirTran, January 19, 2011. Accessed February 16, 2014, http://www.glassdoor.com/Reviews/Employee-Review-AirTran -Holdings-RVW779036.htm.
18. Joyce, Matt. "AirTran Employees Getting New Culture." *Dallas Business Journal*, July 7, 2011, http://www.bizjournals.com/dallas/print-edition/2011/07/08/ airtran-employees-getting-new-culture.html?page=all.
19. Martin, Timothy W. "Southwest Preps for Turbulence." *Wall Street Journal*, August 5, 2011. Accessed April 14, 2014, http://online.wsj.com/news/articles/SB10001424 0531119034545045764879635078335314.
20. Anonymous design specialist (current employee) in Dallas. "The Luv Is Gone." Glassdoor review of Southwest Airlines, May 5, 2013. Accessed September 13, 2013, http://www.glassdoor.com/Reviews/Employee-Review-Southwest-Airlines -RVW2622861.htm.
21. Anonymous flight attendant (current employee). "FUN Work Environment with Great Colleagues. Very Fast Paced Airline with Stressful Situations Sometimes, But Worth It." Glassdoor review of Southwest Airlines, August 1, 2013. Accessed January 25, 2014, http://www.glassdoor.com/Reviews/Employee-Review -Southwest-Airlines-RVW2884154.htm.
22. Personal experience of the author on October 15, 2014. Southwest tweeted in response: "I'm so sorry that our employee fell short of offering the exceptional customer service you (and we) expect." Nothing further was done.
23. Hughey, Cheryl. Interview with the author. Personal phone interview, March 26, 2014.
24. National Weather Service Weather Forecast Office. "Twin Cities Snowfall Records," 2011, http://www.crh.noaa.gov/mpx/?n=mspsnowfall.
25. Nisen, Max. "We've Picked the Coolest Place to Work in Each of New York's Hottest Neighborhoods." *Business Insider*, October 18, 2013. Accessed April 13, 2014, http:// www.businessinsider.com/coolest-places-to-work-in-new-york-2013-10?op=1.
26. Ibid.
27. *Smart Money* Staff. "How Space150 Cultivated a Cool Co. Culture . . . and a Family." *Smart Money*, NBC, August 26, 2014, http://www.smartmoneytalkradio .com/communications/how-space150-cultivated-a-cool-co-culture-and-a-family.

Full disclosure: The team behind this book has retained Space150 for digital advertising work.

28. "The Best Places to Work 2013." *Outside*, 2013, http://www.outsideonline.com/outdoor-adventure/best-jobs/best-jobs-2013@gpkg/best-perks/Best-Perks-Fitness-Plans.

29. Anonymous former Zappos employee. "Great People & Benefits But It Is Like College or High School All Over Again." Glassdoor review of Zappos, November 13, 2014. Accessed December 6, 2014, http://www.glassdoor.com/Reviews/Employee-Review-The-Zappos-Family-RVW5377622.htm.

30. Wooldridge, Adrian. "The Holes in Holacracy: The Latest Big Idea in Management Deserves Some Scepticism" ("Schumpeter" column). *Economist*, July 5, 2014. Accessed July 30, 204, http://www.economist.com/news/business/21606267-latest-big-idea-management-deserves-some-scepticism-holes-holacracy.

The Sixth Rule: Be Boldly Transparent

1. "Interview with Diana Mekota." *Alumni & Friends*, John Carroll University. Accessed May 3, 2014, http://sites.jcu.edu/alumni/pages/interview-diana-mekota/.

2. Cho, Janet H. "Kelly Blazek Returns Her 2013 Communicator of the Year Award After Social Media Backlash." Cleveland.com (*Cleveland Plain Dealer* website), March 5, 2014. Accessed April 3, 2014, http://www.cleveland.com/business/index.ssf/2014/03/kelly_blazek_returns_her_2013_communicator_of_the_year_award_after_social_media_backlash.html.

3. Blazek, Kelly. "Kelly Blazek to Diane Mekota." E-mail posted by Diana Mekota on Imgur. Accessed April 3, 2014, http://imgur.com/gallery/71sQ92K.

4. Gross, Doug. "Kelly Blazek, Diana Mekota LinkedIn Controversy: Nasty LinkedIn Rejection Goes Viral." WPTV.com, February 27, 2014. Accessed April 3, 2014, http://www.wptv.com/news/science-tech/kelly-blazek-diana-mekota-linkedin-controversy-nasty-linkedin-rejection-goes-viral.

5. Cho, Janet H. "Job Bank Head Kelly Blazek Apologizes After Her Rejection Emails Go Viral." Cleveland.com (*Cleveland Plain Dealer* website), February 25, 2014. Accessed April 3, 2014, http://www.cleveland.com/business/index.ssf/2014/02/job_bank_head_kelly_blazeks_sc.html.

6. Blazek. "Kelly Blazek to Diane Mekota."

7. Gross, Doug. "Nasty LinkedIn Rejection Goes Viral." CNN.com (CNN website), February 28, 2014. Accessed April 3, 2014, http://www.cnn.com/2014/02/27/tech/web/linked-in-cleveland-job-bank/.

8. McConnell, Alaina. "Update: Kelly Blazek, Head of Cleveland Job Bank, Writes Scathing Emails to Local Job Seekers." Clevescene.com, February 26, 2014. Accessed April 3, 2014, http://www.clevescene.com/scene-and-heard/archives/2014/02/25/kelly-blazek-head-of-cleveland-job-bank-writes-scathing-emails-to-local-job-seekers.

9. Cho. "Job Bank Head Kelly Blazek Apologizes After Her Rejection Emails Go Viral."

10. Alter, Charlotte. "Anti-Mentor Roasts Millennial Who Contacted Her on LinkedIn. Then Karma Roasts Her Online." Time.com (*Time* magazine website), February 28, 2014. Accessed April 3, 2014, http://time.com/10860/linkedin-rant-apology -kelly-blazek/.

11. Cho. "Job Bank Head Kelly Blazek Apologizes After Her Rejection Emails Go Viral."

12. Light, Mark F. "The Navy's Moral Compass: Commanding Officers and Personal Misconduct." *Naval War College Review* 65, no. 3 (Summer 2012). Accessed August 12, 2014, https://www.usnwc.edu/getattachment/d79951a2-72b6-4181-b735 -5f98fc2ceecb/The-Navy-s-Moral-Compass--Commanding-Officers-and-.

13. "Millennials in Adulthood: Detached from Institutions, Networked with Friends." PewSocialTrends.org (PewResearch Social & Demographic Trends website), March 7, 2014. Accessed April 14, 2014, http://www.pewsocialtrends.org/ 2014/03/07/millennials-in-adulthood/.

14. Frauenheim, Ed. "LinkedIn Referral Policies Could Raise Legal Rift." Workforce .com (*Workforce* magazine website), February 17, 2011. Accessed February 14, 2014, http://www.workforce.com/articles/linkedin-referral-policies-could-raise -legal-rift.

15. Kegan, Robert, Lisa Lahey, Andy Fleming, and Matthew Miller. "Making Business Personal." *Harvard Business Review*, April 2014. Accessed May 5, 2014, http:// hbr.org/2014/04/making-business-personal/ar/1.

16. Anonymous former employee. "Terrible Place to Work." Glassdoor.com review of Bridgewater Associates, March 19, 2013. Accessed March 5, 2014, http:// www.glassdoor.com/Reviews/Employee-Review-Bridgewater-Associates -RVW2477348.htm.

17. Anonymous former employee. "Run Away as Fast as You Can." Glassdoor.com review of Bridgewater Associates, March 22, 2014. Accessed April 15, 2014, http:// www.glassdoor.com/Reviews/Employee-Review-Bridgewater-Associates -RVW3918603.htm.

18. "Featured Guest: Robert Hohman." HRmarketer.com's Conversation Starters— *The HR Market Share Podcast*, June 25, 2009. Accessed February 14, 2014, https:// itunes.apple.com/us/podcast/hrmarketer.coms-conversation/id307448997.

19. Levy, Ari. "Expedia Founder Barton Nears Tech Trifecta with Glassdoor." Bloomberg.com, December 5, 2013. Accessed January 15, 2014, http:// go.bloomberg.com/tech-deals/2013-12-05-expedia-founder-barton-nears -tech-trifecta-with-glassdoor/.

20. "Featured Guest: Robert Hohman."

21. "Can You Trust What You Read on Glassdoor?" Fool.com (Motley Fool website), December 4, 2013. Accessed March 10, 2014, http://www.fool.com/investing/ general/2013/12/04/glassdoor-ceo-on-data-integrity-and-pushback.aspx.

22. McIntyre, Douglas A., et al. "The Worst Companies to Work for in the U.S.: 24/7 Wall St." *Huffington Post*, July 22, 2013. Accessed June 23, 2014, http://www .huffingtonpost.com/2013/07/20/worst-companies-to-work-for_n_3629056.html.

23. Wingfield, Nick. "Employers Sound Off on Company Review Site." *Wall Street Journal*, June 23, 2010. Accessed April 18, 2014, http://blogs.wsj.com/digits/2010/06/23/employers-sound-off-on-company-review-site/.

24. Belkin, Lisa. "Psst! Your Salary Is Showing." *New York Times*, August 19, 2008. Accessed May 27, 2014, http://www.nytimes.com/2008/08/21/fashion/21Work.html?pagewanted=all&_r=0.

25. Eng, Dinah. "Rich Barton's Glassdoor Venture." *Fortune*, January 16, 2013. Accessed March 11, 2014, http://fortune.com/2013/01/16/rich-bartons-glassdoor-venture/.

26. Anonymous former employee. "Turn the Other Direction." Glassdoor.com review of ESRI, March 21, 2013. Accessed March 21, 2014, http://www.glassdoor.com/Reviews/Employee-Review-Esri-RVW2488767.htm.

27. Agha, Laith. "Sausalito-Based Glassdoor to Receive $50 Million in Capital." MarinIJ.com (*Marin Independent Journal* website), December 8, 2013. Accessed March 8, 2014, http://www.marinij.com/marinnews/ci_24673076/sausalito-based-glassdoor-receive-50-million-capital.

28. Associated Press. "Employees Rate Their Employers, CEOs on Glassdoor." CBC.ca (CBC news site), March 29, 2013. Accessed March 29, 2014, http://www.cbc.ca/news/business/employees-rate-their-employers-ceos-on-glassdoor-1.1314945.

29. Smith, Rich. "Reading This Glassdoor Report Could Have Earned You 13% in 6 Months." DailyFinance.com, December 24, 2013. Accessed March 21, 2014, http://www.dailyfinance.com/on/glassdoor-employment-report-big-stock-market-gains/.

30. Pino, Isaac. "A Secret Ingredient for Success at General Electric." DailyFinance.com, January 4, 2014. Accessed May 5, 2014, http://www.dailyfinance.com/2014/01/04/a-secret-ingredient-for-success-at-general-electri/.

31. Anonymous former employee. "Many Kind People, Sadly the Ignorant Victims of a Police State." Glassdoor.com review of Tough Mudder, January 13, 2013. Accessed August 19, 2014, http://www.glassdoor.com/Reviews/Employee-Review-Tough-Mudder-RVW2326189.htm.

32. Anonymous current employee. "Amazing Company and Culture as Long as You're Ready to Work Hard." Glassdoor.com review of Tough Mudder, September 12, 2013, http://www.glassdoor.com/Reviews/Employee-Review-Tough-Mudder-RVW1945230.htm.

33. Schawbel, Dan. "Millennials vs. Baby Boomers: Who Would You Rather Hire?" *Time*, March 29, 2012. Accessed June 29, 2013, http://business.time.com/2012/03/29/millennials-vs-baby-boomers-who-would-you-rather-hire/.

34. Smith, Jacquelyn. "America's 100 Most Trustworthy Companies." *Forbes*, March 18, 2013. Accessed September 19, 2014, http://www.forbes.com/sites/jacquelynsmith/2013/03/18/americas-100-most-trustworthy-companies/2/.

35. "2014 Edelman Trust Barometer." Edelman.com (corporate website), 2014. Accessed April 18, 2014, http://www.edelman.com/insights/intellectual-property/2014-edelman-trust-barometer/.

The Seventh Rule: Don't Kill the Meaning

1. Ariely, Dan, Emir Kamenica, and Dražen Prelec. "Man's Search for Meaning: The Case of Legos." *Journal of Economic Behavior & Organization* 67, no. 3–4 (2008): 671–677, http://people.duke.edu/~dandan/Papers/Upside/meaning.pdf.
2. Ariely, Dan. "What Makes Us Feel Good About Our Work?" TEDxRiodelaPlata presentation, October 2013. Accessed June 21, 2014, http://www.ted.com/talks/dan_ariely_what_makes_us_feel_good_about_our_work#t-81305.
3. Chandler, Dana, and Adam Kapelner. "Breaking Monotony with Meaning: Motivation in Crowdsourcing Markets." *Journal of Economic Behavior & Organization* 90 (2013): 123–133. Accessed March 4, 2014, doi: 10.1016/j.jebo.2013.03.003, http://arxiv.org/pdf/1210.0962v1.pdf.
4. Bunderson, J. Stuart, and Jeffrey A. Thompson. "The Call of the Wild: Zookeepers, Callings, and Double-Edged Sword of Deeply Meaningful Work." *Administrative Science Quarterly* 54 (2009): 32–57. Accessed March 17, 2014, http://apps.olin.wustl.edu/faculty/bunderson/Bunderson%26Thompson(2009,ASQ).pdf.
5. McKee-Ryan, Francis M., Zhaoli Song, Connie R. Wanberg, Angelo J. Kinicki. "Psychological and Physical Well-Being During Unemployment: A Meta-Analytic Study." *Journal of Applied Psychology* 90 (2005): 53–76 (print).
6. Anonymous former Tribune Company journalist. "Ex-Tribune Journalist Says She's Still Trying to Come to Peace with Being 'Put Out to Pasture' in 2007." *JimRomenesko.com* (blog), March 21, 2014. Accessed August 20, 2014, https://jimromenesko.com/2014/03/21/a-journalist-wishes-she-could-come-to-peace-with-being-put-out-to-pasture/.
7. Cartman, Gareth. "The 5 Worst Employee Engagement Strategies Ever!" *Tweakyourbiz.com* (blog), June 19, 2012. Accessed March 1, 2014, http://tweakyourbiz.com/management/2012/06/19/the-5-worst-employee-engagement-strategies-ever/.
8. *Grow Employee Engagement at Your Company*. Culture.fool.com (company video), March 19, 2013. Accessed March 24, 2014, http://culture.fool.com/2013/03/19/grow-employee-engagement-at-your-company/.
9. Ariely, Kamenica, and Prelec. "Man's Search for Meaning: The Case of Legos."
10. "Work as a Calling: Interview with Stuart Bunderson." Organizational Behavior Division of the Academy of Management podcast, February 24, 2009. Accessed March 5, 2014, http://www.obweb.org/podcasts/MikeJohnson/StuartBunderson_02242009_mj.mp3.
11. Bunderson, J. Stuart, and Jeffrey A. Thompson. *The Call of the Wild: Zookeepers, Callings, and Double-Edged Sword of Deeply Meaningful Work*. Video posted by the University of Michigan Ross School of Business. Accessed March 19, 2014, http://rossmedia.bus.umich.edu/rossmedia/Play/0c947592ee3d456d91f3dc385513508d1d.
12. Bunderson and Thompson. "The Call of the Wild: Zookeepers, Callings, and Double-Edged Sword of Deeply Meaningful Work." *Administrative Science Quarterly*.

The Eighth Rule: See Their Future

1. "The Marshmallow Experiment." YouTube video, April 29, 2010. Accessed March 21, 2014, https://www.youtube.com/watch?v=Yo4WF3cSd9Q.

2. De Posada, Joachim. "Don't Eat the Marshmallow." TED presentation, February 2009. Accessed March 22, 2014, http://www.ted.com/talks/joachim_de_posada_says_don_t_eat_the_marshmallow_yet#t-293284.

3. Bourne, Michael. "We Didn't Eat the Marshmallow. The Marshmallow Ate Us." *New York Times*, January 10, 2014. Accessed February 9, 2014, http://www.nytimes.com/2014/01/12/magazine/we-didnt-eat-the-marshmallow-the-marshmallow-ate-us.html.

4. Bennett, Drake. "What Does the Marshmallow Test Actually Test?" *Bloomberg Businessweek*, October 17, 2012. Accessed July 24, 2014, http://www.businessweek.com/articles/2012-10-17/what-does-the-marshmallow-test-actually-test.

5. "The Marshmallow Study Revisited." University of Rochester, YouTube video, October 11, 2012. Accessed March 22, 2014, https://www.youtube.com/watch?v=JsQMdECFnUQ.

6. Ibid.

7. D'Argembeau, Arnaud, Olivier Renaud, and Martial Van der Linden. "Frequency, Characteristics and Functions of Future-Oriented Thoughts in Daily Life." *Applied Cognitive Psychology* 25, no. 1 (2011): 96–103.

8. Schacter, Daniel L., Donna Rose Addis, and Randy L. Buckner. "Remembering the Past to Imagine the Future: The Prospective Brain." *Nature Reviews Neuroscience* 8 (2007): 657–661. Accessed March 31, 2014, doi:10.1038/nrn2213.

9. Walker, W. Richard, John J. Skowronski, and Charles P. Thompson. "Life Is Pleasant—and Memory Helps to Keep It That Way!" *Review of General Psychology* 7, no. 2 (2003): 203–210. Accessed March 15, 2014, http://www.apa.org/pubs/journals/releases/gpr-72203.pdf.

10. Berntsen, Dorthe, and Annette Bohn. "Remembering and Forecasting: The Relation." *Memory & Cognition* 38, no. 3 (2010): 265–278. Accessed March 4, 2014, http://link.springer.com/article/10.3758/MC.38.3.265.

11. Meltzer, Brad. "Do Kids Still Want to Be President?" Parade.condenast.com, January 24, 2014. Accessed February 24, 2014, http://parade.condenast.com/256165/bradmeltzer/do-kids-still-want-to-be-president/.

12. Bernes, Kerry, and Bardick, Angela D. "Occupational Aspirations of Students in Grades Seven to Twelve." University of Lethbridge working paper, 2005. Accessed March 29, 2014, http://hdl.handle.net/10133/1187.

13. Staff, Jeremy, Angel Harris, Ricardo Sabates, and Laine Briddell. "Uncertainty in Early Occupational Aspirations: Role Exploration or Aimlessness?" *Social Forces* 89, no. 2 (2010): 659–684.

14. "When I Grow Up." TV commercial for Monster.com, 1999. Accessed April 18, 2014, http://www.mullen.com/work/monster-when-i-grow-up/.

15. Zack, Jessica. "Scott Adams, Dilbert Creator, Finds Success in His Failures." SFGate.com, January 18, 2014. Accessed April 3, 2014, http://www.sfgate.com/art/article/Scott-Adams-Dilbert-creator-finds-success-in-5156258.php.

16. Muoio, Anna. "My Greatest Lesson." *Fast Company*, May 31, 1998. Accessed July 18, 2014, http://www.fastcompany.com/34136/my-greatest-lesson.

17. Higgins, Monica, Shoshana R. Dobrow, and Kathryn S. Roloff. "Optimism and the Boundaryless Career: The Role of Developmental Relationships." *Journal of Organizational Behavior* 31, no.5 (2010): 749–769. Accessed April 18, 2014, http://onlinelibrary.wiley.com/doi/10.1002/job.693/abstract.

18. Watson, Thomas J. "Thomas J. Watson to Robert and Sherrie Wagner," October 6, 1961. Letter, author's personal collection.

19. Robertson, Jordan, and Michael Hill. "For Tech Pioneer IBM, 100 Years of 'Think.'" NBCNews.com, June 16, 2011. Accessed April 14, 2014, http://www.nbcnews.com/id/43414686/ns/business-us_business/t/tech-pioneer-ibm-years-think/#.U2-3zF63hnI.

20. "The Greatest Capitalist in History." *Fortune*, August 31, 1987. Accessed April 14, 2014, http://archive.fortune.com/magazines/fortune/fortune_archive/1987/08/31/69488/index.htm.

21. Robertson, Jordan, and Michael Hill. "For Tech Pioneer IBM, 100 Years of 'Think.'" NBCNews.com, June 16, 2011. Accessed April 14, 2014, http://www.nbcnews.com/id/43414686/ns/business-us_business/t/tech-pioneer-ibm-years-think/#.U2-3zF63hnI.

22. Martin, Colette. "Mourning the IBM Country Club and End of the Corporate Family." *Forbes*, December 13, 2010. Accessed March 14, 2014, http://www.forbes.com/sites/work-in-progress/2010/12/13/mourning-the-ibm-country-club-and-end-of-the-corporate-family/.

23. Greene, Kelly. "Benefits Leader Reins in 401(k)s." *Wall Street Journal*, December 6, 2012. Accessed April 14, 2014, http://online.wsj.com/news/articles/SB10001424127887323316804578163722900112526.

24. Kamenetz, Anya. "The Four-Year Career." *Fast Company*, January 12, 2012. Accessed April 25, 2014, http://www.fastcompany.com/1802731/four-year-career.

25. Farber, Henry S. "Is the Company Man an Anachronism? Trends in Long Term Employment in the U.S., 1973–2006." Working paper, Princeton University, September 11, 2007. Accessed April 14, 2014, http://arks.princeton.edu/ark:/88435/dsp01ft848q61h.

26. Pearlstein, Steven. "How the Cult of Shareholder Value Wrecked American Business." *Washington Post*, September 9, 2013. Accessed November 11, 2013, http://www.washingtonpost.com/blogs/wonkblog/wp/2013/09/09/how-the-cult-of-shareholder-value-wrecked-american-business/.

The Ninth Rule: Magnify Their Success

1. Variations appear on the Internet from time to time. The subject of the experiment quoted in the chapter is Aubrey C. Daniels from his book *Other People's Habits:*

How to Use Positive Reinforcement to Bring Out the Best in People Around You. New York: McGraw-Hill, 2001.

2. Nash, J. Madeleine. "Addicted: Why Do People Get Hooked? Mounting Evidence Points to a Powerful Brain Chemical Called Dopamine." *Time*, May 5, 1997.

3. Sohn, Emily. "Why Music Makes You Happy." *Discovery Newsletter*, January 10, 2011, http://news.discovery.com/human/psychology/music-dopamine-happiness-brain-110110.htm.

4. Treadway, Michael T., et al. "Dopaminergic Mechanisms of Individual Differences in Human Effort-Based Decision-Making." *Journal of Neuroscience* 32, no. 18 (2012): 6170–6176. doi: 10.1523/JNEUROSCI.6459-11.2012.

5. Salamone, John D., et al. "The Mysterious Motivational Functions of Mesolimbic Dopamine." *Neuron* 76, no. 3 (2012): 470–485. Accessed March 13, 2014, http://www.cell.com/neuron/retrieve/pii/S0896627312009415.

6. Johnson, Steven. *Mind Wide Open: Your Brain and the Neuroscience of Everyday Life.* New York: Scribner, 2004.

7. Arias-Carrión, Oscar, et al. "Dopaminergic Reward System: A Short Integrative Review." *International Archives of Medicine*, published online October 6, 2010, doi: 10.1186/1755-7682-3-24. Accessed March 4, 2014, http://www.ncbi.nlm.nih.gov/pmc/articles/PMC2958859/.

8. "The Deal." *Seinfeld* (season 2, episode 9). Directed by Tom Cherones, written by Larry David, May 2, 1991.

9. These conclusions were drawn from analyzing the responses to each rule for employees at various levels of overall engagement.

10. Jeffrey, Scott A., and Victoria Shaffer. "The Motivational Properties of Tangible Rewards." *Compensation & Benefits Review*, May/June 2007. Accessed March 11, 2014, http://webs.wichita.edu/depttools/depttoolsmemberfiles/psychology/Laboratories/Shaffer/Jeffrey%20%26%20Shaffer.pdf.

11. Kosner, Anthony Wing. "The Sports Car, the Laptop, and the Science Behind the Golden Proportion." Forbes.com, Feburary 22, 2013. Accessed December 6, 2014, http://www.forbes.com/sites/anthonykosner/2013/02/22/the-sports-car-the-laptop-and-the-science-behind-the-golden-proportion/.

12. Fredrickson, Barbara L., and Marcial F. Losada. "Positive Affect and the Complex Dynamics of Human Flourishing." *American Psychologist* 60, no. 7 (October 2005): 678–686, doi: 10.1037/0003-066X.60.7.678.

13. Bower, Bruce. "Ratio for a Good Life Exposed as 'Nonsense.'" *Science News*, August 12, 2013, https://www.sciencenews.org/article/ratio-good-life-exposednonsense. (One of the fools who cited Fredrickson and Losada in his books was the author.)

14. Profile of Marcial Losada on "Meet the Team." LosadaLineConsulting.net (corporate website), undated. Accessed May 17, 2014, http://www.losadalineconsulting.net/#!our_team/cqn6.

15. Brown, Nicholas J. L., Alan D. Sokal, and Harris L. Friedman. "The Complex Dynamics of Wishful Thinking: The Critical Positivity Ratio." *American Psychologist*, online first publication, July 15, 2013, doi: 10.1037/a0032850. Accessed May 17, 2014, http://www.physics.nyu.edu/sokal/BrownSokalFriedmanAPonlinefirst.pdf.

16. Sullivan, Andrew. "Turning Human Beings into 2.9013." *The Dish* (personal blog), dish.andrewsullivan.com, July 22, 2013. Accessed May 17, 2014, http://dish.andrewsullivan.com/2013/07/22/turning-human-beings-into-2-9013/.

17. Zwaan, Rolf. "The Fanciful Number 2.9013, Plus or Minus Nothing." *Rolfzwaan .blogslot.nl* (personal blog), July 22, 2013. Accessed May 17, 2014, http://rolfzwaan .blogspot.nl/2013/07/the-fanciful-number-29013-plus-or-minus.html.

18. "'Positivity Ratio' Criticized in New Sokal Affair." *Discover* ("Neuroskeptic" column), July 16, 2013. Accessed May 12, 2014, http://blogs.discovermagazine.com/neuroskeptic/2013/07/16/death-of-a-theory/#.U117Q163hnI.

19. Fredrickson, Barbara. Author's note in *Positivity*. New York: Random House, originally published in 2009.

The Tenth Rule: Unite Them

1. Drew, Jay. "BYU Football: Coach Changes Mind on Cougars' Jerseys." *Salt Lake Tribune*, August 8, 2013. Accessed August 12, 2013, http://www.sltrib.com/sltrib/cougars/56710353-88/jerseys-players-byu-honor.html.csp.

2. Monson, Gordon. "Monson: BYU's Jersey Fiasco Is Just Bronco Being Bronco." *Salt Lake Tribune*, August 9, 2013. Accessed September 12, 2013, http://www.sltrib .com/sltrib/cougars/56713009-88/players-byu-bronco-idea.html.csp?page=1.

3. Darwin, Charles. *The Descent of Man*, 1879. London: Penguin, 2004.

4. Holt-lunstad, Julianne, et al. "Social Relationships and Ambulatory Blood Pressure: Structural and Qualitative Predictors of Cardiovascular Function During Everyday Social Interactions." *Health Psychology* 22, no. 4 (2003): 388–397.

5. Sebanz, Natalie. "It Takes Two to . . ." *Scientific American Mind* (2006-2007): 52–57.

6. Sebanz, Natalie, Harold Bekkering, and Günther Knoblich. "Joint Action: Bodies and Minds Moving Together." *Trends in Cognitive Sciences* 10, no. 2 (2006): 70–76.

7. Johnson, Steven. "Emotions and the Brain." *Discover*, April 1, 2003.

8. Huron, David. "Is Music an Evolutionary Adaptation?" *Annals of the New York Academy of Sciences* 930 (2001): 43–61.

9. Anonymous. Avis Budget Group advertising tweet on Twitter, November 20, 2014.

10. "The Label Maker." *Seinfeld* (season 6, episode 12). Directed by Andy Ackerman, written by Alec Berg and Jeff Schaffer, January 19, 1995. Accessed June 26, 2014, https://www.youtube.com/watch?v=we-L7w1K5Zo&feature=kp.

11. Wilson, Aaron. "Notarized Documents Show Damien Berry Sold His Super Bowl Ring." *Baltimore Sun*, January 13, 2014. Accessed February 21, 2014, http://www .baltimoresun.com/sports/ravens/ravens-insider/bal-notarized-documents -show-damien-berry-sold-his-super-bowl-ring-20140113,0,5588640.story.

12. Gustin, Sam. "How Ford Earned Its Blue Oval Back." *Time*, May 25, 2012. Accessed July 13, 2013, http://business.time.com/2012/05/25/how-ford-earned-its-blue -oval-back/.

13. LeBeau, Phil. "How Ford Got Back on the Fast Track to Success." NBCNews.com, November 11, 2010. Accessed June 30, 2014, http://www.nbcnews.com/id/40010150/ns/business-cnbc_tv/t/how-ford-got-back-fast-track-success/#.U6iNXl63hnI.

14. "Ford CEO Mulally Leaves Behind Big Shoes for Successor to Fill." *Stateside*, Michigan Public Radio, June 26, 2014. Accessed June 30, 2014, http://michigan radio.org/post/ford-ceo-mulally-leaves-behind-big-shoes-successor-fill.

15. Meier, Barry. "Ford Is Changing the Way It Rates Work of Managers." *New York Times*, July 12, 2001. Accessed March 14, 2014, http://www.nytimes.com/2001/07/12/business/ford-is-changing-the-way-it-rates-work-of-managers.html.

16. "Jacques Knifed." *Economist*, November 1, 2001. Accessed May 16, 2014, http://www.economist.com/node/842705.

17. Hoffman, Bryce. G. *American Icon: Alan Mulally and the Fight to Save Ford Motor*. New York: Crown Business, 2012.

18. Maynard, Micheline. "Ford Brings in Outsider to Help Run the Company." *New York Times*, September 6, 2006. Accessed June 26, 2014, http://www.nytimes.com/2006/09/06/business/06ford.html?pagewanted=1&_r=1.

19. Hoffman. *American Icon: Alan Mulally and the Fight to Save Ford Motor*.

20. Correspondence between the author and Anne Stevens, June 24, 2014.

21. Fernandez, Bob. "Ford Alum to Drive Reading Firm; Anne Stevens Will Be Carpenter Technology CEO." Philly.com (website of the *Philadelphia Inquirer* and *Daily News*), October 19, 2006. Accessed June 26, 2014, http://articles.philly.com/2006-10-19/business/25416635_1_robert-j-torcolini-women-in-top-management-forum-of-executive-women.

22. Hoffman. *American Icon: Alan Mulally and the Fight to Save Ford Motor*.

23. Greene, Aislyn. "Questions for: Alan Mulally." *Puget Sound Business Journal*, December 10, 2010. Accessed June 26, 2014, http://www.bizjournals.com/seattle/print-edition/2010/12/10/questions-for-alan-mulally.html?page=all.

24. Naughton, Keith. "Ford Said to Plan Post-Mulally Era by Promoting Fields." *Bloomberg*, September 12, 2012. Accessed May 4, 2014, http://www.bloomberg.com/news/2012-09-11/ford-said-near-naming-fields-as-coo-in-mulally-succession-plan.html.

25. English, Andrew. "Outgoing Ford Boss Gives Farewell Interview." *Telegraph*, May 26, 2014. Accessed June 26, 2014, http://www.telegraph.co.uk/motoring/car-manufacturers/ford/10850183/Outgoing-Ford-boss-gives-farewell-interview.html.

26. Vlasic, Bill. "Choosing Its Own Path, Ford Stayed Independent." *New York Times*, April 8, 2009. Accessed June 24, 2014, http://www.nytimes.com/2009/04/09/business/09ford.html?pagewanted=all.

27. Howes, Daniel. "Can Ford Keep Transforming After Mulally Exits?" *Detroit News*, June 26, 2014. Accessed July 17, 2014, http://www.detroitnews.com/article/20140626/AUTO0102/306260044.

28. "Ford Motor Company 2013 Annual Report." Ford Motor Company, 2014. Accessed June 15, 2014, http://corporate.ford.com/doc/916/251/ar2013-2013%20Ford%20Annual%20Report%20MR.pdf.

29. "Executive Profile: Alan Mulally." *Bloomberg Businessweek*. Accessed June 20, 2014, http://investing.businessweek.com/research/stocks/people/person.asp?personId=176639&ticker=F.

30. Howes. "Can Ford Keep Transforming After Mulally Exits?"

The Eleventh Rule: Let Them Lead

1. Anonymous current employee. "Show Up, Do Exactly as You're Told, Collect Your Paycheck." Glassdoor.com review of Esri, April 1, 2013. Accessed April 18, 2014, http://www.glassdoor.com/Reviews/Employee-Review-Esri-RVW2521592.htm.

2. Fast, Nathanael, Ethan Burris, and Caroline Bartel. "Managing to Stay in the Dark: Managerial Self-Efficacy, Ego Defensiveness, and the Aversion to Employee Voice." *Academy of Management Journal*, published online before print, September 13, 2013, doi: 10.5465/amj.2012.0393.

3. Taylor, Frederick W. *The Principles of Scientific Management.* New York: Harper & Brothers, 1911.

4. Kanigel, Robert. *The One Best Way: Frederick Winslow Taylor and the Enigma of Efficiency.* New York: Penguin Books, 1997.

5. "Employee Engagement Survey—Sample Survey Questions." Custominsight.com (corporate website), undated. Accessed July 11, 2014, http://www.custominsight .com/employee-engagement-survey/sample-survey-items.asp.

6. "Employee Opinion Survey Demo Results 1." HR-Survey.com, undated. Accessed May 25, 2014, http://www.hr-survey.com/demoRes01.htm.

7. Paquette, Christopher, et al. "Berkeley Lab 2010 Employee Survey." Berkeley Lab and MOR Associates, May 2010. Accessed May 11, 2014, http://www2.lbl.gov/ Ops/assets/docs/surveys/BLES-2010.pdf.

8. Jensen, Bill. "Gallup Engagement: Great, but So 1980s." *Simplerwork Blog,* Simplerwork.blogspot.com, May 30, 2012. Accessed June 3, 2014, http:// simplerwork.blogspot.com/2012/02/gallup-engagement-great-but-still-so.html.

9. "Employee Engagement Survey—Sample Survey Questions." Custominsight.com (corporate website), undated. Accessed July 11, 2014, http://www.custominsight .com/employee-engagement-survey/sample-survey-items.asp.

10. Murphy, Patrick J. "Is It Time for Mutiny?" *Harvard Business Review* (blog), HBR.org, April 9, 2013. Accessed June 9, 2014, http://blogs.hbr.org/2013/04/is-it -time-to-stage-a-mutiny/.

11. Gratton, Lynda. "The End of the Middle Manager." *Harvard Business Review,* January 2011. Accessed July 7, 2014, http://hbr.org/2011/01/column-the-end-of -the-middle-manager/ar/1.

12. Peters, Tom. "Rule #3: Leadership Is Confusing as Hell." *Fast Company,* February 28, 2001. Accessed February 27, 2014, http://www.fastcompany.com/42575/rule -3-leadership-confusing-hell.

13. Buckingham, Marcus, and Curt Coffman. *First, Break All the Rules.* New York: Simon & Schuster, 1999.

14. "Zappos' 10-Hour Long Customer Service Call Sets Record." *Huffington Post,* December 21, 2012. Accessed December 2, 2014, http://www.huffingtonpost.com/ 2012/12/21/zappos-10-hour-call_n_2345467.html.

15. Rosenbaum, Steven. "The Happiness Culture: Zappos Isn't a Company—It's a Mission." *Fast Company,* June 4, 2010. Accessed July 23, 2014, http://www .fastcompany.com/1657030/happiness-culture-zappos-isnt-company-its-mission.

16. "Zappos Family Core Values." Zappos.com (corporate website), undated. Accessed June 26, 2014, http://about.zappos.com/our-unique-culture/zappos-core-values.

17. "Zappos.com." Fortune.com Best Companies to Work For, 2014. Accessed July 13, 2014, http://fortune.com/best-companies/zappos-com-38/.

18. Hannah, E. "Zappos Makes Fortune 100 Best Companies to Work For List!" *Zappos Family* (blog), Zappos.com, January 16, 2014. Accessed June 25, 2014, http://blogs.zappos.com/blogs/zappos-family/2014/01/16/zappos-makes-fortune -100-best-companies-work-*-list.

19. "Zappos Milestone: Timeline." *Footwear News*, May 4, 2009. Accessed June 17, 2013, http://www.wwd.com/footwear-news/markets/zappos-milestone-timeline -2121760.

20. Jacobs, Alexandra. "Happy Feet." *New Yorker*, September 14, 2009. Accessed March 18, 2014, http://www.newyorker.com/magazine/2009/09/14/happy-feet.

21. Holacracy corporate website. Accessed June 23, 2013, http://holacracy.org.

22. McGregor, Jena. "Zappos Says Goodbye to Bosses." *Washington Post*, January 3, 2014. Accessed May 15, 2014, http://www.washingtonpost.com/blogs/on -leadership/wp/2014/01/03/zappos-gets-rid-of-all-managers/.

23. Walker, Tim. "Shoe Firm Zappos Gets a Reboot—with No Managers and No Job Titles." *Independent*, January 18, 2014. Accessed June 19, 2014, http://www .independent.co.uk/news/world/americas/shoe-firm-zappos-gets-a-reboot--with -no-managers-and-no-job-titles-9069451.html.

24. Sweeney, Camille, and Josh Gosfield. "No Managers Required: How Zappos Ditched the Old Corporate Structure for Something New." *Fast Company*, January 6, 2014. Accessed April 14, 2014, http://www.fastcompany.com/3024358/bottom -line/no-managers-required-how-zappos-ditched-the-old-corporate-structure -for-somethin.

25. Denning, Steve. "Making Sense of Zappos and Holacracy." *Forbes*, January 15, 2014. Accessed April 22, 2014, http://www.forbes.com/sites/stevedenning/2014/ 01/15/making-sense-of-zappos-and-holacracy/.

26. Wooldridge, Adrian. "The Holes in Holacracy: The Latest Big Idea in Management Deserves Some Scepticism" ("Schumpeter" column). *Economist*, July 5, 2014. Accessed July 30, 204, http://www.economist.com/news/business/21606267-latest -big-idea-management-deserves-some-scepticism-holes-holacracy.

27. Bowles, Nellie. "Holacracy or Hella Crazy? The Fringe Ideas Driving the Las Vegas Downtown Project." <*re/code*> (online publication), October 3, 2014. Accessed December 6, 2014, http://recode.net/2014/10/03/holacracy-or-hella-crazy-the -fringe-ideas-driving-the-las-vegas-downtown-project/.

28. Rosenbaum. "The Happiness Culture: Zappos Isn't a Company—It's a Mission."

29. Stern, Mark Joseph. "Sin No More: Can Tony Hsieh Turn Downtown Las Vegas into a Family-Friendly Startup Utopia?" Slate.com, December 5, 2013. Accessed June 21, 2014, http://www.slate.com/articles/technology/the_next_silicon_ valley/2013/12/tony_hsieh_las_vegas_can_the_zappos_billionaire_turn_vegas_ into_a_tech_utopia.html.

30. Anonymous current employee. "Socialization over Compensation." Glassdoor.com review of Zappos, March 12, 2014, http://www.glassdoor.com/Reviews/Employee -Review-The-Zappos-Family-RVW3861282.htm.

31. Anonymous former employee. "Culture Can't Be Everything." Glassdoor.com review of Zappos, June 5, 2014, http://www.glassdoor.com/Reviews/Employee -Review-The-Zappos-Family-RVW4352828.htm.

32. Anonymous current employee. "Socialization over Compensation."

33. Anonymous current employee. "Met a Lot of Good Friends. Was Underpaid and Had to Deal with a Lot of Ridiculous Politics." Glassdoor.com review of Zappos, January 8, 2014. Accessed July 15, 2014, http://www.glassdoor.com/Reviews/ Employee-Review-The-Zappos-Family-RVW3509149.htm.

The Twelfth Rule: Take It to Extremes

1. Harris, Dave. "The Background Story." *Dave The Harris* (blog), Davetheharris.com, undated. Accessed August 10, 2014, http://www.davetheharris.com/full-bio/.

2. Lapowsky, Issie. "The Way I Work: Will Dean, Tough Mudder." *Inc.*, February 13, 2013. Accessed May 3, 2014, http://www.inc.com/magazine/201302/issie-lapowsky/ the-way-i-work-will-dean-tough-mudder.html.

3. Parrish, Charlie. "How Tough Mudder Became a Phenomenon." *Telegraph*, July 12, 2014. Accessed August 5, 2014, http://www.telegraph.co.uk/men/active/10959747/ How-Tough-Mudder-became-a-phenomenon.html.

4. Branch, John. "Playing with Fire, Barbed Wire and Beer." *New York Times*, April 28, 2010. Accessed July 12, 2014, http://www.nytimes.com/2010/04/29/sports/ 29mudder.html?partner=rss&emc=rss&_r=0.

5. "Official Tough Mudder Promo 2010." Produced by Nicholas Greene, May 20, 2010. Accessed August 5, 2014, https://www.youtube.com/watch?v=pRwSqrfHdQg.

6. Harris, Dave. "Tough Mudder, Pennsylvania." *Dave The Harris* (blog), Davetheharris.com, May 2, 2010. Accessed August 10, 2014, http://www .davetheharris.com/2010/05/08/tough-mudder-pennsylvania/.

7. Harris. "The Background Story."

8. Widdicombe, Lizzie. "In Cold Mud." *New Yorker*, January 27, 2014. Accessed August 2, 2014, http://www.newyorker.com/magazine/2014/01/27/in-cold-mud.

9. Parrish. "How Tough Mudder Became a Phenomenon."

10. Poynter, Dan, and Mike Turoff. *Parachuting: The Skydiver's Handbook*. Santa Barbara, CA: Para Publishing, 2009.

11. Thompson, Neal. "Ski Movie Mogul Warren Miller Refuses to Go Downhill." SeattleMet.com, November 23, 2011. Accessed August 5, 2014, http://www .seattlemet.com/arts-and-entertainment/articles/warren-miller-ski-film -legend-december-2011.

12. Ariely, Dan. "What Makes Us Feel Good About Our Work?" TEDxRiodelaPlata presentation, October 2013. Accessed June 21, 2014, http://www.ted.com/talks/ dan_ariely_what_makes_us_feel_good_about_our_work#t-81305.

13. Friedman, Milton. "The Social Responsibility of Business Is to Increase Its Profits." *New York Times Magazine*, September 13, 1970.

14. Buchanan, Leigh. "How to Achieve Big, Hairy, Audacious Goals." *Inc.*, November 1, 2012. Accessed August 1, 2014, http://www.inc.com/leigh-buchanan/big-ideas/jim-collins-big-hairy-audacious-goals.html.

15. Whyte, William H. *The Organization Man*. New York: Simon & Schuster, 1956.

16. Anonymous current employee. "Company Is OK." Glassdoor.com review of Gallup, Inc., July 27, 2014. Accessed August 21, 2014, http://www.glassdoor.com/Reviews/Employee-Review-Gallup-RVW4660228.htm.

17. Anonymous former employee. "Tough Mudder Does Not Respect Its Staff." Glassdoor.com review of Tough Mudder, April 16, 2013. Accessed August 5, 2014, http://www.glassdoor.com/Reviews/Employee-Review-Tough-Mudder-RVW2566484.htm.

18. Anonymous former employee. "Facade Failing, Internal Structure Shattered at Best." Glassdoor.com review of Tough Mudder, May 20, 2014. Accessed August 5, 2014, http://www.glassdoor.com/Reviews/Employee-Review-Tough-Mudder-RVW4258497.htm.

19. Anonymous current employee. "Great for a First Job—Just Don't Stay Too Long." Glassdoor.com review of Tough Mudder, January 27, 2014. Accessed August 5, 2014, http://www.glassdoor.com/Reviews/Employee-Review-Tough-Mudder-RVW3595425.htm.

20. Flatley, Kevin T. "Qualifying the Boat: A 'How to' Guide for Qualifying in a U.S. Navy Submarine." *Submarine Sailor dot-com* (blog), April 26, 1998. Accessed August 12, 2014, http://www.submarinesailor.com/stories/Qualifying.asp.

21. McDonald, Bradford N., Captain, U.S. Navy (ret.). Telephone interview with the author, September 11, 2014.

22. Bing, Mark N. "Psychological Screening of Submariners: The Development and Validation of the Submarine Attrition Risk Scale (SARS)." Presentation to the International Personnel Assessment Council, 2003, http://annex.ipacweb.org/library/conf/03/bing.pdf.

23. Whanger, J. C., M. N. Bing, A. America, and J. C. Lamb, "Psychometric Assessment in the U.S. Submarine Force." In Paul O'Connor and Joseph V. Cohn, eds., *Human Performance Enhancements in High Risk Environments*. Santa Barbara, CA: Praeger, 2009, pp. 58–73.

24. Light, Mark F. "The Navy's Moral Compass: Commanding Officers and Personal Misconduct." *Naval War College Review* 65, no. 3 (Summer 2012). Accessed August 12, 2014, https://www.usnwc.edu/getattachment/d79951a2-72b6-4181-b735-5f98fc2ceecb/The-Navy-s-Moral-Compass--Commanding-Officers-and-.

25. Faram, Mark D. "Boosted Bonuses: New Rules Raise Payout Ceiling to $100K." *Navy Times*, April 14, 2014. Accessed August 12, 2014, http://www.navytimes.com/article/20140414/CAREERS/304140031/Boosted-bonuses-New-rules-raise-payout-ceiling-100K.

26. Melia, Michael. "Navy OKs Changes for Submariners' Sleep Schedules." The Big Story (Associated Press website), August 20, 2014. Accessed August 21, 2014, http://bigstory.ap.org/article/navy-oks-changes-submariners-sleep-schedules.

27. *Submarine: Hidden Hunter*. Directed by Matthew Howe. Mount Kisco, NY: The Silver Owl Group, Inc., 2005.

28. Light. "The Navy's Moral Compass: Commanding Officers and Personal Misconduct."

29. Kennedy, Joel. "Fair Winds and Following Seas" *The Stupid Shall Be Punished* (blog). April 1, 2014. Accessed August 12, 2014, http://bubbleheads.blogspot.com.

30. Marquet, David L. *Turn the Ship Around: A True Story of Turning Followers into Leaders*. New York: Portfolio/Penguin, 2012.

31. Anonymous current submarine warfare officer. "Overall, Very Positive. The Navy Has Given Me Enormous Responsibilities and Opportunities." Glassdoor.com review of U.S. Navy. May 6, 2014. Accessed August 2, 2014, http://www.glassdoor.com/Reviews/Employee-Review-US-Navy-RVW4182111.htm.

32. Anonymous current electronics technician. "US Navy Submarine Force—Exceptional!" Glassdoor.com review of U.S. Navy. February 26, 2014. Accessed August 2, 2014, http://www.glassdoor.com/Reviews/Employee-Review-US-Navy-RVW3772166.htm.

33. Kennedy, Joel. "Do Submarine Officers Enjoy Their Job?" *The Stupid Shall Be Punished* (blog). February 11, 2011. Accessed August 3, 2014, http://bubbleheads.blogspot.com/2011/02/do-submarine-officers-enjoy-their-job.html.

34. *Navy Military Personnel Manual NAVPERS 15560D*. Washington, D.C.: U.S. Department of the Navy, August 22, 2002. Accessed August 12, 2014, http://www.public.navy.mil/bupers-npc/reference/milpersman/Pages/default.aspx.

35. McDonald. Telephone interview with the author.

36. Anonymous former nuclear electricians mate. "Nuclear Field EM (Submarine Qualified) Gained Experience and Training, and Had a Little Fun Along the Way." Glassdoor.com review of U.S. Navy, June 29, 2014, http://www.glassdoor.com/Reviews/Employee-Review-US-Navy-RVW4493251.htm.

Handling the Truth

1. Broad, William J., and John Markoff. "Israeli Test on Worm Called Crucial in Iran Nuclear Delay." *New York Times*, January 15, 2011. Accessed June 7, 2014, http://www.nytimes.com/2011/01/16/world/middleeast/16stuxnet.html?pagewanted=all&_r=0.

2. Gross, Michael Joseph. "A Declaration of Cyber-War." *Vanity Fair*, April 2011. Accessed May 25, 2014, http://www.vanityfair.com/culture/features/2011/04/stuxnet-201104.

3. Gilbert, Patrick, and Pete Foley. "Ways to Improve Engagement Using Employee Surveys." *Workspan: The Magazine of WorldatWork*, October 2012. Accessed August 1, 2014, http://www.worldatwork.org/waw/adimLink?id=65382.

4. The author knows this happened, as does a delightful person now at Cargill who once reported to him, because the author did it. He concedes he was an idiot that day.

5. Ryssdal, Kai. "The Hidden Side of Keeping Employee Morale High." *Marketplace* (radio segment and podcast), February 22, 2012. Accessed January 2, 2013, http://www.marketplace.org/topics/life/freakonomics-radio/hidden-side-keeping-employee-morale-high.

6. "The People First Cultural Health Assessment in Action." Lannomworldwide.com. Accessed July 15, 2014, http://www.lannomworldwide.com/people-first-vs-gallup.php.

7. Adams, Scott. *Dilbert* (comic strip), August 29, 2004. Accessed July 29, 2014, http://dilbert.com/strips/comic/2004-08-29/.

8. Hirschfeld, Robert R., et al. "Voluntary Survey Completion Among Team Members: Implications of Noncompliance and Missing Data for Multilevel Research." *Journal of Applied Psychology* 98, no. 3 (2013): 454–468.

9. Saari, Lise, and Charles Scherbaum. "Identified Employee Surveys: Potential Promise, Perils, and Professional Practice Guidelines." *Industrial and Organizational Psychology: Perspectives on Science and Practice* 4 (2011): 435–448.

10. Shirley, Sarah. "Can You Trust Your Employee Survey Results?" Decisionwise.com. Accessed July 20, 2014, http://www.decision-wise.com/can-you-trust-your-employee-survey-results-2/.

11. Anonymous current employee. "Great People That Care, yet Management Invests Absolutely Nothing in Developing or Compensating the Employees." Glassdoor.com review of Right Management, October 12, 2012. Accessed July 12, 2014, http://www.glassdoor.com/Reviews/Employee-Review-Right-Management-RVW2041834.htm.

12. "Techniques to Gain Valuable Employee Feedback." Trilliumteams.com. Accessed July7, 2014, http://www.trilliumteams.com/articles/22/techniques-to-gain-valuable-employee-feedback-

13. "Disciplined Action Planning Drives Employee Engagement." Kenexa white paper, 2006.

14. Zinger, David. "How I Would Change Gallup's Q12 to the Q13." DavidZinger.com, December 15, 2009. Accessed August 5, 2014, http://www.davidzinger.com/employee-engagement-2010-how-i-would-change-gallups-q12-to-the-q13-5532/.

15. Baird, Bruce F. *Managerial Decisions Under Uncertainty: An Introduction to the Analysis of Decision Making.* Hoboken, NJ: Wiley-Interscience, 1989. (The late Dr. Baird was one of the author's most influential professors in graduate school and is remembered fondly.)

16. Marcus, Howard K. "2014 Results: Best Places to Work in Omaha." Omaha.com (website of the *Omaha World-Herald*), May 4, 2014. Accessed July 1, 2014, http://www.omaha.com/money/results-best-places-to-work-in-omaha/article_dd1d8e72-651c-5a67-b098-9fdfc836def4.html?TNNoMobile.

The Profitable Pursuit of Happiness

1. Hogan, Maren. "Employee Engagement Doesn't Equal Employee Happiness." Forbes.com, May 20, 2014. Accessed August 5, 2014, http://www.forbes.com/sites/yec/2014/05/20/employee-engagement-doesnt-equal-employee-happiness/.

2. Kruse, Kevin. "The Difference Between Happiness and Engagement at Work." Forbes.com, December 12, 2012. Accessed August 20, 2014, http://www.forbes.com/sites/kevinkruse/2012/12/21/happy-at-work/.

3. DeWolff, Jeff. "Job Happiness Is the Thing." Wolf Prairie company website, February 21, 2014. Accessed September 3, 2014, http://www.wolfprairie.com/job-happiness-thing/.

4. Crowley, Mark C. "Why Being Engaged at Work Isn't as Simple as 'Being Happy.'" FastCompany.com (*Fast Company* website) September 30, 2014. Accessed October 26, 2014, http://www.fastcompany.com/3036399/the-future-of-work/why-being-engaged-at-work-isnt-as-simple-as-being-happy.

5. Clifton, Jim. "Employee Satisfaction Doesn't Matter." *The Chairman's Blog* (Gallup, Inc., corporate website), June 5, 2014. Accessed August 21, 2014, http://thechairmansblog.gallup.com/2014/06/employee-satisfaction-doesnt-matter.html.

6. Robertson, Ivan T., and Cary L. Cooper. "Full Engagement: The Integration of Employee Engagement and Psychological Well-Being." *Leadership & Organization Development Journal* 31, no. 4 (2010): 324–336.

7. Wright, Thomas A. "More Than Meets the Eye: The Role of Employee Well-Being in Organizational Research." In P. Alex Linley, Susan Harrington, and Nicola Garcea, eds., *Oxford Handbook of Positive Psychology and Work*. Oxford: Oxford University Press, 2013.

8. Feintzeig, Rachel. "Bonuses Are the New Raises." WSJ.com, August 27, 2014. Accessed September 1, 2014, http://blogs.wsj.com/atwork/2014/08/27/bonuses-are-the-new-raises.

9. Robertson and Cooper. "Full Engagement: The Integration of Employee Engagement and Psychological Well-Being."

10. Anonymous current employee. "A Great Place to Learn Grow and Be Happy." Glassdoor review of Amdocs, June 24, 2012. Accessed September 3, 2014, http://www.glassdoor.com/Reviews/Employee-Review-Amdocs-RVW1641383.htm.

11. Anonymous current employee. "I. Couldn't Be Any Happier." Glassdoor review of Optimizely. November 16, 2013. Accessed September 3, 2014, http://www.glassdoor.com/Reviews/Employee-Review-Optimizely-RVW3320995.htm.

12. Anonymous current employee. "Collaborative, Transparent, Wonderful Place to Work." Glassdoor.com review of Okta, March 26, 2014. Accessed September 2, 2014, http://www.glassdoor.com/Reviews/Employee-Review-Okta-RVW3947366.htm.

13. Anonymous current employee. "Happy Staff with Optimistic Future!" Glassdoor.com review of Mauldin & Jenkins, August 19, 2013. Accessed September 2, 2014, http://www.glassdoor.com/Reviews/Employee-Review-Mauldin-and-Jenkins-RVW2951407.htm.

14. DeWolff, Jeff. "Job Happiness Is the Thing."

Appendix

1. While we began our testing with common conceptualizations of engagement, the results of our tests led us to a unique way of thinking and measuring employee engagement. See Step 4 for more.
2. We mirrored our target sample as bulleted as closely as possible, but some countries simply didn't break down their employment numbers according to our criteria. In all cases, however, we were able to compare age and gender in the adult (over 18) workforce. In the United States, we were able to further discern proportions from full-time workers as well.
3. In the United States, we may not consider an organization 500 strong as large, although it is certainly large enough to require formal HR processes, policies, and practices. It is also large enough to demand a leadership hierarchy. However, in other countries and regions surveyed, such as Latin America, there is a higher proportion of small companies; as such, their "large" may be small to the United States, relatively speaking. For the purposes of this research, we drew the line at 500 because we sought to understand engagement in organizations large enough to have standard hierarchies and employee policies and practices.
4. Technically speaking, the factors referred to here are "components," but since the term "factor" is better understood and used in scientific circles, we'll use it throughout this Appendix.
5. We conducted a PCA with varimax rotation due to the truly exploratory nature of this part of the research. It is a data reduction technique similar to an exploratory factor analysis. We used PCA because we sought to discard *a priori* concepts of the underlying structure of the data and begin anew. We examined factors with an eigenvalue greater than 1.
6. Kowske, B. *Employee Engagement: Market Review, Buyer's Guide, and Employee Profiles.* Oakland, CA: Bersin & Associates, August 2012.
7. Macey, W. H., and B. S. Schneider. "The Meaning of Employee Engagement." *Industrial and Organizational Psychology*, 2008.
8. The thirteenth factor had low loadings for all items and largely contained items dropped due to multicollinearity.
9. In our research and in client reports, these rules are likely to appear together due to their belonging to one factor, the result of their high correlation with each other. This is true of any factor we chose to split for practical purposes.
10. A measurement equivalence study is planned for the next wave of international data collection.
11. Scores for each rule were computed by averaging responses to the three statements, using the mean.
12. Scientists: Once items were chosen, we conducted Cronbach's alphas for each factor/scale. Run on the international sample, all alphas are above the industry standard level of "acceptable," 0.70, with the exclusion of one, "Make Them Fearless," which measured at 0.66. Most are in the 0.80 range, with the highest alpha level at 0.88.

13. Krasikova, D., J. M. LeBreton, and S. Tonidandel. "Estimating the Relative Importance of Variables in Multiple Regression Models." In G. P Hodgkinson and K. J. Ford, eds., *International Review of Industrial and Organizational Psychology*. West Sussex, U.K.: Wiley-Blackwell, 2011, vol. 26.

Acknowledgments

It takes more than one person to produce a book like *Widgets*. I am deeply indebted to a large team of insightful and supportive people who assisted along the way. A few instigated the whole thing. Some developed and conducted the cool research. Many gave their thoughtful and unvarnished feedback to early drafts of chapters as they were produced. And a wonderful few kept me sane through the writing process.

No one wrestled with the issues in this book more than Kevin Crowley. He deftly alternated from instigator to editor to strategist to coach. No one was more inside my head as it related to getting *Widgets* well thought through and written. Each chapter in this book was substantially refined through vociferous, constructive arguments in Kevin's office each Tuesday morning over the course of a year. In my career, I've had just three managers who were so supportive and strategically gifted that I could have profiled them in one of my books as great examples to other managers. Kevin is one of those fantastically anomalous few.

Larry Schoenecker saw the potential in this work many years ago. His observations about the changes in the relationship between employee and employer, and his provocative questions, sparked the research that resulted in the book. His vision, strategic insights, and personal support were instrumental in making this book what it is. For the record, the Summer of Love story in the "Be Cool" chapter was included over his objections, which makes its inclusion in my estimation that much cooler. When your 15-year-old occasionally blurts out, "Mr. Schoenecker's cool!" you know you're in rare company.

Author and experienced advisor Mark Hirschfeld added numerous pivotal insights and helped keep my inner cynic under control. When I was most ragged, I envied and often borrowed from his nearly constant zenlike calm. If you were going to trust someone with anything from personal confidences to nuclear secrets (and he's covered precisely that range), no one is better qualified than Mark.

Workplace expert Dr. Brenda Kowske, also an author in her own right, was the voice of authority on "all things science" for this work. It's an expansive jurisdiction, but she oversaw it with an expertise and enthusiasm no one else could replicate. I appreciate that when I was wrong, she correctly me gently by saying, "You're wrong!" There are few things more enjoyable than to watch Dr. Kowske take apart the conventional or accepted ideas she can prove are—her word—"whackadoodle" and replace them with something revolutionary.

Barry Danielson collaborated on much of the early work that resulted in the New Rules studies, including managing the fielding of the 2012 pilot study in the United States. His enthusiasm and drive were crucial in those formative stages.

McGraw-Hill associate publisher Mary Glenn and senior editor Knox Huston pounced on the proposal for this book so forcefully that I knew we'd found the right home for *Widgets*. They have been fantastic collaborators every step of the way. For a fly fisherman trapped in Manhattan, Knox exudes a remarkable calm in managing all the details. Like most authors, I left a trail of errors and confusing bits in the manuscript. Judy Duguid meticulously hunted them down and was the expert who I relied on (or is that "the expert on whom I relied," Judy) to help me not look illiterate. Patricia Wallenburg made sure everything came together as it should on the final pages.

Julie Kline, Ryan Fors, and Andrea Bergeron played a major role in bringing the New Rules of Engagement to life through their design of communications that preceded and influenced *Widgets*. Various sections of the manuscript benefited from scrutiny by Sherra Buckley, Tim Houlihan, Dennis Moynihan, Megan Murry, John O'Brien, Morgen

Paul, Jennifer Ploskina, Betsy Schneider, and Robb Webb. The improvements are to their credit; any deficiencies are strictly on me.

It was once again a delight to work with Barbara Cave Henricks to get the word out about a new book. I'm fairly certain Barbara was one of those kids who, like me, begged her grade school teachers to let her run the mimeograph machine so she could smell the fresh ink. She and the *Widgets* project team at Cave Henricks Communications—Kaila Nickel, Jessica Krakoski, and Kimberly Petty—gave invaluable strategic direction for the book's launch.

John Harasyn, Andrew Ridgeway, Scott Jesser, Ben Schmidt, Tim Dunklee, and Jeff Sorensen at digital agency space150 took *Widgets* and gave it virtual life. They're all nuts (but in a good way, of course). Their enthusiasm, their willingness to push the boundaries, and their creativity made WidgetsTheBook.com and iamnotawidget.com the perfect online counterparts for the book. Greg Harris, Jarah Banks, and Andrew Zetterman made sure all the gears behind the New Rules index rotated in the right directions.

Betsy Schneider, assisted by Kyle Simenson, booked me in all the right places, then moved me around the country like a chess piece to give speeches. They did it in a way that made me feel less like a pawn than that cooler horsey piece that, apropos of my schedule, never travels in a straight line. Sarah Peete joined our team just as things threatened to become disorganized. Chaos cowers when she fires up her computer.

I am grateful to the employees of the Caribou Coffee shops in Excelsior, Minnetonka, Shorewood, and Edina, Minnesota; and Dunn Bros. Coffee in Excelsior; where I often worked undisturbed for several hours at a time. Thanks for the warm smiles, the hot beverages, and the sunny spots by the windows—and for not kicking me out or calling the cops.

My favorite (i.e., only) daughter, Noelle, to whom this book is dedicated, graduated college and became a real employee during the period when *Widgets* was written. When writing about how an employee ought to be treated, I often thought of how I would like to see her regarded. I bounced many questions and observations off her to make sure the book would resonate with her fellow millennials. She instigated our muscling through a turning-point Tough Mudder as *Widgets* was being formulated. Hypothermia never felt so good. From the beginning, Noelle has cheered on my book writing. Her perspective only becomes more valuable over time.

My son and scuba partner Parks takes me seriously but never lets me take myself too seriously. Although he is a far faster runner than I am, he willingly hung back during several key races we ran while *Widgets* was being written, yelling in my ear to "Take It to Extremes." His mixture of idealism and candor were inspirational to me, and his reactions to draft chapters spot on when formulating the advice in this book.

Some of the biggest dopamine rushes of my career were dropping into the occasional bookstore with my son Charlie and having him insist on pulling the store's inventory of my books so I could sign them. His tremendous encouragement, the hope of seeing his excitement at fresh ink on the shelves once more, his perfect tweak of this book's subtitle, and his inspirational intensity on the lacrosse field and the ice of a hockey rink helped shoot this one into the net.

This was the writing of the third book through which my wife, Nora, has had to suffer, and therefore the second blatant violation of her declaration, "Well, we're not going through *that* again." She even willingly descended into Endnote Hell with me during the final weeks of manuscript prep. She was once again exceptionally understanding and patient with my persistent level of distraction.

Many people who wished not to be named confided their best and worst moments at work. I greatly appreciate their trust, and I hope that *Widgets* carries to leaders and managers the message these employees—these people—would most want them to hear.

—RGW
Excelsior, Minnesota

Index

About the Author

RODD WAGNER IS ONE OF THE FOREMOST AUTHORITIES ON EMPLOYEE motivation and collaboration. His books, speeches, and research focus on how human nature affects business strategy.

Wagner is a confidential advisor to senior executives on the best ways to increase their personal effectiveness and their organizations' performance. His work has taken him to a fiberglass factory in Brazil, a vehicle engineering facility in India, a paper warehouse in Poland, a home improvement store in Wales, a medical device design site in Germany, a pharmaceutical firm in Switzerland, the Pentagon, and the aircraft carrier *USS Nimitz*.

Wagner is currently vice president of employee engagement strategy for BI Worldwide. He was previously a principal of Gallup, research director for the *Portland* (Maine) *Press Herald*, an editor and crime reporter for *The Salt Lake Tribune*, and a radio talk show host.

Wagner's books have been published in 10 languages and his work featured in *The Wall Street Journal*, *ABC News Now*, Businessweek.com, CNBC.com, and the *National Post* of Canada. None of this got a rise out of his children, who were only impressed when one of Wagner's books was parodied in *Dilbert*. He is a passable fly fisherman, persistent 5K runner, and enthusiastic youth lacrosse coach who lives in relative tranquility with his family near Minneapolis.

His blog can be found at WidgetsTheBook.com. He tweets under the name @Rodd_Wagner.